IN THE MINISTER'S WORKSHOP

BOOKS BY HALFORD E. LUCCOCK

Never Forget to Live

365 Windows

In the Minister's Workshop

IN THE MINISTER'S
WORKSHOP

BY HALFORD E. LUCCOCK

ABINGDON PRESS
NASHVILLE • NEW YORK

IN THE MINISTER'S WORKSHOP

Copyright MCMXLIV by Whitmore & Stone

ISBN 0-687-19374-5

Library of Congress Catalog Card Number: 44-6948

PRINTED AND BOUND AT NASHVILLE,
TENNESSEE, UNITED STATES OF AMERICA

FOREWORD

THE PURPOSE OF THIS BOOK IS SHARPLY LIMITED. ITS THEME IS NOT primarily the content of the minister's message. As the title indicates, it is concerned with the problems of the preacher's workshop. It undertakes the practical task of trying to bring some specific and concrete help in the craftsmanship of the making of sermons.

Parts of the material in the book have been given as lectures on the Alden-Tuthill Foundation at the Chicago Theological Seminary and on the Earl Foundation at the Pacific School of Religion.

I am greatly indebted to my colleague Professor Raymond P. Morris for making the index and to Mr. Ronald Sleeth for the typing of the manuscript.

HALFORD E. LUCCOCK

Yale University Divinity School

CONTENTS

I. BEHIND THE MINISTER

===

H E SEEMED TO BE THE CHANNEL OF A COMMUNICATION, AND NOT THE
source of it." These words, written by Walter Bagehot after hearing a sermon preached by Frederick Denison Maurice, are more than
a perfect tribute to a great preacher. They describe all true preaching.
In real preaching, the preacher is a channel, not a source. That truth is
pictured in the word commonly used for the sermon—"message"—
something sent, through a channel. It is the prophet's charter. "The
word of the Lord *came*." As the Old Testament prophets reached back
into the dim, shadowy realm of inspiration, they were conscious, not
of their own wisdom or wit, but of something spoken and heard.
"Thus saith the Lord God of hosts, Go . . . and say." [1] "Thus shalt
thou say unto him, The Lord saith thus." [2] The primary fact about
preaching is that which is behind the preacher—the reality of a God
who speaks. Any discussion of preaching which does not begin there,
might as well not begin at all.

At an ordination service a few years ago the preacher who gave the
charge to the young minister pleaded eloquently for consecration of
mind and energy, and ended up with the exhortation, "Now go out
and give to your preaching all that is in you." It was a fitting word
for the occasion, persuasively spoken; yet it would be hard to conceive
a better definition of just what preaching is *not*. It is not giving all that
is in us; it is giving that which is not in us at all. It is the preacher's
presenting himself and all that he is and has as a channel for something that is not in him, the grace of God. The first words of the
Bible are the first words of preaching: "In the beginning God."

This primary truth is set here in a primary place. First of all, because
it belongs here. It is the only true north on the preacher's compass.

11

There is another reason, however, for the stress in these first few pages on the preacher as a channel of a communication whose source is not in himself but in God. That reason is that this book is to be occupied with the quite secondary matters of the craftsmanship of sermon making, and to a lesser degree with some of the content of the preacher's message. This focus on craft and technique needs no apology. It is part of a minister's reasonable service, a measure of his consecration. If we concentrate our attention on this realm, it is done with the emphatic and continual understanding that skills of any degree are secondary matters. These may be the branches of preaching; they are never its roots. So if what is primary in preaching, the God behind the preacher and the religious experience out of which true preaching flows, receives but scant attention in these pages, that omission is deliberately made, with the remembrance that, compared to it, all else is a minor affair. All the skills and tricks of a public speaker's toolbox cannot make one vital word out of a spiritual vacuum. In one of her sonnets Edna St. Vincent Millay has expressed the feeling with which the present volume is undertaken:

> I know I am but summer to your heart,
> And not the full four seasons of the year.[3]

There has been no lack of opulent treatment of the full four seasons of the minister's life, including that springtime of the spiritual life which is hidden with Christ in God.

Here in these chapters, then, the field is the sharply limited, stoutly fenced one of some craftsman's problems in the making of sermons—how we may strive to give the sermon what a bird has, a sense of direction and wings; how it may acquire carrying and explosive power—in a word, the details of a dedicated workmanship. Our concern is how we may keep ourselves oriented to experiment in the shaping of more effective sermons, in the bettering of marksmanship, in the closer relevance of sermon to people, so that preaching may bring the result that followed the first Christian sermon at Pentecost—men earnestly asking, "What shall we do?"

The whole conception of a person as a channel through which a reality beyond the self communicates a revelation is one that has found memorable expression in the other arts. Rodin has put it clearly in regard to sculpture. He wrote that

the search (of the mature artist) is to express, not himself, but his sense of something that exists in himself, something not personal but universal. What that something is has never been clearly defined; it has been felt as the reality behind appearances. To express not his own feeble or defective emotions, but his conception, his apprehension of that reality, felt through his emotions—that is the object of his search.[4]

How close this comes to Brooks's "Preaching is truth through personality"!

For the artist who works in words, that sense of a reality which enters the mind and spirit from outside is expressed by Robert Louis Stevenson in a familiar purple passage in his letters—legitimately purple; for while purple is not to be splashed inadvisedly, but reverently and discreetly, nevertheless it is in God's spectrum. Recovering from a severe illness, he wrote to W. E. Henley:

After this break in my work, beginning to return to it, as from light sleep, I wax exclamatory, as you see.

Sursum Corda:
Heave ahead:
Here's luck.
Art and Blue Heaven,
April and God's Larks.
Green reeds and the sky-scattering river.
A stately music.
Enter God.   R. L. S.

Ay, but you know, until a man can write that "Enter God," he has made no art![5]

Those are gorgeous stage directions: "A stately music. Enter God." And the preacher's sustaining faith may be that, no matter how small the stage on which his drama is played out, or how remote from thronged centers, there may be a "stately music" and "Enter God." It is supremely true of preaching that art begins with "Enter God."

13

When there is no stately music coming from off stage, when there is no "Enter God," preaching becomes a trivial matter, either of the pulpit living on its wits or of the sterile repetition of a mechanical tradition.

Where does a sermon begin? It begins where a river begins—in the sky. "Freely ye have received, freely give," is an ultimate fact of geography. The preacher is the herald of a revelation, the carrier of a communication from a God who has disclosed himself.

> Behind the dim unknown
> Standeth God within the shadow.

These words are not only the expression of Christian faith in a time of adversity; they are an imaging of the preacher's proclamation. Behind the word is the Word. Himself confronting the reality of God, the preacher in his message confronts men with the revelation of a God who has unveiled himself. When preaching does not begin with that apprehension of reality, it soon becomes a sorry bankruptcy of ingenuities. A suggestive picture of beginning at the wrong end is found in a criticism of a volume of stories which Richard Curle sent to H. G. Wells. Mr. Wells wrote him: "You are drunk with Conrad. You have got a style before you have got a story, and God help you." [6]

A style before a story—how often has that verdict been justified in the history of preaching! The story comes first. The revelation is a story in three chapters: "The Word was made flesh"; "If any man . . . open the door, I will come in"; "Other foundations can no man lay than that is laid, which is Jesus Christ." When any style takes precedence before that august story, it becomes a supreme impertinence.

But when the story, the revelation, the God behind the preacher, is communicated through the channel of the preacher's personality and word, then there is the recurring miracle of preaching. Look at another picture from Stevenson's letters. In a letter written in 1875—the same letter in which he wrote, "I've been to church, and am not depressed"—this follows:

In church, old Mr. Torrence preached—over eighty, and a relic of times forgotten, with his black thread gloves and mild old foolish face. One of the nicest parts of it was to see John Inglis, the greatest man in Scotland, our Justice-General, and the only born lawyer I ever heard, listening to the piping old body, as though it had all been a revelation, grave and respectful.[7]

Very evidently Stevenson missed something vital here. His novelist's eye caught the details of gloves and face. But the major thing may have eluded him, as it often did. We cannot go back to the Edinburgh church on a Sabbath morning in 1875. We do not know "old Mr. Torrence." But we do know that, times without number, a "piping old body" has *been* a revelation. And it may well be that the "greatest man in Scotland" saw what Stevenson missed, that before him was a revelation of something that lay beyond the "old body," that the man was an incandescence. It has been so. The wonder of it is all wrapped up in the words, "He that receiveth you receiveth me."

II. THE MINISTER HIMSELF

IF THE PREACHER IS NOT THE SOURCE OF HIS MESSAGE BUT A CHANNEL FOR God, then he himself is a primary matter—his inner life; the flavor, the color, the fire, the music, that make him himself; his capacity to absorb spiritual truth and experience, which will determine his capacity to transmit them.

This whole basic realm lies outside the focus of this volume. And here, as earlier, the indulgence is craved of stressing with insistence, that the deliberately limited field of the minister in his workshop, his craft of every sort, is a distinctly secondary one. Far more important than what the minister can do about his sermons is what he can do about himself. In the present chapter effort is made to express in brief compass the place of the preacher, not as an artisan of sermons, but as a personality so tempered that he may be an unobstructed channel of communication. Here also is a swift glimpse of the increasingly complex and difficult settings in which the minister is placed in these years. Even the most hurried glance at the demands on the minister's personality, mind, and energy is more than a bit terrifying. Some of these demands are noted here, not to induce the paralyzing luxury of self-pity, but rather that clear-eyed look at the task for which Jesus pleaded so earnestly with his disciples: "For which of you, intending to build a tower, sitteth not down first, and counteth the cost, whether he have sufficient to finish it? Lest haply, after he hath laid the foundation, and is not able to finish it, all that behold it begin to mock him, saying, This man began to build, and was not able to finish." [1]

1. The minister's own religious experience is the incomparable source of preaching. It is the prelude to preaching, the sort of prelude which Jesus gave to his own disciples. His first word to them was not

"Go" but "Come." He said to them, "Come ye . . . apart . . . and rest a while." Stand where I stand. See what I see. Hear what I hear. Jesus' prelude to preaching—the same yesterday, today, and forever—is, "Freely ye have received, freely give." Oscar Wilde once said a true thing about the preacher, without having any idea of what he was saying. It is one of the many ironies of his life that his cleverest epigrams, set off like verbal fireworks, have deep and permanent meanings of which he was no more conscious than if he were doing automatic writing. Here is one: "I have put my genius into my life; I have put only my talent into my books." It was a sorry "genius" that Wilde put into his life. But the order of importance is correct, an order which no preacher can ever dare forget. Life is more than meat—and more than sermons. The best of one's life, his genius, must go into living, into receiving, into being. After that priority has been granted, talent comes in for its legitimate contribution. Among the many things which preaching shares with painting is the truth that the main thing about an artist is not his brushwork but his personality, in the deepest sense of the word.

Robert Frost has traced the source of a poem to its secret springs in the poet's own experience. "A poem is never a put-up job," he writes. "It begins as a lump in the throat, a sense of wrong, a homesickness, a lovesickness." [2] Granted that this is not the last word to be said about poetry. It is at least a true word. And is it not true of preaching as well as poetry? A sermon is never a "put-up job"—if it is a real communication of life through life. If it does not begin, in Frost's phrase, with a lump, it is too smooth. One of our present-day poets, Josephine W. Johnson, in a poem picturing vividly a first need of life in a sophisticated world, has written, without intention, a prayer for the modern preacher—for that first need of his life, an amazed wonder of vision:

> This is the trouble with us all:
> That we see under the shell, and we see under the inner shell,
> And we see under what lies under what lies under,
> And we cannot look at each other without laughing.

. . . .

Grant that some shadow of awe,
—Some gold fog of marvel—
Cover for once this terrible sun of our eyes![3]

What a first word for an age prone to bow down at the shrine of psychology and technique! John knew that "gold fog of marvel"— "Behold, what manner of love"!

This primacy of a minister's experience is all the more to be stressed because of the terrifying truth that the ministry is distinguished from every other profession by the fact that it must be an incarnation. The minister must not only *do;* he must *be.* Our gospel is that of an incarnation; our practice must be an incarnation—infinitely less than that Word which became flesh, but real notwithstanding. Unless there is in the preacher a word which becomes flesh, there is no redemption.

2. The variety and magnitude of the demands on a minister's mind, heart, time, and strength expose him to the danger of leading a minimum spiritual life himself in a time of maximum demand. The need for inner replenishment is a recurring one inherent in the very nature of the minister's work. He is to be a forth-giver, a giver of faith, hope, and courage. He may be so burdened that there is no renewal. The yawning pit which Paul discloses is always at the side of the road: "Lest . . . when I have preached to others, I myself should be a castaway." That danger comes not only in spite of having preached to others but, ironically, because of it. For in the process of coming face to face with a truth in experience or of catching sight of some gleaming word from the Bible or other literature, he may not take it for its heartening or rebuke to himself; he may miss all that and merely give a collector's chortle, "What a good idea for a sermon!" Thus he may become like a town baker who himself starves to death.

Consider, for instance, the preacher's need for inner capital—for opulence, really—in the one matter of bringing to people courage for living. There is and will be a literally immeasurable need in multitudes of people for courage for living, for one day, for one year, five years, twenty-five years. Every pastor knows the truth of Chekhov's word: "To keep another going is a million times more tiring than to keep oneself going." That is true in spiritual mechanics as well as in

18

physical, though the "million times harder" is poetic license. One of the supreme "preacher's parables" among the parables of Jesus is that of the friend at midnight, with its haunting confession of inner bankruptcy: "A friend of mine in his journey is come to me, and I have nothing to set before him." Every Sunday friends, known or unknown, come to the preacher from journeys, often hard and rough—journeys through the week that have led through a dark woods or a dry desert —and without a renewed larder he may have to say, "I have nothing to set before them." That tragedy of empty shelves may accompany all the marks of outward success.

3. The minister must have some resources to repair the constant attrition of life. We have heard much from the military standpoint of a "war of attrition." The minister's whole life is a war of attrition. It is the bearing down of repetition, a major danger of a calling which is full of recurring items. The mind and temper are worn down by the attrition of the same thing over and over again. There are many things a man can stand with equanimity once and twice; but when they occur the third time, to say nothing of the five-hundredth time, he is grieved, his spirits are frayed, worn down by the friction of attrition. The minister has his being in a state of attrition. So much of his life, if he holds to his task in season and out of season, follows the pattern of that figure of Greek mythology Sisyphus. Sisyphus rolled a heavy stone up to the top of a hill, only to have it roll down again and the whole labor start anew. It gives us a picture of the Rev. Mr. Sisyphus rolling the stone up through the week to the hilltop of Sunday, then starting at the bottom again on Monday. No wonder that a spirit of futility develops. Vachel Lindsay has given a sharp and painful picture of the wearing down of the spirit that comes to a preacher, although he was writing of his experience as an itinerant lecturer. "You see, Louis," he wrote to Louis Untermeyer, "it is so easy; the house half full, the check promptly paid, everybody pleasant, and nobody giving a damn." [4] It might be a picture of the eleven o'clock Sunday morning service, with the one exception that often the check is not so promptly paid. The wearing down of the spirit through repeated effort which seems to have the pall of a comparative futility over it, is something the preacher must be ready to meet.

But there is an attrition of spirit which comes from deeper causes than these. The minister of today who has any sensitiveness at all is exposed to the despondency coming from the calamity that has over-taken so much to which he has given his life and which he holds most dear. The highest seems to be at the mercy of the lowest. He must work in a "world he never made"; and his mind would be deadened if, occasionally at least, he did not have a swift wonder whether God ever made it. He has worked for peace, to find his world engulfed in a war whose waste runs beyond the bounds of human thought. He has worked for the extension of human welfare, to find himself between one world-wide depression and another that looms ahead. To many observers, the forces of economic and social reaction seem to gather strength even as the need grows for generous and farsighted action. The influence which the life and work of a parish may bring to bear on international events seems dim and uncertain. All that opens the door to a numbing chill of futility. Dr. Albert Schweitzer has a notable word for this part of a minister's experience. Writing from Africa on his return from his first furlough, contrasting the partial chaos and breakdown of his work there with the zest and joyful hope in which the work opened, he says, "The prose of Africa is heavy on me, and it will be a long time before it passes." The prose of the world, and of the parish, lies heavy on the minister.

Some may strongly deplore what may seem to be black funeral wreaths over the preceding paragraphs. They may sound like a sigh of defeatism, or enervating self-pity. Yet it is hard to see how any necessary scrutiny, even though very fragmentary, can be made of the demands on the minister's mind and spirit without facing with level eyes these liabilities. True, there is a luxury of despair which must be resisted. There is a perverse titillation of the mind in the abandonment to despair, in saying with Shakespeare's Richard II:

> For God's sake, let us sit upon the ground
> And tell sad stories of the death of kings.

That is a Black Death for a minister or for anyone. The demands on the preacher—the ups and downs of a parish Sisyphus, the attrition, the lurking mood of futility—are not here listed to induce any clerical

"Woe is me." They are introduced merely as evidence in the witness box to the truth that the minister's first equipment for preaching, beside which all else is trivial, is replenished resources in his own life and fresh, firsthand experience of the riches of the grace of God. Mr. Chesterton has said that our world is full of people who "know the last word about everything and the first word about nothing." It is a bad state to be in. Techniques may be a last word about preaching. But the first word, the indispensable word, is that grace of God by which the inward man is renewed day by day and out of whose fullness the mouth speaks.

III. SERMONS ARE TOOLS

A NY DETAILED CONSIDERATION OF THE PREPARATION OF SERMONS IS FELT
by some to be a very minor affair, especially when the urgency of
the preacher's message is felt compellingly. This is particularly true
in years when the need of a devastated world for a redeeming word
and act makes the preaching of that word a momentous thing.

An entering student at a theological seminary at the beginning of
the second World War expressed that opinion frankly when he asked
the Dean to be excused from taking a required course in preaching.
"Monkeying with sermon outlines," he graciously explained, "and all
that one-two-three stuff is fiddling while Rome burns." And who will
say that he was entirely wrong? Certainly Rome was burning. And
just as truly any kind of "fiddling" is not only a slim refuge but an
impertinence in a crisis.

If any apology for attention to preaching skills were needed, it is
found in the fact that it is just when the compelling urgency for
getting a thing done is at its greatest that the concrete means for its
accomplishment assume the greatest importance. This is true in any
realm. Begin with football. A team comes within a few yards of the
goal posts. In the minds of thousands of spectators on the grandstand
is one thought and in their throats one shout, "Touchdown!" A fine
idea, but just how is it to be done? Touchdowns are not achieved by
shouting; they do not grow on grandstands; they come from acquired
skills, from the grueling repetitions of exercises on hot September and
October afternoons. Are there any techniques good enough to do the
job? And which is the one to use? It can all be put into a formula:
The importance of specialized skill varies directly with the urgency
for accomplishing a great achievement.

Look at it in medicine. A person is desperately sick. The sands are running out. The family and friends wring their hands and beg, "Oh, doctor, do something!" Again a fine idea. But just what? It is not a matter of urgency for realizing the crisis or of the vehemence of the desire to save. It is a matter of the resources of technique. The need is for a past history of what the theological student just mentioned would put under the general head of "fiddling." The long, tiresome hours of clinic and laboratory, the endless repetition and experiment and practice, the skilled co-ordination of hand and eye—these are called for.

Come into the very field of preaching, that of public speaking. Recall the truly appalling urgency which rested on Mr. Winston Churchill in June, 1940. An imminent invasion, the issue of which no one knew but all could fear, placed upon him the necessity of playing the role of an Atlas, of getting under a whole nation and literally lifting it up to a new level of fortitude and faith and the will to endure. That is what he did. He did it in real part by a workman's skill with words. There were other elements, of course, in that miracle of 1940—the character of the British people themselves and the personal stamina of Mr. Churchill. But to a large degree Mr. Churchill could bring what the urgency of the crisis demanded—the superb technique of a man who had worked for a lifetime with words. The Nazis had talked much of secret weapons, but England had two secret weapons which the Nazis did not know. One was Gibbon. The other was Macaulay. Mr. Churchill had learned a craftsman's way with words and sentences from both of them. When he was a young army officer in India, he gave long hours to both of these favorite authors. They helped to give a rhythm to his speech which in a real way matched the rhythm of the pulse in men's bodies. They helped to impart a lapidary precision to his fingers when he wrote. When the British came to "their finest hour," they responded to a technique adequate to the urgency. Anyone could have shouted, "Let us be brave." It was the artist who could etch an unforgettable picture in the minds of millions, the picture of a defending army giving ground but never giving up: "We shall defend our island, whatever the cost may be, we shall fight on the landing grounds, we shall fight in the fields and

23

in the streets, we shall fight in the hills; we shall never surrender."[1]
It was the artist who lifted a nation to its feet.

Come up to the highest illustration of technique. A long time ago
in Palestine there was need for a truth to be spoken with carrying
power. Here was the situation: "Now, all the publicans and sinners
were drawing near unto him to hear him. And both the Pharisees
and the scribes murmured, saying, This man receiveth sinners and
eateth with them." [2] That "murmur" was like the noise of a sea; it
has resounded in all times and all centuries, the harsh murmur of self-
righteousness and a loveless contempt. There was need for a crushing
rebuttal. Anyone could have said, "You ought not to show scorn or
indifference to the erring." That would not have carried ten feet or
ten years. Then the supreme artist spoke, painting truth in a picture
that will last as long as time: "What man of you, having a hundred
sheep," and "A certain man had two sons." The common people heard
him gladly for many reasons, but one reason was that his words were
shaped with the consummate skill of an artist. Perhaps to some it
may seem less than reverence to think of the Son of Man as an artist.
But if that is left out, one factor in his many-sided personality is left
out.

So today the very urgency for bringing a saving word to a perishing
world, engulfed in disaster through a highly organized skepticism
concerning Jesus as a guide for life, brings an intensified demand for
the most effective technique possible as a precision tool for the message.
The sensitive hearing of this demand has to be preserved amid the
din of world calamity, when the very capacity to feel the woe of humanity tends to make all else seem insignificant. Hawthorne, in the
midst of the Civil War, gave a sharp expression of the feeling which
sympathetic response to a great convulsion brings to the worker in
ideas and words. He wrote:

The present, the immediate, and the actual have proved too potent for
me. It takes away not only my scanty faculty, but even my desire for imaginative composition, but leaves me content to scatter a thousand peaceful
fantasies upon the hurricane that is sweeping us along with it, possibly
into a limbo where our nation with its polity may be as literally the fragments of a shattered dream as my unwritten romance.[3]

24

That was an ultimate blue to one who watched and felt his country's agony in 1864. And every minister whose mind is a sensitive plate, as it ought to be, to the tensions and fears of his generation knows that feeling of the relative unimportance of any skill. In these years the same trinity, "the present, the immediate, and the actual," is potent with us. But about it there are some valid things to be said. For one thing, the preacher is not concerned merely with what Hawthorne was impelled to throw to the winds, "imaginative composition" and "peaceful fantasies." He is the servant of a word relevant to every occasion. God and his will, as well as "block busters," are also "the present, the immediate, and the actual." We may likewise remember that in the midst of the vast mechanical upheaval of the Civil War one of the most powerful forces at work was the skill and art of the spoken and written word of Abraham Lincoln. Never since they were first written has there been a more overwhelming urgency to the words, "Study to shew thyself approved." For without a mastered craft, words become dull tools, just the instruments of a stale and vague rehash of generalities.

Of course, a caution is needed all along through these chapters, one which should be repeated at the risk of causing weariness. There is a very great danger of placing far too much reliance on the sermon in itself and alone. A sermon is like a brick: it fulfills its function only as it is placed in relationship, in a structure. On this point Gaius Glenn Atkins speaks with his usual wisdom: "Preaching is having a hard time just now because too heavy a burden has been put upon it in our evangelized Protestantism; preaching was never meant to carry out the program of an institutional church; it was never meant to do the whole work of making religion real." [4] That remembrance must be the backdrop of all thinking about sermons; otherwise there is a fatal distortion. Preaching, separated from its roots and accompaniment in the life of a parish and community, becomes an aerial plant with a faint color and deficient life. The sermon has true meaning when it is seen as one of many agencies of the spiritual life. When it alone is used to build, the building sags. George Bernard Shaw once drew a picture of the variety of a minister's tasks, a picture reflecting scorn and what was intended to be a withering sarcasm. "The average clergyman," he wrote, "is an official who makes his living by christening babies, marrying adults, conducting a ritual, and making the best he can, when he has any conscience about it, of a certain routine of school superintendence, district visiting, and organization of alms-giving, which does not touch Christianity at any point except the point of the tongue." There is, of course a point in Shaw's picture, even though the details of a minister's work seem to be assembled merely as a "build-up" for the sarcastic turn of the last words. However, Shaw does something he does not realize; he gives an impressive picture of the variegated demands on a preacher and the wide-spreading range of the life and work of a parish. His very words, so far from showing a parish touching Christianity only at the point of the tongue, portray it as touching life helpfully at many vital spots—truly an unintentional picture of the channels of service through which the Christian impulses of a congregation flow, of which preaching is just one agency in co-operation.

To the stress on the need for a dedicated workmanship—a need which is intensified with the urgency of a world situation—there must be kept open the other side of the ledger to preserve a balance. That is, the very real dangers to a preacher's potential effectiveness which lie in a preoccupation with technique must be kept in high visibility. For technique, when it ceases to remain a servant and becomes a master, when it ceases to be a means and aspires, often with a fatal success, to become an end in itself, has slain ten thousand preachers. Browning's familiar words may serve as a motto for this needed warning, a very lighthouse set amid hidden reefs:

> There burns a truer light of God in them,
> In their vexed beating stuffed and stopped-up brain,
> Heart, or whate'er else, than goes on to prompt
> This low-pulsed forthright craftsman's hand of mine.
> Their works drop groundward, but themselves, I know,
> Reach many a time a heaven that's shut to me.[5]

It can all be put into one sentence, certainly worth remembrance. It is this: Jesus went from the carpenter shop into the ministry; there is danger that the preacher may reverse the process and go from the ministry into the carpenter shop. That is, he may become less and less concerned with the high commission felt in the opening words of Jesus in Capernaum, "The Spirit of the Lord is upon me, because he hath anointed me to preach the gospel to the poor," and more and more concerned with the T square, the slide rule, the hammer and nails, of a literary carpenter shop.

The histories of all the arts fairly shout over the centuries this danger of decadence when an interest in form displaces content and soul. None shouts louder than the history of preaching. This degeneration has been pointed out often in the realms of painting and music. For instance, Greek drama, German music, and Italian painting have often served to illustrate the risks of art. They all started with a strong religious impulse. They gradually acquired a technique adequate to express it. Then the technique became an end in itself, the religious impulse was lost, and art declined into triviality. English preaching in the eighteenth century is another striking example. Preaching can become, and often has become, a classic tragedy in four acts—the deep religious impulse, the acquired technique, the means becoming an end, triviality. Chesterton's lines might well be given a place on every parsonage study wall:

> When folks have lost the dance and song
> Women clean useless pots the whole day long.

How much pot cleaning there has been as a prosaic substitute for the dance and song of a herald of good news!

For a chief concern with technique becomes so insidiously a substitute for the real thing in any art. Walt Whitman said it crushingly when he remarked to Thomas Bailey Aldrich, a fair representative of a time of poetic triviality, "I like your tinkles, Tom." That is what they were, mostly. That word "tinkles" rings a bell in the mind. It echoes the very word in the King James translation of the thirteenth chapter of First Corinthians, "tinkling cymbal." That strange mixture of mingled wisdom and exhibitionism, George Moore, expressed the same danger when he wrote of Guy de Maupassant's stories that they were merely "carved cherry stones." Whatever that may lack as a criticism of De Maupassant, it has a terrible appositeness as a descrip-

tion of many sermons at the eleven o'clock Sunday service—a display
of "carved cherry stones," skill diligently applied to miniature themes
or content. A similar figure appears in Van Wyck Brooks's description
of a Boston painter—Appleton, of the age of the epigoni, or successors.
He had studied in Italy, but "his little talent had petered out in a
passion for painting pebbles, which he gave his friends to use as paper-
weights." [6] That is a sentence to remember. It has the same alliteration
as "Peter Piper picked a peck of pickled peppers," but carries a bit
more significance. "A passion for painting pebbles." We may well ask
on our knees, "Lord, is it I?"

A perverted devotion at the shrine of method will take the place of
genuine creation. Hasn't it done so with Sinclair Lewis, to mention
one of scores of examples that spring to mind? A talent that once
created, dwindling to a remarkable skill of caricature repeated like a
vaudeville artist doing the same juggling act over and over again.
Rodin, whose biography merits so richly the attention of a preacher,
traveled in the other direction. Replying to one who asked what ideal
he was striving for in art, he replied: "When I was young I strove for
beauty in form and line. What I seek for now is life." A true progress
to artistic maturity. So we may, in all high seriousness, listen to the
severe word of Jesus, applied to the danger of technique: "If thy hand
cause thee to stumble, cut it off." If the skill of the hand displaces or
obscures the message of the apostle—cut it off. For "it is good for thee
to enter into life maimed, rather than having thy two hands to go
into hell." [7] For a consuming interest in doing a "nice little turn" in
the pulpit may lead to that ultimate bankruptcy so well described by
Carl Van Doren, writing of the forgotten Clyde Fitch, an acknowledged master of dramatic technique in the 1890's. He had a fine command of the technique of the drama, brilliant wit, fine imagination.
Only one thing was lacking: "He had little or nothing to say." [8]
Shakespeare said it all, as he frequently did, in putting into the mouth
of Hamlet's mother addressing Polonius, "More matter, with less art."
Every preacher should be a pair of brothers, Moses and Aaron—Moses
with the message of God in his heart and mind, Aaron with the
skills of speech.

Preaching is frequently, and often validly, criticized for lack of

28

emotional daring. There are no indiscretions, no lift from the ground, just a careful pedestrian trudge. In a later chapter we shall look at one of the dangers lurking along the path of even very useful life-situation preaching—preaching which is liable to become so largely psychological, good counsel on the management of life. It may be skillfully constructed and lack any powers of flight. True writing, says Christopher Morley must have the power "to set fire to that damp sponge called the brain." It must have a certain lyric ecstasy that is not the gift of any literary artisan's technique. H. H. Asquith, the British prime minister, said once in explanation of going to hear Silvester Horne so often, "He had a fire in his belly." Not very elegant words, perhaps, but certainly biblical and clear. No one who heard Silvester Horne deliver that last glorious swan song, completed a few days before his death, his Beecher Lectures on Preaching at Yale, *The Romance of Preaching,* will have any doubt about the "fire." "Poetry," says one critic, "comes from anger, hunger, and dismay." That is far too narrow to serve as an explanation of the genesis of poetry. But it does chart the precedence of a genuine emotion over technique.

Of course, emotion, like all powerful things, carries its own dangers with it. One of these is that fervor as a chief reliance opens the door to insincerity. It gets to be like a drug—heighten the dose, if necessary, to secure the desired effect. Joseph Conrad has given a classic analysis of the process:

In order to move others deeply we must deliberately allow ourselves to be carried away beyond the bounds of our normal sensibility—innocently enough, perhaps, and of necesstiy, like an actor who raises his voice on the stage above the pitch of natural conversation—but still we have to do that. And surely this is no great sin. But the danger lies in the writer becoming the victim of his own exaggeration, losing the exact notion of sincerity, and in the end coming to despise truth itself as something too cold, too blunt for his purpose—as, in fact, not good enough for his insistent emotion.

Another druglike danger of reliance on emotion is that it becomes a deceptive substitute for hard work.

So there are dangers on both sides. Indeed, much of a preacher's lifelong course is a cruise in the Strait of Messina, a tacking passage between Scylla and Charybdis. The navigation calls for courage and skill. But that is one of the risks which make it an exciting voyage. Let no fear of the jutting rock of the false use of emotion or the danger to one's integrity of an impassioned ardor keep a man from the employment of that indispensable means of waking the dead, a headlong expression of passionate conviction. For, after all, the preacher, if he is really doing his job, delivering his message and not conducting some highly original fantastic legerdemain, is not saying anything new. The needs that he meets are old; the remedies that he brings, if he is not a charlatan, are old. That master of prose in our time, E. C. Montague, puts this with pertinence: "The minds of Vergil, Sophocles, Shakespeare and Dante and Goethe seem in the main to have brooded over just those staple things that have elicited less memorable expressions from Smith, Jones and Brown. What distinguishes a real artist is *intensity* of reaction." [9]

What a preacher brings to a people is a personal intensity which results from being possessed by a Person and a gospel, an available reserve of sheer intensity of perception and emotion. What shall it profit a man to gain a whole world of method and lose his own intensity of grasp and giving?

IV. AN ART IS A BAND OF MUSIC

ONLY A SMALL PART OF THE FIELD OF THE PREACHER'S CRAFTSMANSHIP has been traveled over when we become sharply aware of the pitfalls of a distorted preoccupation with any technique. Personal and professional calamity impends when a means becomes an end. Yet we dare not forget that the end depends on the means. A consideration of ends without attention to means is pure sentimentalism.

What often fails to receive attention at anything like its true value is the recognition of what a deep and lifelong interest in the technical side of his art will do for a preacher, in the sustaining of enthusiasm and vivacity, in preventing the calamity which has overtaken so many preachers when the toil of sermon making becomes a chore, "stale as the remainder biscuit after a voyage."

Robert Louis Stevenson well expressed this preserving function of an interest in art: "An art is a band of music." Who ever proved that up to the hilt more than he? It was a resource that even a lifetime of fighting hemorrhages could not deplete. The band of music still played in the last days; and it was not a death march when, an exile in the South Pacific, his voice completely gone, he learned the deaf-and-dumb alphabet so that he could dictate a last novel to Isobel Strong. It is right at that point of a workman's joy in his job that one of the most significant dividing lines runs between ministers. We read in the Book of Acts of Paul's meeting a certain group who had never heard of the Holy Ghost. There is a true parallel in the company of preachers who have never so much as heard of another holy spirit, the thing that keeps a true maker of any sort—artist, musician, sculptor, architect, skilled artisan—renewed in the inward man—an interest in the craft itself, in the overcoming of the particular obstacles, in the

31

creation of beauty and of the form that fulfills the function. That will carry a man through the inevitably recurring low tides of the spirit when even the sense of the presence of God recedes.

An art is a band of music. Without its accompaniment on the professional march many a man in the pulpit moves with the heavy, mechanical trudge of Kipling's soldier—"Boots—boots—boots—boots—movin' up an' down again."

Without a truly re-creating interest in the technique of creation the minister may be haunted with a dire apparition following him: "I have a little shadow that goes in and out with me"—the shadow of next Sunday's sermon. He may even feel,

> And my soul from out that shadow
> . . . .
> Shall be lifted—nevermore!

We are assured, "Ye shall know the truth, and the truth shall make you free." It is also true that a serious interest in the practice of art, restlessly experimenting to find a better medium and method, will make a preacher free—free from a fatal ennui that can strike at the mind and soul.

That is the glory of teaching, found—not rarely, thank God, but often—in a teacher whose interest in his professional task is a life preserver of the spirit, whose reward is not in any prestige or money but in the thing in itself—the miracle of communication. Bliss Perry has given a memorable picture of a great teacher transfigured by that absorbing interest, Louis Agassiz: "Louis Agassiz, whose gift for research was doubted by no one, but who was never happier than when he was standing in front of a blackboard in a crossroads schoolhouse before an audience of farmers, armed with a clam-shell and a piece of chalk."[1] Shining armor—a clamshell and a piece of chalk! In that picture change the country schoolhouse to a country church, leave the audience of farmers just the same, substitute a Bible for the clamshell—and you have the preacher, sustained not by any insignificant paraphernalia of his profession but by the thing in itself.

For it is only through a maker's joy that one comes into a strange mystery of preaching: its excitement in the effort of accomplishing an intricate task. The more lethargic and unpromising the audience, the greater the excitement of the preacher. It is just "the given" with which he has to deal. A sermon is like a wrestling match, or rather two wrestling matches, first with an idea and then with an audience, with the absorbed tenseness of those first moments which will determine whether one can get an effective hold on idea or on people.

There is a further mystery about preaching, a providence of God without which we would all droop and faint, in that blessed illusion that if we do a creditable job one time out of twenty, we are buoyed up by the feeling that this one achievement is our true form. A merciful cloud blots out the nineteen misfires. That same joyous illusion operates notably in golf. A man may go around the course with a sum total of a hundred more-or-less dub shots. And then comes the miracle —a clean, hard drive which sends the ball singing on its flight, making a celestial music to which only a golfer's ear is attuned. Then he lifts his head, squares his shoulders, feels the equivalent of a *Te Deum,* and says, "Now I am hitting my stride. That is my true form!" And the memory of that one shot puts to flight any painful recollection of the ninety and nine hooks and slices and divot digging. That sustaining mystery of preaching—call it illusion if you will—is a special grace by which the preacher is enabled to obey the command, "Be not weary in well doing." But it is present only when one has a craftsman's interest in his tools and tasks.

This preserving interest in an increasing skill is not at all unrelated to the content of the message. It is inseparable from a real feeling of the momentousness of the message. Henry James put this concisely in his dogma that "what is merely stated is never really presented." That ought never to be absent from a minister's mind and conscience. If the difference between those two verbs "stated" and "presented" could be clearly seen and strongly felt, the persuasive power of ten thousand pulpits would be vastly increased in effectiveness. It is so easy to "state"; it is so hard to "present." Merely stating a truth, from "Honesty is the best policy" all the way up or down the scale of acknowledged axioms, can be done in one's sleep, and is frequently so done. The soporific qualities of merely "stating" surpass those of laudanum. But to *present* a truth, a persuasion, a warning, or an appeal; to

33

sharpen its form so that it can etch itself on the mind; to give it the mobility of surprise, so that it gets past the guards which the minds of a congregation raise; to breathe into words the very breath of life so that they become a living soul—that is so difficult as to deserve the toil of years. One of the frankest personal revelations of the cost and reward of a command of words is that of J. B. Priestley in his filling in of the phrase "engrossed by an art." "The difference between us," he writes, referring to some early fellow practitioners of writing,

was not in ability, but in the fact that while at heart they did not really much care about authorship, but merely toyed with the fascinating idea of it, I cared like blazes. And I suspect that in any form of art, it is this caring like blazes, while you are still young, that counts. Because, you care and the dream never fades, other things, looking like those gifts of the gods, are added unto you. The very passion of the heart draws power. In some mysterious fashion, I suspect, you orientate your being so that such gifts as observation, invention and imagination are pulled your way. This explains why certain actors, from the Irving of yesterday to the Laughton of to-day, who begin with the gravest natural disadvantages, with obvious weaknesses of appearance, gait, voice, have ended as masters of their art. A mere desire for the rewards, no matter how constant and burning that desire may be, will not do the trick. You have to be fascinated from the first by the art itself, engrossed and spellbound, and not simply dazzled by the deceptively superior life of its successful practitioners. In this matter you have, in short, to be pure in heart before you can be blessed.[2]

The goal, the effective presentation of a true word which can set men on their feet, even when its setting is of the simplest, is so great as to deserve any extent of discipline and sacrifice. That goal is movingly pictured in David Morton's conception of how great a thing a poem may be; it applies as truly to a sermon:

> To make a small sound
> In a large place,
> So that, for miles around,
> It being of such grace,
>
> All other sound is stilled,
> Though a moment only,

And all the air is filled
With the grave and lonely

Listening to a word
Wherein is drowned
All else, and nothing heard
Save this small sound.[3]

All of this, of course, compels the enlargement and deepening of
that word "craft" as commonly used. It must include the "spirit in
which" as well as "the means by which" a given article is produced.
That was true of skilled handworkers, silversmiths, pottery makers—
of many artisans. It is supremely true of the artisan of the words of life.

Now to conclude this chapter on a very practical level. The consideration to follow does not move on the heights of prophecy, but it
grazes closely a matter of great concern to every preacher—his possible
length of service in a parish. One legendary figure of literature ought
to be well remembered by every preacher. She is Scheherazade, the
ingenious raconteur who told the stories which make up the *Arabian
Nights*. The origin of the stories is traced to the pleasant custom of
a caliph who married many brides successively and always beheaded
them the next morning. Finally he married Scheherazade, who was
very evidently much more than a "glamour girl." She had wit and
resourcefulness. She told her lord and temporary husband on her
wedding night a story of such enthralling interest and suspense that
the execution was postponed for a day that the caliph might learn
"what happened next." The next installment was equally gripping
and unfinished. So the execution was again deferred, to be followed
by a thousand and one nights of storytelling. A life preserved by the
sheer interest of a story! That is not a cynical picture of the situation
of the Protestant minister. His life is prolonged in a parish, the writ
of execution is stayed by the pulpit-supply committee, the overhanging
sword is held back, by the sheer interest of the preacher's story in the
pulpit. Character, sympathy, faithfulness all count. But in so many
churches the execution, in the form of a desire for a new minister, is
postponed through the minister's skill as a Scheherazade, the sustaining of the desire to listen again. On the other hand, many a pulpit

committee, growing tired of a twice-told tale, stirred to no expectation by the plot of the story, has ordered the execution at dawn.

Van Wyck Brooks has put this true state of affairs into words of personal confession: "Every day I begin my work with the same old feeling, that I am on trial for my life and will probably not be acquitted." [4] The minister is truly on trial for his life, and acquittal will come partly through a retention and increase of skilled workmanship. Let him who in jaunty complacency has no fears aroused by the story of Scheherazade remember the word of Joseph Conrad, "The stuff that comes easy is dull reading." And we may add an ecclesiastical postscript, "dull hearing."

One of the priceless equipments of a preacher is a limp, of the sort that Jacob got from wrestling with an angel. Toiling at a craft with intensity is wrestling with an angel of the Lord.

V. THE IMPORTANCE OF PREACHING

"HOW SHALL THEY BELIEVE IN HIM WHOM THEY HAVE NOT HEARD? AND how shall they hear without a preacher?"[1]

These words of St. Paul's express an early estimate of the importance of preaching, words which might well be dusted off and traced again in illuminated letters. It is a matter which is often taken for granted by both clergy and laity. But taking anything for granted is always equivalent to laying it out for burial. There is recurring need, never more intensified than today, to be newly seized with a sense of the indispensable place of preaching, that it may exorcise the evil spirit of apology which so easily besets us and dims the native resolution of both pulpit and pew. So much in our years of world convulsion conspires to induce an inferiority complex in the preacher. A periodical recently published a cartoon of a little man on a parade ground, with a gigantic tank in front of him and another executing a flanking movement, apparently with him as the objective. Under the drawing was the legend, "I feel sort of out of things." It was not surprising. In a day when great impersonal forces are driving down the main avenues of life, it is but natural that many in the church should be oppressed by a feeling of being off on a side street speaking in a muffled voice that cannot be heard above the din of engines and clashing armor. When the church calls to this onrush of a mechanized world, "Is it nothing to you, all ye that pass by?" the answer is, quite audibly, "Nothing."

But that is not all of it. This feeling of comparative futility, of being reduced to a "bit" part in the world's drama, is not due entirely to the great preoccupation of war. It existed before the war. It comes also from the pressure of the bewildering variety of the assault on the senses and attention which the modern world makes. Coleridge's ancient mariner felt the competition of distracting noise:

> The Wedding-Guest here beat his breast,
> For he heard the loud bassoon.

The bassoon has been particularly loud in recent years. Often it has been a literal, physical bassoon, swing music, calling youth like the flute of the Pied Piper. Always it has been a figurative bassoon, whose notes beat on the ears and minds of an audience which a speaker is trying to hold with a story of great matters.

The preacher must be baptized into a new conviction of the importance of preaching in a world increasingly distracted. He needs Paul's overpowering sense, expressed in the passage just quoted, of being the trustee of a word of salvation in a world increasingly damned. The relationship of that word to our world was strikingly drawn in blazing letters over a hundred years ago by a German Jew who saw with a penetrating eye, Heinrich Heine. He wrote in 1834: "Should that subduing talisman, the cross, ever break, then the old stone gods will rise from the long-forgotten ruins and rub the dust of a thousand years from their eyes, and Thor, leaping to life with his giant hammer, will crush the Gothic cathedrals." Was ever a prophecy more literally and tragically fulfilled? The cross did break for multitudes in Europe, and Thor crushed the Gothic cathedrals. That sentence of Heine's might well be carved on a plaque to be set in the rebuilt cathedrals of Coventry and Cologne. For it affirms the basic moral and spiritual reality of the world. It affirms that the proclaimer of "the talisman of the cross" is not marooned off on a side road but is in the very center of all the world's conflict and traffic. But if there is no undebatable compulsion to proclaim God's imperishable word, there will just be a rear-end action in a defeatist mood.

Every great movement in history has been prepared for and partly, at least, carried through by preaching—the beginning of the Christian church, the Crusades, the abolition of slavery, the Reformation, the Evangelical Revival, the labor movement, Marxian Communism, German Nazism. Not, surely, always Christian preaching, but preaching as a powerful instrument. For years we have been living in a world noisy with sermons. They blare through the radio, they shriek from headlines, they are dropped by the ton as leaflets over cities. They often go under the head of "psychological warfare"; but they are preaching, arguments, persuasions, appeals for conversion. They are major instruments. "Ideas are weapons." One fear that grips the hearts of multitudes today in America is that while possessing an amazing effectiveness of technical achievement in war—in the heaven's above, the earth beneath, and the waters under the earth—the United States may fail in the realm of the warfare of ideas, fail to sound any saving word in a doomed world.

Preaching, if it is to have adequate depth and height and breadth, must be theological preaching. Indeed, there is no other kind that is much more than a respectable embellishment of a comfortable life.

This has been expressed with rugged force in the challenge to the church: "If you have anything peculiarly Christian to say at this hour, for God's sake say it! But if you can do nothing but mouth over the slogans of the street corner, or the usual banalities of the Chamber of Commerce, for God's sake, keep still!" Those are rough words, but so were many of the words of Paul, and of Jesus. If preaching is not basically theological, not the proclamation of a God who has acted, but merely an anthology of moral maxims, it soon comes to resemble the description of Matthew Arnold as "a mournful evangelist who had somehow contrived to mislay his gospel." It is seductively easy to mislay a gospel. The old distinction, made again and again, is always valid and of first importance, that preaching should be a sector of truth and not an arc. An arc is a portion of the circumference of a circle; a sector is a V-shaped wedge in a circle, which includes a portion of the circumference but goes by radii to the center. "Arc preaching" deals with a segment of the circumference of life; "sector preaching" includes circumference but goes to the center. A true, as well as clever, description of preaching that stays on the circumference is found in the oft-quoted remark of Arnold Lunn: "There is no market for sermons on the text: God so loved the world that he inspired a certain Jew to inform his contemporaries that there was a great deal to be said for loving one's neighbors." Paul did "sector" preaching; he dealt with the varied circumferences of life in the

39

Judean and Greco-Roman world—family life, the care of children, eating and drinking, the treatment of slaves—but from that circumference he drove a wedge of thought deep to the center, to the unveiling of God in Christ.

No mere arc on the circumference of life today, no matter how surely drawn, is adequate in a world waiting for the relating of life to central reality, to God. Many strange voices outside the pulpit, often clear outside the church, are expressing in clear words that need. Listen to two of them, representing a larger company. Here is William Rose Benét, the poet: "It is up to writers today to show us clearly what God we have today and why we should not serve both God and mammon. It is up to them to keep clearly before us the highest aspirations of the human spirit." Here is another "guest preacher," Walter Lippmann. He has never been regarded as one of the twelve disciples, and we are not baptizing him now. He is merely making a sound historical generalization in a column entitled "The Forgotten Foundation":

The liberties we talk about defending today, were established by men who took their conception of man from the great central religious tradition of western civilization and the liberties we inherit can almost certainly not survive the abandonment of that tradition. And so perhaps the ordeal through which mankind is passing may be necessary. For it may be the only way in which modern man may recover the faith by which free and civilized people must live.

The needs of men are not to be met with "ten-minute ideas," sermons fashioned on the model of a small-time package of bright, vivacious radio comment or a spread of boldface type on a newspaper page. Without a solid core of theological conviction and proclamation the preacher will soon become like that pathetic creature of Greek mythology, Tithonus, who was changed into a grasshopper. An equally sad figure, the Reverend Dr. Tithonus is also fairly familiar, the preacher who has no august revelation to set forth in coherent continuity and so spends his pulpit life hopping about in a delirious zigzag, a homiletical grasshopper.

When a metaphysic is lacking, all one can do about the evils of the world is to report them. That, in a sentence, is a real part of the story of much twentieth-century fiction. There has been acute observation, a skilled realism that even surpasses Zola, an ardent sympathy that matches Hugo. Yet, with all metaphysic, all theology, lacking, often the most that can be said is a tearful "Too bad." True, during the depression years of the 1930's the last chapter of many novels called the comrades to the barricades; but there was no deep ground for hope, and the motivation was thin.

A dominant mood of today, one of the most evident moods of our time, furnishes a fertile field for a message with metaphysical and theological depth to it. That mood is the hunger for affirmations, a natural accompaniment of a time of upheaval. It is strongly felt and expressed in many ways and fields in America today. It is the outstanding present mark of literature in the United States. For a score of years we have been living on a diet of realistic criticism (outside of that reading public who never vary the menu of romance). It has been a searching, probing, of national ills—political, social, economic. Scores of minor Goethes have pressed with exploring, diagnostic fingers, saying, "Thou ailest here and here." And, like all good medical examinations, it has been of enormous value, a moral asset of immense worth. But with the stern and frightening challenge of the whole democratic theory and process which the rise of Nazism has brought, a new evaluation of the American heritage has been made. It is always when a tradition is threatened that its nature and worth are re-examined and assessed in more positive terms. In days of danger man cannot live on criticism alone. He must ask, "Is there any good in our heritage?" This is the ultimate reason for the flood of historical novels, novels of celebration of American values of other periods, words of affirmation. This is the reason for a score of anthologies of democracy, its definitions, its notable expressions, its history and contributions to society. Life in a difficult time needs positive affirmations for its sustenance.

It needs to be said, in passing, that there is very great danger to human freedom and social progress in the overindulgence of this hunger for affirmations. It may result in the suspension of critical faculties altogether, in the glorification of the *status quo*.

41

But the mood is a real one. And it is felt in the whole realm of religion. The question arises from deep sources: Is there anything to which a person can cling securely? Are there any affirmations in which life can be rooted? That makes a genuine "teaching situation." It makes a great opportunity for preaching with affirmative religious content. The words of Max Lerner serve as a weather vane showing the direction of much present-day thinking: "The only kind of a tract for the times that is worth the ink and paper it costs, is one with a long-range philosophy about men's purposes and motives."

In the face of that hunger for affirmations that reach to the center of reality, preaching cannot be trivial without meeting a deserved contempt. A preacher toying with a minor theme merits the judgment of Conrad on Henry James, "A hippopotamus chasing a pea." Any kind of verbal acrobatics is a dark betrayal of a man asking for bread to live by. Emerson's *Journals,* that vast quarry of wisdom for a man who seeks to bring truth to bear on life, has one entry which puts sharply the need of preaching for momentous content. On June 18, 1843, he wrote: "Webster gave us his plain statement like good bread, yet the oration was feeble compared with his other efforts, and even seemed poor and Polonius-like with its indigent conversations. When there is no antagonism, as in these holiday speeches, and no religion, things sound not heroically."

Here are two things necessary if "things" are to sound heroically in the pulpit—"antagonism" and "religion." It is sobering to think that a man may preach for a lifetime with fair outward success without either an indiscreet and unyielding antagonism to the powerful evils which maim and strangle lives, and without real religion, getting along with a flow of moral chatter as a substitute.

Nor can the deep needs of men today be met with the competent accomplishment of routine. Brooks Atkinson made an acute comment on a certain actor's performance of *Hamlet* several years ago, a comment that has sharp pertinence for the preacher: "It was not powerful enough to hold the play together. He was lucent and tame on a wild and whirling occasion." Surely the world has come upon a wild and whirling occasion; to be lucent and tame is not enough. Routine competence in the presence of a cataclysm does not have the

42

dimensions of a needed response. "Our business is not as usual," advertises the telephone company during the war. It is far more true of the church. One of the greatest risks the churches run is not the advent of a new age of persecution—the facing of dungeon, flame, and sword —no thing so heroic; for that would bring its own access of strength. It is rather the more deadly danger of not being able to rise out of a routine, both in pulpit and parish life, that has formed like a hard shell. H. G. Wells has put this shell of routine, deadening the higher centers of the brain, in the petulant protest of his croquet player:

> I don't care. The world may be going to pieces. The Stone Age may be returning. This may, as you say, be the sunset of civilization. I'm sorry, but I can't help it this morning. I have other engagements. All the same—laws of the Medes and Persians—I am going to play croquet with my aunt at half past twelve today.[2]

That was the compelling imperative—croquet! And many a preacher has gone off to play croquet with many an aunt, not at twelve-thirty, but at the hour of divine service, Sunday after Sunday.

Three other matters may receive brief mention here. Each will be given only the most cursory glance, but each is worth pondering. The first is a bit of counsel for the advocate of a cause which comes from the history of that whole art of persuasion and argument which is now commonly gathered under the head of "propaganda."

That history, from its very beginning until the present, stresses the superior power of positive affirmation over negative refutation. In military language, it is the superior power of offensive thrust over defense. Let the advocate, in the main, state his case affirmatively, again and again, and refuse to be drawn off the major battlefield into bickering disputations devoted to refuting the charges of the enemy. For that surrenders the initiative to the opponent. It puts him in the center of the stage. It creates the impression in the minds of the hearers that the opponent's objections have the advocate worried to death and that the opponent's criticisms are far more important than the advocate's, or the preacher's, positive declarations. In the warfare of the spirit and mind as well as in that of armies this wisdom holds: Choose your own terrain and hold the initiative.

Take but two examples out of scores that might be summoned: The preaching of Phillips Brooks was a far more powerful force for Christianity than the hundred and one vehement refuters of Robert Ingersoll. The preaching of John Wesley was far more powerful than Bishop Butler's careful refutations of the objections to revealed religion in his *Analogy*.

George Creel writes, out of considerable experience in propaganda:

St. Paul, Thomas Paine, Woodrow Wilson and other great masters, avoided a state of perpetual dither by paying no attention whatsoever to what their adversaries were saying or doing. Instead of that they concentrated on the preparation and presentation of their own case, taking infinite pains to rest it on the hopes, aspirations and ideals common to all peoples.[3]

Mr. Creel has mentioned St. Paul. He was a great disputant. But recall how his writings bear out the clear triumph of his positive affirmations over negative refutations: "But we preach Christ crucified, unto the Jews a stumblingblock, and unto the Greeks foolishness [the overtone says clearly, 'Never mind about that'] but unto them that are called, both Jews and Greeks, Christ the power of God, and the wisdom of God."[4] And again, recall that superbly positive manifesto, "I determined not to know anything among you, save Jesus Christ, and him crucified."[5]

Recall the preaching of Jesus. He was a consummate debater. Occasionally we find him in skillful fencing with lawyers intent to trap him. What attorney for the defense ever turned the tables on a prosecutor in a courtroom as deftly as did Jesus when he shifted from defense to offense, with the foxy quibblers who set a trap before him, by asking about the authority of John the Baptist. He seized the initiative in his question, which shifted the whole ground: "I will also ask of you one question."[6] The case against him collapsed like a punctured balloon. Yet how small a part of his preaching that mastery of argument occupied! "Thou hast the words of eternal life," men said to him, great positive words: "Come unto me, all ye that labour"; "Blessed are the poor in spirit"; "the kingdom of heaven is like . . ." In this respect, as in others, he is the great teacher.

Another matter is one of "the pretty ways of providence"—one of the evidences, numberless as the sands of the sea, of the truth that "he that loseth his life . . . shall find it." They are to be found in every field of activity. They gleam with peculiar brightness in the field of preaching. The supreme way in which one may "find himself" as a preacher is to lose himself in a cause. The passive voice comes first, in religion as in art. One must be possessed before he can possess. He must be laid hold upon before he can lay hold upon others with the most enduring grip. It is an abiding paradox that forgetting oneself, losing oneself, being mastered by a great cause, is the one sure way to the mastery of a means. On a very practical line, this truth gleams in the formula for a successful book of travel or adventure given by Stewart Edward White: "Forget writing, have a whopping good time, and then come back and write about it." With due substitutions, that formula stands for the highest kind of adventure writing, that of the adventures of the soul. The words of a pulpit are often pallid things devoid of blood, nerves, and sinew because the man who utters them has never had "a whopping good time" in his own self-forgetting adventures in the grace and will of God; thus he has never reached the highest level of skill by the winding road of indirection.

In both poetry and prose this access of art which comes with being absorbed in a great cause is evidenced in the development of several New England writers after their conversion to the abolition of slavery. Van Wyck Brooks thus gives his witness to the wonder of finding life by losing it:

In this Abolitionist campaign, which was dividing households, as the Unitarian movement had formerly done, the orators especially had found a cause. They were in need of a cause, for the tale of the Revolution and the patriot fathers had grown rather stale, flat and thin. Eulogies of Washington and Adams, profitable to Edward Everett, rang hollow in the ears of the new generation. What was the meaning of these declamations, this cant about the inalienable rights of men in a country where it was known that Jefferson's nephew had chopped a slave to pieces with an axe, where beating, branding, mutilating slaves, selling them, kicking them, killing them was all in the nature of the situation? The ancient art of oratory, the pride of ancestral Boston, had become an abuse. It was breathing out its vacant life in words, empty as a cloud, cold as the frozen Frog Pond; and suddenly, as if by a blood-transfusion, its slow pulse began to beat again. Oratory once more possessed a function. It touched the springs of action, for the voices of Charles Sumner and Wendell Phillips were voices to which Boston was obliged to listen. Their doctrines, their ideas were scarcely new. What was new was their personal style, their passion, their conviction, their sense of fact.[7]

The third matter is a true word to be said, perhaps not of vast importance, but one which will meet a real need in some quarters in helping the parish pastor to fortify himself with a heightened estimate of his function. Any sensitive pastor with a keen realization of the range and complexity of the field that he covers must feel at times a numbing hesitancy at not being a specialist in the fields in which he is set to furnish guidance. He can look over their extent and well say, "Who is sufficient for these things?" His fields range from biblical criticism and the history of doctrine to social security and international organization. To the pastor's dismay, often, to this empire has been added of late years the vast quicksands of psychiatry, with many a bog for the overconfident.

Consequently, there is real need for a fresh recognition of the function of the general practitioner. That is what the parish minister is. It is a high and indispensable role. It is a function which no specialist in a particular field of knowledge fulfills. All the professions might well take a warning from nature, from the many species which became extinct by overspecialization. A noble model is the general practitioner in medicine. There, at his best, was a doctor who did not make up by bedside manner what he lacked in learning and skill, but a man who was a specialist in the *practice* of medicine, who treated the whole person. Many a person has died in the best-equipped hospitals of the world, not because he did not have half a dozen competent specialists, but because he had no physician. One of the most interesting trends in current medical thinking and practice is the new recognition of the importance of the general practitioner, evidenced by the reshaping of the curriculums of medical schools that the general physician's needs may be placed more nearly at the center. It is part of the general trend of revaluation of the curriculums of professional schools from the starting point of job analysis, what the graduate has to do. This has been long overdue, particularly in theological seminaries. Dr. Harvey Cushing, shortly before he died, made a notable plea for the earlier introduction into the curriculum of the medical school of bedside practice, and a greater centering of the teaching and clinical work around the bedside practice of medicine.

In the pulpit the popularizer fills an indispensable function. "Popularizer" is a noble word which has fallen on evil days by base usage; but it has recovered some of its glory from the spirited plea which James Harvey Robinson has been making for "the humanization of learning," particularly in historical writing. Too much history has been written by highly trained bores; too much knowledge has been sealed deep in pyramids of pedantry. The true popularizer is not a vulgarizer in the usual meaning of that term. The *vulgarisateur,* to give him his formidable title, is, in the words of Sir Charles Oman, "the man who proposes to make history, religion, science, or art easily comprehensible to the multitude by leaving out all their problems and uncertainties." [8] Such is not the general practitioner of the pulpit.

We are sadly familiar with the charlatan writer with a gift for making everything simpler than anything really is. There is one sense of the word, indeed, in which the pastor-preacher is engaged in a very "vulgar" task, the high and holy meaning in the statement that Wycliffe and Tyndale translated the Bible into the "vulgar" tongue. The preacher is the interpreter who has specialized in people, who knows them so well that he can throw up a highway for truth in their minds. A classic picture of this high function is found in the familiar words of Matthew Arnold:

The great men of culture are those who . . . have laboured to divest knowledge of all that was harsh, uncouth, difficult, abstract, professional, exclusive; to humanise it, to make it efficient outside the clique of the culti-vated and learned, yet still remaining the *best* knowledge and thought of the time, and a true source, therefore, of sweetness and light.

Let the parish preacher commit those words to memory, so that he need never be browbeaten by any pundit who has no conception of the difficulty and importance of his work.

There is an impressive picture of the preacher's field as general

47

practitioner in the "Prologue for the Theater" at the beginning of
Goethe's *Faust*. Goethe applies it to the dramatist's art, but it is just as
relevant to the pulpit. A poet is talking to the manager of a theater,
and the manager seeks to bring home to the latter the kind of people
for whom he is writing. Only look, he says, for whom you are writing.
One is wearied and bored; another comes from some sumptuous banquet; and, worst of all, many come from reading the newspapers.
With confused and scattered minds they come. They are half-cold,
half-raw; and then after the play they go into the darkness, one to a
game at cards, another to a wild and sensual night. Such, says the
manager to the poet, are the people you have to impress.

Leave out the "wild and sensual night" from that picture drawn
by the theater manager and you have a fair description of the congregation everywhere. The minister has to seize the attention of many
who are not primarily interested in religion; he must furnish quick
and effective first aid to the imagination even of those who have a
genuine interest. To build a personal bridge to people over which
spiritual traffic may pass is a difficult task of engineering.

Another, more homely, analogy for the realization of the role of
the general practitioner in a parish pulpit is to think of him as one
who breaks up currency bills of large denominations into smaller
units which can circulate readily. A five-hundred-dollar bill is a valuable thing to have, but a bit difficult to spend in a grocery store. It
needs to be converted into forms which can be spent without calling
in the police. The *New York Times,* on May 31, 1943, contained a
news story of the plight on the day previous, Sunday, of a merchant
seaman who had just finished a trip on a ship loaded with explosives.
For that dangerous service he had just been paid his bonus in two
five-hundred-dollar bills. (Why that particular form of a cruel practical joke was chosen by the paymaster remains shrouded in darkness.)
The sailor arrived at the police station asking for food. He displayed
the authentic five-hundred-dollar bills but explained that, since all
the banks were closed and he was a complete stranger, he could buy
nothing. A great theological truth, or a sociological or economic truth,
is frequently like a thousand-dollar bill, of immense value but awk-
ward or impossible to make use of for the daily needs of life. There

48

is a text in the Agrapha which images this high functioning of the preacher, "Be good moneychangers."

Let no pastor, then, in depreciation of his own role, bend low before any research scholar. The body is more than raiment, and the creative use of truth a more difficult task than the assembling of information. Stephen Leacock, who has worked in both fields, thus measures the relative difficulty:

Many of my friends are under the impression that I write these humorous nothings in idle moments, when the wearied brain is unable to perform the serious labors of the economist. My own experience is exactly the other way. The writing of solid, instructive stuff, fortified by facts and figures, is easy enough. There is no trouble in writing a scientific treatise on the folk-lore of Central China, or a statistical inquiry into the declining population of Prince Edward Island. But to write something out of one's own mind, worth reading for its own sake, is an arduous contrivance only to be achieved in fortunate moments, few and far between. Personally, I would sooner have written *Alice in Wonderland* than the whole *Encyclopaedia Britannica*.

VI. PREACHING TO LIFE SITUATIONS

WHAT IS POPULARLY CALLED "LIFE-SITUATION PREACHING" IS BEING SO widely, and often so effectively, practiced today that to discuss it at any length seems like carrying a very superfluous cargo of coals to Newcastle. But one sad, characteristic item of war news from England in 1940 may bear a bit on the subject. The story recorded the sinking of a British cargo ship off the east coast of England, concluding with the sentence, "The vessel was loaded with coal and bound for Newcastle." If, in the years of war, ships have literally been carrying coals to Newcastle, perhaps that may serve as a justification for a few more words on a well-worn theme. For this approach to the making of sermons has been a great advance in the effectiveness of preaching. It is a field of such rich promise that without some careful notice of it no exploration of the minister's sermon workshop could be anything but partial and inadequate.

What is written here is set down with the remembrance that the whole subject is more than a twice-told tale, the A B C of modern preaching, a method of sermonizing which has been employed in thousands of pulpits with rich fruitfulness. The hope here is not to disclose anything new but haply to bring some persuasion to a more diligent practice in preaching which meets people at the point of experience which they have reached.

The life-situation sermon is one kind of a sermon. Later on some consideration will be given to the liabilities of preaching to life situations. One danger only need be mentioned here, that the hot zeal of a new discovery may lead some preachers to regard it as the only kind of preaching. Thus one good custom may corrupt the pulpit. In the pages which immediately follow, attention will be given to two types of sermons: one begins not with subjects but with persons in the

50

situation which surrounds them; the other begins with an idea but arrives at persons as its destination.

Little time need be spent on a description of the sermon which originates in the experience of the people to whom it is preached, with the specific aim of bringing help to that situation. The largest service which can be rendered in connection with this whole subject is to direct the reader to the article by Dr. Harry Emerson Fosdick, "What Is the Matter with Preaching?" which contains the most illuminating and persuasive, as well as the most compact, discussion of this type of preaching which has ever been published. The article appeared in *Harper's Magazine,* July, 1928, and has since been reprinted as a pamphlet by the Riverside Church, New York. It richly deserves that overworked word, a "must" for the preacher. One sentence from it indicates the heart of this whole approach to preaching:

Start with a life issue, a real problem, personal or social, perplexing the mind or disturbing the conscience; face that problem fairly, deal with it honestly, and throw such light on it from the spirit of Christ, that people will be able to go out able to think more clearly and live more nobly because of that sermon.

Look at two New Testament instances of life-situation preaching. One is that moving passage in Matthew: "But when he saw the multitudes, he was moved with compassion on them, because they fainted, and were scattered abroad, as sheep having no shepherd. Then saith he . . ." [1] The steps are clear: He saw clearly, as he stood by the roadside, the plight of the people, their situation; he entered sympathetically into their experience; from that understanding his utterance came. The other instance is the preaching, to a congregation of one, of Philip to the Ethiopian treasurer. We read: "And Philip ran thither to him, and heard him read the prophet Esaias, and said, Understandest thou what thou readest? . . . Then Philip . . . began at the same scripture, and preached unto him Jesus." [2] Philip began at the exact spot which the treasurer had reached in his experience; and from that experience and interpreting it, he brought the resources of his gospel to bear upon it. It is a perfect picture of life-situation preaching.

It is preaching which starts where people live. It shares with the

51

whole modern movement of education in bringing teaching closer to experience. Look at the contrast between most elementary-school education of today and that of forty years ago. The teaching of geography, for instance, used to begin in a singsong chant—not too unlike the repetitions of Mohammedan children learning the *Koran* by rote. The child in Indiana began with this incantation: "Indiana is bounded on the north by Lake Michigan and Michigan, on the east by Ohio, on the south by Kentucky, on the west by Illinois." Selah! It was not even as closely related to the child's experience as the words "Eenie, meenie, miney, mo"; for that formula, while a bit obscure, had utility—and magic. You could start a game with it.

But now for the child in school, geography begins where he lives, with a map of the back yard or of the schoolyard, or with a trip to the nearest hill. So in arithmetic. It does not begin with the sacred tables of the Law—the multiplication tables—but in a play store, where pupils buy lollypops. It lies close to experience, not only lighting up the dark mystery of figures, but strengthening the motivation toward mathematical speculation. Arithmetic and grammar are brought into the child's activities at the point where he needs them for the working out of something in which he is interested. Effective preaching follows the same general model; spiritual truth is brought to bear at the point in experience where a particular need is felt. It is all wrapped up in the dictum of the Dewey pedagogy, that thinking begins with a felt difficulty.

To put it in another way, preaching to life situations is not preaching on a subject so much as it is preaching to an object. A theological student reported not long ago that, on going into a strange church in which he was to preach, he found in the pulpit a little framed card with the question, "What are you trying to do to these people?" He confessed that he found it a very embarrassing question because, on running over his sermon in his mind, he concluded that he was not trying to do anything specific—he was just preaching. It is frequently an embarrassing question and always a good one to ask oneself.

There is an eloquence, heightened by its colloquial language, in the words of that strange and eccentric preacher, Casey, in Steinbeck's *Grapes of Wrath*. He comes to the abandoned land in Oklahoma from which the people have been tractored out and sent on that tragic Pilgrim's Progress on roads leading west to nowhere. He says: "Somepin's happening. I went up an' I looked, an' the houses is all empty, an' the lan' is empty, an' this whole country is empty. I can't stay here no more. I got to go where folks is goin'." That, clearly, is a true apostolic commission. The preacher must say: "I can't stay in any place which is empty, devoid of people. I can't stay with merely academic or historical questions. I got to go where folks is goin'." This preaching starting from where people are and are going carries into the field of persuasion the sound and ancient practice in house building, that, no matter how fine the view from the rear, a house should front on a road. That is where people pass.

A war always dredges up essential facts about people and about every profession. The second World War has been a gigantic scoop shovel bringing into view many truths about human life easily forgotten or disregarded in more placid days. As was true in the first World War, the gathering by the draft of great cross sections of the men of Great Britain and the United States has recalled anew the great gap that exists between much conventional preaching and the everyday life and interests of masses of people. A British officer, not a chaplain, has put the case for life-situation preaching with an urgency coming out of actual experience. He writes:

Not one preacher that I have heard starts where his listeners actually are. As I sit among the troops and listen to our real godly chaplain, I feel that it is because he hasn't the dimmest, foggiest idea of what an ordinary soldier thinks about and is that he fails to strike a single responsive note.[3]

Commenting on this, Dr. J. H. Oldham adds words of great insight:

What I am concerned about is a new approach,—that instead of starting out with Christian doctrine as something fixed and settled, that needs only to be taught and applied, we should begin at the other end, and set ourselves patiently to learn what are the real needs of men today and at what point and in what way the Gospel has something to say that those addressed recognize to be relevant.[4]

This approach is not as new as Dr. Oldham's words seem to indicate. But they do set forth as powerfully as direct words can say it the demand and opportunity for preaching which starts with the plight and predicament of people.

This approach makes of the sermon a means but never an end. Is there not an arresting meaning for the preacher in the words of Jesus, spoken in an entirely different connection: "The kings of the Gentiles exercise lordship over them; and they that exercise authority upon them are called benefactors. But ye shall not be so: but he that is greatest among you, let him be as the younger; and he that is chief, as he that doth serve"? [5] How many times have we seen or read about the "great ones" high and lifted up in the pulpit (recall that terrible phrase from another day, "princes of the pulpit"), lording it over their subjects in the pew with an onrush of overpowering oratory or by turning on the charm of personality. In either case the interest centered on a display of ability more than on the lowly serving of those sitting at meat in the pews. Jesus said, "It shall not be so among you." One way of guarding that it shall not be so is to keep the present need of any sort of people, rather than the exhibition in the pulpit, in the focus of attention. The only way to true greatness in the pulpit, as in all other realms, is the paradoxical way of making oneself the servant of a particular task. The history of literature is full of demonstrations of this truth. Whenever a writer conceives of himself as writing for posterity, he becomes a wooden thing, in spite of talent. When he has written for a particular contemporary audience, trying to meet it with a specific service, he finds life and length of days. Posterity is a perverse mistress to work for. She rarely pays any attention to what was written especially for her, but she is often curious about what was written in supreme unconcern for her. St. Paul wrote great literature, not because he said, "Go to, now; I will write an ode to love which will go ringing down the centuries; watch me carefully," but because he had his whole mind, with all of its endowments, intent on the task of making Christ formed in the lives of those to whom he wrote and spoke.

This kind of preaching, where the particular object is the main thing, cuts across the traditional classifications of sermons into doctrinal, biblical, ethical, or topical, as Dr. Fosdick has so clearly shown. It may be three of them at once. It may fall into any classification because it employs doctrine, or Bible, as a means of making life more abundant, not for the primary purpose of inculcating doctrine for its own sake or of teaching the Bible—just as a physician's purpose is not to empty his medicine chest, but to cure a sickness. In the treatment of doctrine, for instance, life-situation preaching follows the wisdom of one who advised, "Always get ahold of a doctrine at its preaching end." There is a preaching end of every great Christian doctrine—many ends. If someone raises the objection, "Suppose you can't find a preaching end to a doctrine?" the answer is, "Then it isn't an essential doctrine." There is much suggestion for preaching in the Negro spiritual, "Swing Low, Sweet Chariot." Let the chariot of truth swing low from the sky till it touches the earth and human life on the earth closely. The Epistles of St. Paul are full of the sweet chariot swinging low, of doctrine grasped at the preaching end. The love of Christ which passeth knowledge is brought into the guidance of the relation of husband and wife; the incarnation interprets the ethics of eating or not eating meat; the resurrection becomes part of a financial collection, interpreting and urging the duty of sharing, not only meeting it on the level of earth but lifting it to the plane of heaven.

The observation of Professor T. H. Robinson on the teaching of Jesus in the Sermon on the Mount is relevant in this connection. He writes: "The Sermon on the Mount is not so much a detailed statement of Jesus' essential principles as a series of illustrations of the way in which they will manifest themselves in life." Surely that is grasping doctrine, "essential principles," at the teaching and preaching end.

There is a rich suggestiveness for all this in the old Anglo-Saxon development of the "kenning," a primitive kind of metaphor found in compound nouns which described a thing in terms of its use. There is much primitive poetry in some of these.

Thus a name for the sea was "sail road"; a ship was a "sea horse"; the sword, a "warrior's friend"; muscles were "bone lockers"; the sun, "a sky candle"; and, most beautiful of all, the word for wife was "weaver of peace." This Anglo-Saxon practice of building words, "kenning," throws a rich shaft of light on both theology and preaching, defining a thing in terms of its use in human life.

Let us try to look at this matter more concretely. The specific procedure of life-situation preaching is seen when we examine the differences between the traditional pedagogy—that associated with the name of Herbart, for instance—and that of John Dewey. The Herbartian method of teaching consisted, roughly, of five steps:

1. Preparation
2. Presentation
3. Comparison
4. Generalization
5. Application

Expanding a bit, the first step was the preparation of the mind, accomplished in different ways, for receiving the new idea or information. Then there was the presentation of the new knowledge to be added to what one already had. Then followed the comparison of the new idea or knowledge with other ideas, showing its relationship, truth, or fitness. Then came the generalization or conclusion as a result of the discussion and presentation, to be followed at last by the application of the new truth to life.

Contrast this with the method of John Dewey. Here also there are five steps, but with a very different starting point and order:

1. A felt difficulty
2. Location and definition of the difficulty
3. Suggestion of possible solutions
4. Development by reasoning of bearings of suggestions
5. Further observation and exploration leading to acceptance or rejection of the solution

Preaching which begins with the problems bothering people, or the predicaments they are in, follows the model most noticeably in beginning with "a felt difficulty." This is basic in Dewey's educational theory. He says that real thinking begins with "a felt difficulty." We can easily see the truth of this in the commonest actions. We rarely think about our automobile engine when the car flows on like a song. It is when it is mysteriously stricken with something more complicated than a flat tire or an empty gas tank, when it goes dead and won't start at all, that we really begin to think about it—about what makes it ever go, as well as what makes it stop. The dead engine is a deeply "felt difficulty" and a compulsion to thinking. We see this in a larger field in the fact that there was more real thinking about the economic system during the years of the depression, from 1930 until 1939, when the second World War put a very deceptive and temporary suspension to the depression, than ever had been before in the history of America. Millions looked in baffled despair at a dead engine, and began to think about it. Ten million unemployed made a "felt difficulty." Often the first real thinking a person ever does about immortality begins with the sharply felt difficulty of the loss of a loved one.

A second step is the location and definition of the difficulty. What causes it? Where does it come from? Indeed, these two steps may be likened, in a homely but rather true analogy, to a visit to the dentist. That begins certainly with a "felt difficulty." You go to the dentist to have him find and locate the difficulty—which tooth is it, and what is the matter? Then there follows in the procedure the suggestions of different solutions that have been offered or might be applied—the same step here, it will be noted, that is in the Herbartian model. Then, after further consideration of the suggestions, we reach what corresponds to the fourth step in Herbart—the generalization, or the accepted solution.

Compare these two procedures in a sample basic theme. Take Paul's word to the Philippian jailor, "Believe on the Lord Jesus Christ." Under the traditional method the development would unroll, in a general way, somewhat as follows:

1. The preparation. This would be the story of Paul's coming to Philippi, imprisonment, the earthquake, the fright leading up to the jailor's question.
2. Presentation. What belief in Jesus is.
3. Comparison with other leaders and ways of life.
4. The generalization that there is no other way to salvation: "I am the way," and so forth.
5. Application to some aspects of life.

Now look at the other method, dealing with the same material and reaching the same conclusion:

1. The felt difficulty—there is a great lack of wholeness, of peace and power, in modern life—described so that many will recognize that they feel that lack.

2. Location and definition. Where does the difficulty come from? Here would appear whatever the preacher wishes to stress—for instance, lack of inner security, of commanding purpose, of outgo from life.

3. Possible solutions. Ways of escape which people try, in the distraction of pleasure, in the evading of fundamental questions, in work.

4. These do not save, do not bring wholeness into life.

5. Receiving and following Christ has saved from the things which destroy life—the "war in the members," selfishness, and so forth.

Notice some differences. The sermons begin in different places—the first in Greece; the second in Pontiac, Michigan, Riverside, California, Rural Route 1, Irene, Nebraska—that is, wherever the congregation is listening. The first sermon begins in the first century and, as ordinarily preached, is likely to stay there fifteen minutes; the second begins in the twentieth century at the present hour. The sermon on the Herbart model runs the danger of postponing the application to life until the end, when the attention limit has been passed and alertness lost; and the real heart and point of the sermon reaches a distracted and exhausted audience. There is a tide in the affairs of a sermon which, taken at the flood, leads on to fortune; omitted, the peak of opportunity is passed.

In sharp contrast to this, the sermon on what has been called the Dewey model begins with the application, the point where there is a need or an already awakened interest. It is the delayed application, or even its omission, which leads to that most fatal comment on preaching: "What of it? What difference does it make?" Too often the end of a sermon has been something like this: "Well, my time has gone by; I leave you to make the application for yourselves. Let us pray." Thus the main reason for preaching the sermon at all comes in as a postponed afterthought. This has even been defended in one of the most ill-considered things a very able preacher, Edward Everett Hale, ever said. Speaking once to ministers, he said: "The conclusion is written to apply to the congregation the doctrine of the sermon. But if the hearers are such fools that they cannot apply the doctrine to themselves, nothing you can say will help them." So? It is evident from his words that Dr. Hale was thinking of the old-model sermon, where the practical application was tacked on like a little unimportant caboose at the end of a long train. Jesus did not teach after that fashion. Neither did Paul. Nor did Brooks or Robertson, to name no living preachers among many who might be named.

All this is not to say that a vast sum total of effective preaching and teaching has not been done in what is here called the traditional form. It is being done now and will be done in the future. The contrast is made not to say that the second style of approach is the best or the only kind to use. The purpose has been to examine in some detail *one* style of productive sermon.

Preaching which begins with life situations and is carefully aimed at them, starts with the great initial advantage that it presents something for which the need is felt. It begins with an understanding of a problem, or of a pressure under which people live. And very often it elicits the response from the pew, "If you've got anything to say about that, go ahead; that's where I live." Then the sermon gives a sound like that described in a line by Archibald MacLeish, the sound of "the sharp, clear stroke when the axe goes into living wood."

There is a visual picture of experience-centered preaching in the Nativity story in Matthew, a story deserving to be kept in the preacher's imagination and memory. It is that part of the story about the star which moved in the heavens until it stood over the stable in Bethlehem: "And, lo, the star, which they saw in the east, went before them, till it came and stood over where the young child was." That is a perfect picture of the movement of a fruitful sermon—a great truth, set in the heavens, moving across the sky before the eyes of men, and then brought close to life till it stands over a basic human experience, such as the birth of a child. So often the star of a great truth is visible, but it does not reach the stable and interpret the experience there. It remains remote. It is a case of

> Twinkle, twinkle, little star,
> How I wonder what you are,
> Up above the world so high,
> Like a diamond in the sky.

We may well give our sermons this Bethlehem test: Does the star that we have seen stand over a human experience?

59

Look now at some things which this kind of sermon leads the preacher into, and also at some common pitfalls from which it saves him.

For one thing it sharpens the evangelistic point and edge of preaching. It relies on the sharp particular persuasion rather than the easily dulled general appeal. It gives to the great words of evangelism, "Repent and believe," the force of specific content, the persuasion to turn from some particular destructive and unChristian way of acting and thinking, and the persuasion to accept the Christian faith at a localized point where the need for its resources is evident. Evangelistic preaching, as that high term is frequently used, has often been debased into what someone has described as a "bunch of borrowed illustrations tied up in baby ribbon." Carlyle once commented on a sentimental and inadequate book about Margaret Fuller that if you seek a fact in it, "you are answered (so to speak) not in words, but by a symbolic tune on the bagpipe, symbolic burst of wind-music from the brass-band." [6] Wind music from the brass band is not a means of effective evangelism.

This kind of preaching will also help to meet the amazing range and sum of need disclosed in the correspondence and contacts of almost everyone whose name is before the public in any continuous manner. A columnist, for instance, no matter what the field in which he writes, gets a flood of mail on personal questions. If he tried to answer it, he would have to become a pastor in spite of himself. Even mail-order houses get a large amount of letters which, as an accompaniment to orders for overalls or preserving jars, ask for counseling in the management of life, letters that would demand a skilled personal counselor or pastor to answer. People flock to physicians when their deepest need is for pastoral ministration, for religion as a personal experience. This all shows an immense need and reaching out on the part of many who have no church connection or pastor to whom they can turn for light on their own problems and for specific help with which to meet them. There is a multitude far greater than is usually realized who, like the company on which Jesus looked with compassion, are distressed and harassed. To meet that variegated need

60

calls for the truth and resources of religion brought to bear in specific terms at the point of concrete needs.

Akin to this is the service which life-situation preaching renders both preacher and congregation in keeping in remembrance the needs of individual persons in an age of great movements involving nations and continents and billions of people. Unless the preacher has a microscopic eye for individuals, as well as a telescopic vision of world trends, his preaching will be fragmentary and come to be very thin. This is due not merely to the fact that it is through individuals that a leverage on the world, if any, is to be obtained, but to the fact that the intense, personal needs of individuals go on just the same in a time of world disaster as in time of peace. In fact, the personal needs are in most cases multiplied and sharpened. Fiction speaks movingly of how the persistent needs of individuals go on in the midst of war and a world stood on end, specific plights that are not to be met by general orations. Sidney Carton, in the time of the French Revolution, still had his own private tragedy in his lack of discipline and self-control. And poor, tawdry Scarlett O'Hara in *Gone with the Wind* had an inner trouble that did not come from Sherman's invasion of Georgia and would not have been changed by any military victory—a degeneration of personal integrity.

Turning in another direction, look at some common pitfalls of preaching from which the sermon which starts where people are in their experience helps greatly to save.

It saves from the fog of vague generalities, from the preaching that is largely spraying the universe with words. Many sermons have been like the miracle of Mohammed's coffin, suspended between heaven and earth, and actually touching neither. Life-situation preaching at least carries an "earth indicator," that useful instrument to an aviator "flying blind" which shows in what direction the earth is. It is an equally useful instrument in a pulpit flight.

Preaching with a specific aim at the problems of people does another great service. It helps to save from the very real danger, especially in a time of crisis, of preaching practically the same sermon every Sunday. And who will say that has not been an immense liability of the war years? Certainly not the students who have had to sit in college chapels

61

and listen to sermon after sermon from visiting preachers on either "The Defense of Democracy" or "The Spiritual Aspects of the War." Occasionally different texts were used, and some sermons were longer than others. But aside from that, they might have been turned out from the same assembly line in a mass-production factory. Great themes, undeniably, which must be preached upon. But after the fifth repetition the mind puts up stout defenses. In some colleges when the audience discovered that the preacher was not "defending democracy," no matter what his subject, be it vegetarianism or life among the ancient Hittites, he was greeted with a sigh of thanksgiving. Two hundred years before Christ some representatives of Carthage who visited Rome reported to their countrymen: "In the Republic yonder all the Senators together have only a single dinner service. Wherever we were invited, we again came across it." Since the beginning of the war the same preaching dinner service has appeared again and again in many pulpits. Continual flogging of the same issues, no matter how great, is too much like the speech which John Quincy Adams gave on slavery in 1830. It lasted one hour a day for a month.

It has been proved paradoxically true that the only way to have a variety of sermons is to have them all preached by the same man.

But there is also much danger of repetition in the parish pulpit—this for reasons which reflect great credit on the preacher and which evidence his alert awareness of the greatness and urgency of world crises. There is light which must be thrown on the world's disaster and sin from the gospel. There is compelling need for sermons on the theme, "Seek ye the Lord while he may be found, call ye upon him while he is near," with an international application now while there is fleeting opportunity to seize this sorry scheme of things entire and make a more Christian order. But unless the sense of great issues is coupled with an equally vivid sense of people and their predicaments, with a knowledge of and sympathy for the bewildering range and variety of the needs, anxieties, and disturbances of individuals, the preacher's range will be sadly limited and his ministry circumscribed. He will become a pulpit piano tuner, continually striking one note instead of playing on the whole gospel keyboard. The habit of beginning with people and situations becomes the preacher's salvation.

In this connection how deeply impressive are the personal ministries of Jesus to individuals in the very shadow of the cross. As he set his face steadfastly to go to Jerusalem, moving close to the crisis, not only of his own life, but of all history, even that did not become a preoccupation to excuse him from the roadside cry of individual need. One instance will suffice. As he came to Jericho on the last, long mile to Jerusalem and the cross which he could see so clearly, a blind man by the wayside (there is a pathos in the very phrase; he had been crowded off the main highway of life—a mere "wayside" object) cried piercingly, "Jesus, thou son of David, have mercy on me." And even in that momentous hour, when in a supreme way eternity was to intersect time, he stopped and stood at attention with that priority which he always gave to an individual in need and asked, "What wilt thou that I should do unto thee." [7] In that question is there not an echo for the preacher standing amid great occasions and issues: "Go, and do thou likewise"?

Another service which preaching to people in definite situations renders to the minister is that it helps greatly to keep him from moving away from his basic and original material. That material is human experience, felt and seen from the midst of it. To move away from it is perilously easy; a minister's very success in preaching may push him into a barren desert. The parallel field of literature has many warning tragedies of success. In that book so well worth careful study by every public speaker and writer, *The Summing Up,* by W. Somerset Maugham, in which he gives his literary credo and experience, he moves searchingly into the question of moving away from a writer's "original material." He raises a common question. Why are the later novels of an author so often greatly inferior to his earlier ones? The answer he gives is that it is not due so much to the frequently ascribed causes—that he has "written himself out," or that his head has been turned by success—but that he loses touch with the human material, which is the seed plot of true and great writing. He says:

Success . . . often bears within itself the seed of destruction, for it may very well cut the author off from the material that was its occasion. He enters a new world. . . . He grows accustomed to another way of life. . . .

63

The new world into which his success has brought him excites his imagination and he writes about it; but he sees it from the outside and can never so penetrate it as to become a part of it. No better example of this can be given than Arnold Bennett.[8]

The difference is between the knowledge and sympathy with which Bennett portrayed the life of people in the pottery towns, which made the *Old Wives' Tale* one of the great novels of the twentieth century, and the succession of pot boilers which came from his later years. But Maugham could have found a nearer example than Arnold Bennett in himself. His greatest novel, *Of Human Bondage,* was the one that had deepest roots in life, in his experience in the hospitals of London where he gave life to bedrock people, the people he knew in slums and hospitals when he was a down-at-the-heels medical student and a starving writer. So a teacher can move away from his life-preserving original material in the class room and dwindle down into a mechanical figure in a downtown supervisor's office, spinning out of his own dried-up insides lifeless courses of study to be applied in what has become a completely unknown country to him. And so a preacher may move away from the mother earth of people, from what ought always to be a Holy Land to him, and grow deaf to roadside cries, some so faint that only the sensitive ear may hear, cries of life under pressure.

What can be done to prevent this degeneration, which often masquerades under the disguise of a call to the preacher to do business in great waters? It is too great a thing to be snared in any little "sure fire" formula. Fundamentally, salvation comes from living with people, both actually and also in the habitual movements of the mind. In the chapter which follows, a glance will be taken at the subject of people as a source of sermons. Here is stressed only the elementary but basic necessity of knowing people. T. H. Huxley once said that the only way to know how a crayfish sees is to be a crayfish. The only way a pastor can know how a person sees and feels is to become that person, in so far as he can do that vicariously, by the means of precise knowledge and a consecrated imagination. There is no other way in which a preacher can know where the nerves and muscles and tendons of life lie than the hard way by which a surgeon learns anatomy.

Put two men on the witness stand. The first is James Denney of Scotland, who came to the study of the New Testament with the heart and mind of a pastor and always felt the confining wall which teaching threw up about him. He wrote in one of his letters:

When I was a minister one of the things I felt most constantly was the amount of sorrow there is of every description under apparently placid surfaces often; and I many a time regret that the kind of situation I now have tends to put this out of mind, and wish I had a congregation again— not that I have any morbid interest in pains or griefs, but just not to be so far away from what is too terribly real to so many.[9]

The second witness is that strange and pungent genius, John Jay Chapman. Concerning Josiah Royce he wrote in 1897:

I hear he is going abroad. I am awfully glad. Let him have no money. Let him come in grinding contact with life. Let him go to Greece and get into a revolution, somewhere where he can't think. Let his mind get full of images, pains, hungers, contrasts—*life, life, life.* He's drawing on an empty well.[10]

However inadequate, or even false, that might be concerning Royce, the words do describe a preacher's danger, "drawing on an empty well."

If a man is to read the invisible ink in minds, he must look at life before he talks about it. There is a sure insight in a few lines of Thornton Wilder's play *Our Town,* where a girl who comes back from the grave is appalled at the blindness to people with which so many, even with love in their hearts, stumble through the years. She cries passionately, though none can hear her:

EMILY: Oh, Mamma, just look at me one minute as though you really saw me.

. . . .

EMILY: I can't go on. Oh! Oh. It goes so fast. We don't have time to look at one another.

That sort of "looking" at people appeared in the reports of a few students in a theological seminary who were asked by a teacher to take as close a look at their congregation and community and write down what they saw. Here are a few people in particular predicaments:

A woman school teacher who had been in the same place for a dozen years and saw no chance of getting out. Her enthusiasm was going stale; the zest of life had oozed out. Only one vista ahead—

> And tomorrow and tomorrow and tomorrow and
> tomorrow
> There's this little street and this little house.[11]

A mother with two sons in the army—one in Iceland, the other she knew not where.

A girl who had come up through the church school and young people's group, deeply disturbed by the feeling that adherence to the religious standards of personal conduct were "keeping her out of things" and, to be frank about it, spoiling her chances of marriage.

A man confessed he got nothing whatever out of prayer.

The parents of two sons who were drifting away from the church and showed no interest in what the parents cared most about.

A man, a trustee of the church, whose increasing business success was displacing what had been a real interest in the spiritual life.

That tragic figure, to be found in so many parishes, a woman dying of cancer.

Such are to be seen everywhere if we have eyes instead of spectacles. "Who," we may well ask, "is sufficient for these things?" No one. Our sufficiency is not of ourselves. The point stressed here is that, with this clear sight of some people sitting in front of him, the pastor would surely have more color, warmth, and directed aim. In his first pastorate, at West Roxbury, Massachusetts, the young Theodore Parker preached a sermon on "The Temptations of Milkmen." Why not? There were several in the congregation.

Here are some things which pastors have done to help preserve the sense of human situations. Many have done the same or similar things, but here are three personal recordings:

Dr. Albert B. Coe has written of going often into his church on a weekday when it was empty, standing in the pulpit and looking out at the pews remembering the particular people who sat in them, the Joneses here, the Browns to the left, the Robinsons farther back. The sermon would be put to the test of the pews; where would it touch the people who sat in them? Then he would see not a blurred mass of people in a churchly fog but individuals sharply etched—"Each face, dear God, a world!"

Carl Knudsen, of Plymouth, Massachusetts, has described almost the identical practice:

On Saturday evenings I often make a secret retreat to the silent auditorium of our church, turn on a light over the pulpit, leave the rest of the room in darkness, and then sit in a pew for a period of quiet meditation. At such times my soul is often deeply touched with an awesome feeling of reverence for the man in whose accustomed place I happen to sit. He will be in church the next morning. He will look toward that pulpit for something high and holy, something to steady him in faltering moments, a sturdy faith that will give quality and worth to life itself. The effect on me is one of oppressive humility. Am I a channel through which his needs can be met? With that humility comes an extraordinary sense of sympathy for the layman. With Ezekiel I can say, "I sat where he sat." I have tried for the moment to put myself in his place.[12]

The same spirit is felt in the deeply moving picture which Dick Sheppard gives of a night spent in the parish limits of St. Martin-in-the-Fields, London, shortly after he had been called to be vicar but before he had taken up his work. He was looking at his parish, trying actually to see it:

Wandering from place to place in the parish and neighborhood. I went into many a strange building until then unknown to me and talked to all who would talk to me. I was in a casualty ward at Charing Cross Hospital, without being a casualty, and in the courts at Bedfordsbury, as well as in several public houses, for the first time; and thinking in those days that the Embankment was in the parish, I spent several hours on its benches, ending up in the early morning in a coffee stall close to the church.

I had always loved the bustle and stir of central London but it was this night's impressions that persuaded me that no square mile could provide a more thrilling and adventurous pitch for a parson's job, if only . . .

When at the vicarage, I loved to awake at that hour (as dawn broke) and go to my window and look across at Trafalgar Square, for it seemed to me that it was then, in the stillness, that the needs and longings of those who lived in the shadows of the church, could, so to speak, be held up before God.[13]

The same test of one's preaching, not in the physical location of the layman, but in the study, is found in Dr. Fosdick's description of his usual revision of a written sermon, not for the purpose of polishing phrases—quite the contrary—for the purpose of discovering where, if at all, an interest in words has subordinated an interest in people. He writes:

Uniformly I am through with my manuscript on Friday noon. The next stage is one of the most important of all, for, fearful that in working out my subject I may occasionally have forgotten my object, and may have got out of the center of focus the concrete personalities who will face me on Sunday, I sit down on Saturday morning and re-think the whole business as if my congregation were visibly before my eyes, often picking out individuals, and characteristic groups of individuals, and imaginatively trying my course of thought upon them, so as to be absolutely sure that I have not allowed any pride of discussion or lure of rhetoric to deflect me from major purpose of doing something worth while with people. This process often means the elision of paragraphs that I liked very much when I first wrote them, and the rearrangement of order of thought in the interest of psychological persuasiveness.[14]

One procedure which is indispensable in helpful life-situation preaching, and which should never be allowed to escape from the foreground of the mind, is that of bringing some solution, some practical suggestion, bearing on the problem raised. Diagnosis, no matter how brilliant, without therapeutics, is an affront, both in the consultation room and in the pulpit. Imagine a physician, after taking X-ray pictures and going through other clinical explorations and tests, looking up brightly and saying, "Well, its fine weather we've been having, isn't it? Glad to have seen you. Goodbye!" Absurd, of course, but a great many sermons approach that futility of diagnosing an ill, with little if any offer of concrete suggestions for meeting it. Every preacher knows how easy that kind of sermon is, and the curiously deceptive feeling it gives that one has actually done something about it. The diagnosing of an evil, whether it is the international order or the overcoming of the habit of worry, which offers nothing more than a vague reference to "the need for the spirit of Christ" is pretty close to zero in the cure of souls.

A story that comes from the early days of Fabian socialism in Great Britain has a real contribution to make to preaching. H. G. Wells was waxing eloquent in a high, squeaky voice. He declared dramatically, "Something must be done about the unmarried motherhood of England." Bernard Shaw interrupted the flow of eloquence by asking, "What, for instance?" "What" is a good word in a pulpit lexicon. There is no mental picture of more value for a preacher to carry than that of a man of a slightly cynical temper in the back pew of the church asking, "What, for instance?"

A real help in this is the habit, referred to earlier, of "backing into" a theme or a sermon. That is, keep the end in view as well as the beginning, letting the solution develop concurrently with the description of the problem. If the cure proposed is not as strong as the disease, then the sermon is not ready. Plant the problem in the mind and let its treatment grow there, for weeks, months, or even years. It is good to think and talk about getting down to people's needs, but let us keep the question staring at us, "Getting down *with what?*" A novelist's word on writing detective stories puts this whole thing concisely. Pamela Hansford Johnson writes warningly:

A novel of mystery of monstrous shadows and forebodings is easy to begin and not so easy to conclude. The time comes when the author must open the cupboard and let his skeleton out with a clatter, and, after so much preliminary, it has got to be an impressive skeleton. If it isn't, bang goes atmosphere, bang goes plot, and bang goes book.

Without any loss of point this counsel on craftsmanship to mystery-story writers can be transferred to preaching. There comes a time in a sermon to a specific situation when the cupboard must be opened and the constructive treatment or action in that situation disclosed. If it is not relevant or adequate—bang goes sermon!

69

This focus on the situations in which people are found, and the desire and ability to bring spiritual resources for meeting them, can be greatly helped by the preacher's reading. A cloud of witnesses surrounds us—people in real-life experiences, in fiction, drama, biography, and history. The personal contacts of anyone with actual experience are necessarily circumscribed. No one but Baron Munchausen ever saw everything personally. But the vicarous adventuring in other people's lives may bring back a rich cargo of insight and wisdom, that is, if it is done in the domain of real literature and not in the romance which is merely the mental equivalent of a sleeping powder. The questions can be asked: What was really the matter with this person or that? Why didn't life add up to more with him? What was the flaw? What was the real trouble with Becky Sharpe or Paul Dombey, Sr., or a hundred others in the dramatis personae of literature and history and biography.

Another field with treasure hid in it is that of the rapidly growing literature of psychology written in readable style, of genuine worth. We are not advising excursions into the dismal swamp of Dale Carnegie, or journeys into the "streamline your mind" school of thought—if "thought" is the proper word in that connection. The field in which real treasure is hid is that of the description of the way in which the mind and the emotions of people work, the kind of scientific work done by G. W. Allport or W. H. Burnham, to name but two. A growing knowledge of this field of the mind and personality and the emotional drives will furnish specific aid in the management of life.

Mention of fruitful reading in this field compels the brief notice of one type of reading genuinely helpful to the preacher in the matter of method and shaping of sermons arising from experiences in life and aimed at bringing help for meeting them. That is the study of sermons which have effectively done that particular thing. The purpose of this, of course, will not be to use the material or to plagiarize but to learn from the workmanship. To be sure, the reading of sermons ought to have a minimum place in a preacher's reading; otherwise he will go on a "soft" diet mentally, lose his teeth, and spend the rest of his life munching at prepared foods. The greatest danger of plagiarism is not so much ethical as psychological; it leads to mental paralysis, crutches, and eventually the wheel chair. Yet a man with an adult mind ought to have no greater difficulty in resisting the desire to steal another man's product than he has in restraining himself from stealing the diamonds displayed on a jeweler's store counter. There is frequently a good deal of pose about the preacher who draws himself up in a noble gesture and says, "I *never* read sermons." That declaration leaves the way open to a natural comeback, "It might be a good thing if you did." The man who has no keen interest in the best work in his profession lacks much of a true vocation. Who ever heard of a musician who never attended concerts, or an actor who never went to plays? The very phrase "a busman's holiday" has expressed an engrossing professional interest. What would we think of a physician who never attended clinics or read medical journals?

Surely a preacher can look at a task skillfully done as a gallery of medical students watch a surgeon operate. One should be able to do that without succumbing to the motives of a pickpocket. The work of a great host of living preachers is vastly worth studying in this field of preaching.

Here, in conclusion, is a very small sample case opened for the benefit of any who may desire examples of the subject of this chapter. They are just recollections, imperfect and partial, of the themes of sermons recently preached by several different men. They have at least the virtue of having stuck in the mind like burrs.

A sermon in a small-town church on the text, "The sin which doth so easily beset us." Here we are, said the preacher, a company of comfortable middle-class people. What sins beset us? Not drunkenness, adultery, or theft. Here are some: the complacency of the comfortable, the chloroform of like-mindedness. What else?

A sermon imbedded in an address by Dr. John A. Mackay of Princeton—on the people who have been baptized into Christ but have never been enthralled by him. This may not seem like a particularly concrete life situation. But how many people there are in an average church in just that condition; what a world of difference between the two verbs "baptized" and "enthralled"! How to get people to move from one verb to the other?

A sermon by a young minister, just a few years out of the seminary, on the present-day danger of life's becoming a drizzle of complaints. A sermon for days of rationing. Jesus said, Do not ask what ye shall eat and wherewithal ye shall be clothed. How strange that sounds in a day of scarcity, ration points, and rules.

71

So many people can scarcely talk of anything else. If we are not spiritually vigilant, life can be engulfed in a petulant and enervating whining. In many homes it comes close to being true that

> This is the way the world ends
> Not with a bang but a whimper.[15]

A sermon by Dean Robert R. Wicks, timely and courageous, on the great threat to the future which lies in an economic and social conservatism—a position that so insidiously becomes the native climate of the mind and spirit of so-called "strong" churches.

The dangerous habit of saying "No." This has been touched, in one way or another, by several preachers. We need to learn to say "No" if we are not to be flattened out and if life is to have protecting walls behind which individuality may develop. But the habit grows. We say "No" to so many things that we are in danger of saying "No" to everything. Thus we incapacitate ourselves for self-commitment and the true life found in it.

The chapter on "Getting Oneself Off One's Hands" in Dr. Fosdick's *On Being a Real Person* meets a specific problem which everyone faces.

The Archbishop of Canterbury, William Temple, in his little book *Basic Convictions,* speaks to an easily besetting sin, what he calls the "Pharisaism of the publican," the disposition to thank God not that we are not as other men but that we are as other men.

VII. PEOPLE AS A SOURCE OF SERMONS

THE CONCERN OF THIS CHAPTER, THAT OF PEOPLE AS A SOURCE OF SER-
mons, is a field without fences. It includes, of course, the whole
range of what has been glimpsed in the preceding chapter on life-
situation preaching. But it includes much more. It is far more than
just starting the sermon with particular problems and predicaments;
it is a sense of people which permeates all varieties of sermons, a quality and flavor evident both in the inner spirit and in the visible and
audible word. It comes from living with people, and issues in what
Emerson called "writing that is blood-warm." That phrase "blood-
warm" brings to remembrance a strong conflict which went on in the
mind and writing of Emerson—a conflict worth noting by any speaker
or writer. There are so many pungent evidences in Emerson's *Journals*
and *Essays* not only that his warmest admiration went out spontaneously to writing that had its source in people but that he did that kind
of "blood-warm" writing himself. Here, for instance, is a characteristic
sentiment:

I ask not for the great, the remote, the romantic; . . . I embrace the
common, I explore and sit at the feet of the familiar, the low. . . . What
would we really know the meaning of? The meal in the firkin; the milk
in the pan; the ballad in the street; the news of the boat; the glance of
the eye; the form and the gait of the body.[1]

"Blood-warm" stuff, surely, yet there are large tracts of abstract
writing which justify the shrewd comment of Margaret Fuller that
"he failed to kiss the earth sufficiently." Living with people, both
actually and in the social use of the imagination, to such an extent
and so genuinely that they become a source of preaching, is, for the
preacher, kissing the earth, a deeply religious practice.

How continuously Jesus did it. So much of his preaching, in the reports of the Synoptic Gospels, not only proceeds *to* persons but came *from* persons. Is it not quite probable that he had seen prodigal sons go up from Nazareth to Jerusalem and then come home again? Hugh Martin picks a few samples thus:

A long line of unemployed waiting for a job, men who turned a pretty penny on an investment, and those who went bankrupt, a hold up on a lonely road, profitable and unprofitable agriculture, a clever embezzler who makes friends to help him when he gets fired, the stupidity of silly girls who never get to a wedding party.[2]

Jesus never seemed to be satisfied with less than a personal touch with those whom he wished to help. He did not stay upon a mountain receiving reports and issuing orders. Again and again in the Gospels we read sentences like "He came down with them" and "When he came into the house." He did not conduct a correspondence school. A scrutiny of these personal contacts of Jesus makes one risk with confidence a generalization to the effect that when one gets from experience something that fits one life at a point of concrete need, he has something of universal value. The only truth which has no universal value is one which starts with the universe.

G. K. Chesterton once observed that if he had the direction of the church, he would have young preachers start in as bishops and then gradually work up, as their competence was demonstrated, to the high office of parish priest. There is far more than whimsey in that "first shall be last" suggestion. The parish priest has the most difficult and important task, just in the degree that he comes into living contact with people. This truth finds specific illustration in the experience of John Angell James, of Birmingham, England, who made an ascending progress, through pastoral contact with people, from the inflated rhetoric so omnipresent in the early part of the nineteenth century in England, when Burke, Gibbon, and the polysyllabic Dr. Johnson set the pace for orators, up to the human quality of his later years. He made the discovery that preaching without the humanizing experiences of the pastorate was a danger, not only to the diction, but to the soul, of the preacher. For seven years, beginning at a time when his fame made him one of the most popular preachers of Great Britain, from 1834 to 1841, he withdrew from all external engagements and gave himself to the regular work of a pastor. These, as his great successor R. W. Dale has pointed out, were his greatest years. He lived with people. They became a main source of his preaching instead of a blocked little tributary. The Birmingham mechanic increased, and Edmund Burke decreased.

When people become a major source of preaching, like the Ohio River pouring into the Mississippi to make it a larger servant of the life of the nation, preaching takes on a new interest and even excitement. Douglas S. Freeman, in his book *Lee's Lieutenants,* pictures something very akin to this excitement of pastoral experience. He describes what is to him the greatest joy of historical writing: "A writer . . . can ask for nothing more interesting than to begin with a score of names in printed military dispatches and then to work over historical materials of many sorts until names become personalities . . . and reports take on the sound of a voice." He played the role of the Angel Gabriel, calling forth the resurrection in a military cemetery. That can be a preacher's thrill, when names come alive into people, when they walk out of a church roll and ask in a living voice, "Have you got anything for me?"

All this is so obvious that the vexed query arises, "Why reiterate it line upon line?" A good answer to that was made some years ago: "If ye know these things, happy are ye if ye do them." One excuse for not doing them is the intangible feeling that preaching is something fenced off from other writing, a sort of esoteric verbal hocus-pokus off by itself. Preaching is related to all creative writing in that its sources of strength lie in a knowledge of people. A preacher's strength does not reside, like Samson's, in his hair (though many a bald-headed preacher might write feelingly, even a bit enviously, on hair as a pulpit asset) but in his hands which grasp other hands. Sherwood Anderson has put this forcefully in a reply to the usual letter from a student asking him how to write:

Too often the student thinks of writing as some sort of clever trick. It isn't that. If it is anything, it is a way of life. I think if I were a student I would not spend much time thinking of how to write, but would spend my time thinking of people, trying to enter into their lives. You do not really get anything out of life unless you continually give, and writing is nothing but giving yourself to others.[3]

Sherwood Anderson may seem a strange conscript for even a very temporary instructor in preaching; but in these words he is not far from the kingdom of the pulpit, or even, for that matter, from the Kingdom of God.

The realm of painting brings its own eloquent persuasion on this point. When the artist turns his back on things seen, on the real world, then painting languishes, no matter how involved the skill may be. People are a source of painting, just as the accurate knowledge of anatomy is a source of medical skill. Edith Hamilton, discussing the differences between the art of the East and that of the West, points out that a Fra Angelico in Italy and a carved or painted monster God in India are alike in that they have both lost their source in real life:

Winged angels radiant against a golden background, a many-handed God, both belong to the same conception of the world. The artist has turned his back on the things that are seen. He has shut the eyes of his mind. The art of the West, after Rome fell, and the influence of Greece was lost, went the way of the East as all else did. Pictures grew more and more decorative. The flat unreality of the primitive developed into the flat unreality of the stylized, until at the Renaissance the visible world was rediscovered with the rediscovery of Greece.

In Florence, where great painters had great minds, the beauty of the real world was discovered and men painted what they saw with their eyes. Italian painters found the law of perspective, not because Signorelli was a greater painter than Simone Mattini but only because he and his like were looking at real things, and desiring to paint realities and not heavenly visions.[4]

This rediscovery of the visible world must be a recurring process in a preacher's life, like seed time and harvest. For the preacher, growing blind to the human models all about him, may go "the way of the East" into the "flat unreality of the stylized." For that reason Giotto (1276?-1337?) may be called the "preacher's painter"; for with him people, rather than the canons of an established school, became the vital sources of painting. He actually looked at them, long and closely and with artistic integrity. Thomas Craven thus assesses both the sources of his achievement and his service to art:

Giotto took the art of painting from the cobwebbed cellars of medievalism into the daylight where he might observe the actions of men as they went about their business. He was a painter of many experiences, but he retained, in his maturity, that extraordinary freshness of vision which is the special property of children and poets. He was a religious painter, after the custom of his time, but the first to connect dramatic stories with living people; the first to give movement to figures; and to make the sacred matter of art incontrovertibly real and true by portraying it as one who believed in the miracle of life.[5]

That was a great step in the Renaissance, when art came up out of the cellar into the daylight where it could observe people.

Take two others who might be called "preacher's painters" in that they are worth a preacher's careful and loving study because of their strong sense of people and skill in portraying them. They are Pieter Brueghel the Elder (1520?-1569), and William Hogarth (1697-1764).

Brueghel's name has not lived on the lips of multitudes as have those of Rembrandt or Frans Hals. But he deserves immortality and has much to give to the worker in words who seeks to portray human life, whether novelist, poet, or preacher. Brueghel is notable for painting the actuality of life, not by a brushwork equivalent of photography, but by catching the spirit and form of the person seen. A striking estimate of Brueghel as a model for preachers, particularly for preachers seeking to interpret life in a time of tragedy, is that of J. B. Priestley:

He does not create a charming little refuge for sensitive but rather tired souls. He is an artist from and to the people. His art is not aristocratic but essentially anonymous and democratic, what films would be if they really were works of art and not products of a cynical industry. . . . And we writers, if we do not wish on the one hand to whisper to a few, or on the other hand merely to tickle the mob, could find in him an inspiration. He had as we have a desperate, foundation-cracking world as his scene and background. Then as now in man's spiritual life the seas were dark and heavy and the steering-gear had nearly gone. There was still colour and gaiety in the foreground, but in the background it looked as if doomsday were breaking.[6]

77

William Hogarth was a contemporary of John Wesley and had some important traits in common with him. In many way as unlike as two men living in the same place and time could be, both had a formidable realism. Both had a piercing eye; both put people in the center of their world and work; both revolted from the sham that was in the prevailing traditions, Hogarth in the field of painting, Wesley in that of the church. Both looked long at London and actually saw the people caught in its narrow and vile streets. They saw the cruelty, grossness, fights, drunkenness, and riots, the misery, and filth. Hogarth painted it with an artist's terrible realism. Wesley saw men and women with an equally terrible religious realism, which makes him no antique stranger to the dominant religious emphasis of our time, with its realization of man's evil, actual and potential. In these words one student of the eighteenth century, Louis Kronenberger, pointed out the source of Hogarth's art in people:

Then Hogarth, a man of the people, with as strong an interest in people of every kind as any painter has ever displayed, burst upon London. He looked around with a piercing eye, and recorded what he saw into vivid and imaginative designs. Life did not embarrass or intimidate or unbalance him; flaring, swarming, roaring, it fed and nourished him and drove him on.[7]

To be cast in the role of a teacher of preachers would have greatly shocked Hogarth, but enough evidence can be brought to prove him guilty of the charge. Hogarth's paintings in such series as "The Rake's Progress" or "Marriage à la Mode" were never "pretty"; but they had tremendous power in conveying impressions of actual London life. That ought to be a part of the goal of a preacher, to acquire a Hogarthian power—to move among people until he knows them (a costly undertaking that, to be paid at the cost of each of the senses, sight, hearing, smell, taste, touch); to find his themes, as Hogarth did, in real people, and to open the doors of his mind, and of his sermons, to life as it comes "flaring, swarming, roaring" in. That would at least save us from a neat sterility; for when people drop out of the center of our world, we get to feeding on our own notions rather than the stuff of life. And let us not forget that a real part of what many today are

78

disposed to think of as "crude evangelism," in its portrayal of the actualities of life, giving it a leverage on the conviction of sin, was in the tradition of Hogarth.

With preaching, as in painting, there is no technique about this which will go into a convenient book of rules. The paralyzing thing about any book of rules is that it becomes so insidiously a substitute for ongoing life and learning from fresh experience. The dependable resource is a matter of orientation of the mind, an unsleeping consciousness of people, the habitual sounding of an alert in the presence of people, something like a woodman's eye for tracks or movements in a forest. One might say, without too much of the fantastic, that there are really four trinities for a preacher to keep in mind: first, that of Father, Son, and Holy Ghost; second, Abraham, Isaac, and Jacob, representing the variety of persons in the Old Testament, who come close to lives today and have an immortality in recurring human experiences; third, Peter, James, and John, representing a similar wealth of persons in the New Testament; and fourth, Tom, Dick, and Harry, a never-to-be-forgotten trinity standing for the varied people among whom the preacher lives and to whom he speaks. A man may be a formidably orthodox Trinitarian in his theology and preaching, and still be curiously ineffective if he forgets or denies that other trinity of Tom, Dick, and Harry around him and in front of him.

One practical help in keeping this orientation of the sermon toward people is to keep in mind the different folks who were in Paul's congregations, the equivalent or parallel of people today in their nature or needs. Here only a few are named; the whole "Who's Who" among Paul's friends and hearers, as found scattered through the Book of Acts and the Epistles, is worth patient investigation. There is, thank God, Lydia in most congregations (and outside of them), the person just at the point where the mind and heart may be opened to the gospel, like Lydia the seller of purple, "whose heart the Lord opened." There is Demas, at a very different point, just ready to throw it all up and revert to the world. There are the tough skeptics Agrippa, Festus, and Gallio. (Often they are not in the church building. But frequently they are in the back pews; and sometimes walking impressively down the aisle and taking up the collection; or in the meeting of the board of trustees, having brought a wet blanket along.) And then there is Eutychus; and let us never dare forget him, just on the point of going to sleep, perhaps well on his way. These and a score of others are in our congregations; if we can really see them, it will help us to speak not as one beating the air. It will enable us to speak sometimes the word that seems to have a person's name written on it.

Look for a moment at what this habit of finding a source of sermons in people will do for the preacher. For one thing, it will give him a sort of human screen through which to pass his material. It will give him a new basis of selection, help him to choose the things which have a human destination and origin. An interest in scholarship, essential and laudable as it is, may lead the preacher to misjudge the preaching worth of his various kinds of material and leave out those human things, often homely and never seeming of overwhelming cosmic importance, which give wings and direction to the word and carry it to its mark. How much of the fascination of Jesus' speech lay in the things which, in their distorted views of relative importance, many would have thrown out! We may all be deeply grateful that the Synoptic Gospels were not edited by a committee on the state of the church. They would have bleached all the color out of Jesus and left a sort of first-century John Stuart Mill.

Again, a vivid sense of people furnishes the "spark" in preaching, as necessary to forward movement as the spark plug in an automobile. Phyllis Bentley, writing of the novelist's wakefulness when "on the job," gives very practical wisdom for the preacher.

To go for a walk when you're not writing is simply exercise. But to walk when you are actually on a job is astonishingly different.

Neckties, scowls, frowns, smiles—very small details, ordinarily invisible. When I'm not writing I don't give a thought to neckties; a stranger frowning as he walks along a road is simply a stranger frowning. But when I'm writing my indifference vanishes. Perhaps it is because I'm more alive, in any event every incident is grist. A necktie sloppily tied comes to my eye as a gift. I think, "Sam wore that same kind of tie, and made the knot the same way before running to the mill that night." Sam, of course, being a character in my book. It is helpful, even exciting, to discover this detail.

It is no good trying for that same alert reaction when you are not

80

actually at work. You could fill a hundred notebooks with such detail, and I know from experience that the contents of those notebooks would be like gasoline pouring through a carburetor with no spark to ignite the fuel. The job is the battery that puts detail to work.[8]

The job, which for the preacher is the person, is the spark that puts detail to work. Here is the same truth, in terms dealing directly with preaching, put by Gaius Glenn Atkins:

The supporting substance of all preaching is the preacher's gospel, his peculiar mediation of the meaning of religion for life. The elastic freshness of preaching is in its sensitiveness to changing needs. There will be enough fluid variation in what he is responding to to make every Sunday a surprise. There are not often, save in the preaching of the rarely gifted, unusual elements of novelty. The newness is in something the congregation supplies, something in the hearing of the recipient soul. What was commonplace the Sunday before has suddenly caught a new significance through an experience unknown before. Life has turned another facet to the light and the sermon shines for a moment in that reflection. But how can that happen save through the ripened intimacy of preacher and people? [9]

This sense of people helps to keep alive what must never be absent from true preaching—a constant remembrance of the burden and mystery of life. Such remembrance will not mean that all the preacher's words come out of a dark cloud. But it will help to exorcise the demon of triviality and that painfully bright "cheeriness" which is the most grievous burden to be borne by a person carrying heavy burdens of trouble or bewilderment. Jesus said often, "Be of good cheer"; he never used the Aramaic equivalent of "cheerio." That rare preacher, A. J. Gossip, unconsciously reveals one of the secrets of his own power when he describes the awareness of people with their unvocalized needs which must be caught by pastoral clairvoyants if they are to be heard at all:

The mass of suffering in a congregation hidden away behind the quiet faces in the pews, is almost unbelievable. But the average preacher seems not to be very sensitive to it, or to get dulled and deadened to it as the years go on; he can talk to people at their wits' ends with their whole souls crying, Why and why and why? in a glib, complacent, non-understanding way that does not help, but maddens.[10]

Turn now in another direction and look at some things which "people as a source of sermons" saves the preacher *from*.

It helps to save him, for one thing, from what Carlyle called "the big bow-wow strain" (and of which, incidentally, he was so prodigious an exemplar). The preacher needs to guard against the type of speech, usually in generalities, which affects a hearer like a heavy truck passing by in the street; it assaults the eardrums and then is gone by. But when one is talking to a person, when his theme has been born alive from people, a straining imitation of Demosthenes becomes a childish impertinence.

A sense of people leads one out of a hectoring pomposity into a tender searching of hearts. And there is a long distance between the two.

This also helps to save the preacher from talking to himself, from conducting a dramatic monologue in the pulpit after the manner of Macbeth, "Is this a dagger which I see before me?" Once when Hilaire Belloc was making a political speech, someone from the back of the hall, hoping to disconcert him, shouted, "Speak up!" Without being upset at all, Belloc called back in his high, fluty voice, "It's all right. I'm only talking to myself." Belloc may have been able to do it; most preachers cannot without reducing their audience to a total of one.

Another service of keeping open the source of preaching in people is that it helps greatly to keep an audience from "passing out" under the ministrations from the pulpit. A sermon may be compared to a surgical operation. In fact, it really is an operation—on the head. In a hospital two people are engaged in the operation—the surgeon who does the job and the anesthetist who, among other things, sees that the patient does not pass out while the operation is going on. Otherwise the classic verdict would have to be rendered, "The operation was successful, but the patient died." The preacher must combine the functions of both the surgeon and anesthetist. He must perform the operation—in his case, preach the sermon—and also keep a quick, watchful eye on the pulse and breathing of the patient—in his case, see that the

82

audience does not go to sleep or, its polite equivalent, into mental wanderings. A preacher ought to be able to say with conviction, "This one thing I know, the glassy stare which comes into the eyes of a congregation when it is not paying attention." Some ministers never master this double role. They can be having a marvelous time all by themselves up in the pulpit, speaking like Hamlet in the graveyard scene (except that Hamlet had still alive three gravediggers in his audience), and not be at all conscious of the fact that the audience passed out of this world ten minutes ago. A focus on people helps the preacher to become a watchful anesthetist.

It may be said, in passing, that a great help in the role of watcher is a sense of humility. If, instead of feeling strongly the privilege an audience has of hearing him, the preacher has a real feeling of grateful wonder that anyone should listen to him for five minutes, the Lord is with him. Blessed are the poor in spirit, for theirs is the kingdom of the pulpit.

The habit of finding sources of preaching in people also helps to save from swinging censers of protestant incense. By that phrase is meant holy generalities that have no more specific content than incense fumes. Browning writes of "good, strong, stupefying incense smoke." The stupefying effect (without the fragrance) can frequently be felt in Protestant churches when laudanum words and sentences from the pulpit are addressed to space in general. A phrase frequently heard over the radio at the conclusion of a broadcast from an overseas country is well worth a preacher's attention. It is the phrase, "I return you now to New York." The sermon ought to end up with that. After the truth has been presented and explored, the sermon should return the hearer to his own country, where the truth is to find its expression and implementation. Jesus often did the equivalent of that. At the end of a discourse or an act of healing he would say, "Go back to your own home." "Go, and do thou likewise." He "returned" them, for the carrying out of the truth, to Capernaum, Jericho, or Jerusalem.

The last word on this belongs to Mother Goose, quite a source of folk wisdom:

> As Tommy Snooks and Bessie Brooks
> Were walking out on Sunday,

IN THE MINISTER'S WORKSHOP

Said Tommy Snooks to Bessie Brooks,
"Tomorrow will be Monday."

Now that remark has usually been taken as an example of an ultimate low in social conversation. But compared to many conversations which we have heard between young people, it appears to be rather meaty. For preaching, it ranks high. It is a high achievement when the truth brought by the preacher in his message is shaped and spoken with consciousness that "tomorrow will be Monday." For that is the test of preaching—*Monday*. "By their fruits ye shall know them." The true test is not, How beautiful does it sound on Sunday? but, How available will it be on Monday; how will it undergird a person for the strain of Monday's load; how will it rebuke a person for Monday's temptation to pride and self-righteousness and self-seeking; how strongly will it carry over to be a challenge and persuasion to the hard struggle to bring Monday's world more into harmony with Sunday's truth and with the purpose of Him who rose on a Sunday morning?

VIII. SOME DANGERS IN LIFE-SITUATION PREACHING

SOME OF THE DANGERS CONNECTED WITH PREACHING TO LIFE SITUATIONS are so visible as to need scant attention. Nothing that follows here takes back a word that has been said in the preceding two chapters on the necessity of preaching to people at the point of experience which they have reached. The cautions merely chart some reefs along a necessary voyage.

One of these is the elementary danger of the lack of variety in preaching. One good custom, no matter how vital and central, may corrupt the pulpit and rob it of any surprise, thus dulling the message. The sword of the spirit is robbed of its thrusting and cutting power when wielded with just one motion endlessly repeated. The wise thrush may sing the same song twice over; but the preacher, by repetition, may easily lose the first fine careless rapture. We are told to bring out of our treasury things new and old; that applies in preaching, surely, to form as well as to content. One-crop farming exhausts the soil, and one-crop preaching exhausts the audience. If it is all one-crop sermons—personal problems—the fertility becomes depleted. The familiar paraphrase of the statement in the Gospels, applied to some contemporary preaching, "Without a problem spake he not unto them," has sharp point. Indeed, that statement in regard to Jesus' use of parables can be very misleading if taken literally. Jesus used parables; but how much else he used! The variety of form matched the variety of content. The good seed, scattered widely, was not all one-crop seed.

An equally obvious danger is that the preaching may become wooden, in spite of the fact that, theoretically at least, it is designed to bring help to persons in a particular experience. A preacher may, by diligence, make a list of 129 stock life situations and say to himself, "Go to now, I shall preach Sunday on Number 67 and the following Sunday on Number 119." The whole thing may get mechanical. Some preachers who fall into this groove come to look restlessly for new "situations" when they have run through most of the common human perplexities. Their minds gladden at the discovery of a new disease, out of which they can make a sermon. They get to be like the Concord physician pictured in Emerson's *Journals,* who rubbed his hands when describing a case and said with warm enthusiasm, "The most correct apoplexy I ever saw! Every symptom perfect!"

But some liabilities in life-situation preaching, when it threatens to become the sole way of dividing the truth, are deeper and more hidden. The greatest of these can be put into one sentence. There is the danger of slurring two major things in Christian preaching. The first is the presentation of God, and of communion with God, as inherently the greatest experience of life, and the august prophetic demand for repentance for sin, individual and social. The second is the compulsion to become a co-worker with God in his kingdom on earth. We may fail to confront people with God, high and lifted up; and we may fail to confront them with the social implications of the Christian gospel.

One pitfall is that the preacher may unconsciously substitute psychology for religion. In his sincere effort to bring help to the practical management of life, the psychological mechanisms involved may overshadow, or even blacken out, the religious experience.

The vocabulary may undergo a change, often subtle and unconscious; the "complex," the "sublimation," the "phobia," may fall on the ears more frequently than "the grace of God." Jesus, Paul, and John may even become a corroborating footnote to a more ascendant trio, Freud, Adler, and Jung. The preacher who was commissioned to be a herald of the gospel, a witness, may dwindle into an amateur psychiatrist.

The danger of making a merely instrumental use of religion is a real one, and never more real than in a time which might be called an age of psychology. Religion is prostituted when it is regarded as a means of accomplishing something else, no matter how good or great that desired end may be—whether a release from worry, or the creation of a socialized economic order, or winning a war. Religion is not a means. It is an experience so commanding in itself that it needs no justification on the ground that it brings about beneficial results in life. That sort of prostitution of an end into a means goes on all the time. We see it frequently in regard to prayer. Do you have nervous indigestion? Try prayer. Troubled with insomnia? Try prayer. Thus man's greatest experience is treated as a sort of glorified aspirin tablet. The highest exercise of the soul is degraded to the level of a corner drugstore. Of course, a vital religious faith and communion with God in prayer have had tremendous effects in life. Faith and prayer have enhanced mightily both physical and mental well-being. But that is not the reason for prayer. When we treat religion as a way of achieving any kind of by-product, we are still on the level of Simon the Sorcerer, who saw in the gospel Paul preached merely a superior kind of conjuring trick. That instrumental use of religion is not a necessary accompaniment at all of preaching aimed at helping to meet the predicaments and perplexities of people. Yet the danger is present in a constant stress on the practical benefits brought by religious faith, and against it men must watch and pray.

Another liability is that the preacher may desire to be so "practical" that he becomes merely didactic, pedestrian, moving on the horizontal level of earth and never going down deeper than six inches below the surface. To use a sea figure, he may never get "out of soundings." When a ship has beneath her keel more depth of water than can be plumbed by the lead line, the vessel is, in mariner's language, "out of soundings." Preaching that never gets "out of soundings" is not a faithful stewardship of the deep mysteries of God. There is an unmeasurable deep to human life, and sermonic voyages which never dare beyond the shallows which can be measured with moralistic homilies on "How to Do This" and "How to Do That" fail to bring the greatest resource for life's deepest need. The words "Be still, and know that I am God" do not furnish us with a neat little list of "four ways to overcome an inferiority complex." But they do something more—because they do something deeper. If out of a productive stillness one comes to a real knowledge of God, he is set free from the preoccupation with self which is one root of an inferiority complex.

These words in the preceding sentence, "preoccupation with self," suggest another danger in concentration on life-situation preaching. It may serve to focus people's attention on themselves and their own problems and ailments. Thus may be fostered an enervating self-concern which shuts one out from the salvation which comes from finding life through losing it. A preacher may, with mistaken motherly solicitude, hover over a congregation, take its pulse and temperature, and whisper anxiously, "How are you feeling now, dear?"—when all the time the principal ailment of the people may be fatty degeneration of the will. Thus the last state of that congregation becomes worse than the first. Its mind is never lifted up for any great length of time from a preoccupation with ailments by the sounding of the truly redeeming challenge, "If any man will come after me, let him deny himself, and take up his cross, and follow me." The Good Physician used shock treatment and radical remedies. He practiced moral surgery: "Go thy way, sell whatsoever thou hast, and give to the poor"; "Let the dead bury their dead"; "Pluck out thine eye." These are not little pills or a gentle massage. They are words of life, stern, demanding, yet leading to salvation.

Now, of course, this picture is an extreme one; it is not the result of faithful experience-centered preaching; but it *has* happened when that becomes a sort of monomania; it *can* happen anywhere. Two other traps, covered with camouflage, to be watched for with the prayer "Good Lord, deliver us" may be charted. One is the obvious fact that continuous preaching on overcoming particular difficulties may suggest to people problems that never bothered them before. They are pushed by repeated shoves from a healthy extrovert quality of mind into an inordinate introspection. There may easily develop results like those of patent medicine advertising; after reading again and again of the terrible plight of Mrs. X, whose heart beat faster after running up only two flights of stairs, we detect a "flutter" unnoticed before. Many parents will remember the "Goops" of Gelett Burgess a generation ago. They were mythical little creatures, born out of the artist's imagination as a means of teaching good manners

88

to children. The approach was that of warning by horrible example. The little figures, mostly oversized heads, were shown doing all sorts of wicked things distressing to godly parents; and the moral was always, "Don't be a Goop." But many parents who had cried, "Here is help from heaven," and put these highly moral treatises, illustrated with fascinating detail, into the hands of their children, received a shock. The bright young child readers had suggested to them glorious possibilities of distressing behavior they never dreamed of before, such as throwing ink bottles at the wall-paper and pulling the tablecloth off the table. The Goops, instead of raising a moral shudder, became heroes of great resource and persuasive educators in wickedness. A trivial illustration, of course, but it does present a possible unexpected result of too continuous negative suggestion of things to avoid. Another point for watchfulness which has been often marked is that there are not enough particular problems to serve as the chief or only themes of the pulpit. A year has fifty-two Sundays. *Caveat praedicator.*

One of the most threatening aspects of this whole subject is that concentration on particular personal problems furnishes to the preacher a wonderful means of escape from the hard, dangerous business of facing the realities of the social world. It furnishes an insidious and respectable excuse for never dealing with controversial questions, an alibi which has been eagerly and often unconsciously seized by many pulpit defenders of the economic or international *status quo,* or by those ministers who never look over the parish fence. The minister becomes in some respects like the physician sarcastically portrayed in a recent novel, "A benevolent soother, tirelessly scattering sedatives and sunshine, courage and quinine, aspiration and aspirin, love and liniment." Jesus could have avoided controversial questions; in doing so he would also have avoided the hard climb up the hill of Calvary; he would also have avoided being the world's Redeemer. When a minister makes such an escape from costly struggles with the dark powers blighting and maiming mankind, he not only goes into a spiritual degeneration but also makes impossible a thoroughgoing ministry to individual need. If he does not face the social roots of individual problems, he condemns himself to the superficial role of healing slightly his people's diseases. It is hard to think of a common

89

personal predicament which does not have a root in the injustices and social sins of our time. Try it. The ax must be laid to the root of many an evil tree; it is not enough to pick some poisoned leaves off the branches. It comes close to the conscience with both rebuke and heartening that Jesus assumed two kinds of ministry. He stood before scores of individuals with the question in his heart and on his lips, "What can I do for you?" He also stood before the most powerful forces of his time and place and said: "Ye are . . . outwardly . . . beautiful, but inwardly are full of dead men's bones," and "Woe unto you, . . . for ye devour widows' houses." Jesus escaped from nothing except from the failure to do the will of Him that sent him.

One who preaches in a manner that might merit that beautiful tribute from seventeenth-century England, "He spoke to my condition," should remember what may seem a paradox, that the aims of practically helpful preaching are sometimes accomplished not by the specific application of truth but by the inducing of moods and the communication of emotion and experience. Consequently a plea for the intangible element in preaching, as part of the full cycle, is justified.

A clear illustration of this, which carries its own persuasion, is found in the two kinds of art. There is art as imitation and art as communication. These may also be called representational art, that is, the copying of nature, or of those who have copied nature, and nonrepresentational art, which does not seek to imitate or reproduce appearances but to communicate the personal experience of the artist when he was confronted by the object. To make the immediate parallel to preaching, the sermon corresponding to the art of communication, or nonrepresentational art, is not one which outlines the ethical duties of a situation or gives four ways of overcoming worry or presents five marks of a Christian society. It rather communicates the experience of a man who has seen Christ.

Take poetry as imitation or representation of a high order:

> I know a bank where the wild thyme blows,
> Where oxslips and the nodding violet grows,
> Quite over-canopied with luscious woodine,
> With sweet musk-roses and with eglantine.

So, in *A Midsummer Night's Dream*, Shakespeare brings the very sight and smell of the wild flowers of the Avon at Stratford.

But there is another kind of genuine poetry which does not aim to represent exactly or in detail at all, but shows how a thing affects the writer.

Thus Lascelles Abercrombie, in a poem on a storm, writes:

> And then a hundred beasts of wind leap howling
> And pounce upon the roof with worrying paws!

That would not fit into a meteorological report. Winds have no "worrying paws"! Yet how wonderfully and accurately the lines convey the impression the storm makes on one, the very experience of the storm!

Again, there is Carl Sandburg's well-known poem in which he pictures the fog looking over the harbor like a cat on its haunches.

In the name of common sense, the fog doesn't do anything of the sort!

Exactly! It is not common sense; it is poetry—the nonrepresentational poetry of communication. It does communicate the impression the fog makes. A. E. Housman, in *The Name and Nature of Poetry*, writes: "The *name* poetry is indifferently applied to include both poetry and verse, but it is the nature of poetry to transfuse emotion, not transmit thought, but to set up in the reader's sense a vibration corresponding to what was set up in the writer."

The pertinence of this to preaching needs no heavy laboring. Think of what an accurate description of much of St. Paul's preaching that phrase of Housman's is: "To set up in the reader's soul a vibration corresponding to what was set up in the writer." Paul used the very idea in saying to Agrippa: "I would to God, that . . . not thou only, but also all that hear me this day, might become such as I am, except these bonds." Paul was yearning to "set up a vibration" corresponding to what was set up in him by Christ. So to the Galatians he writes, "My little children, of whom I travail in birth again until Christ be formed in you," and to the Ephesians, "For this cause I bow my knees unto the Father, . . . that Christ may dwell in your hearts by faith."

There is, then, the practically effective preaching, in which Paul is only the first of a long line of truly apostolic successors, not made up of practical details, but communicating, "What Christ means to me." A fatal weakness in preaching is manifested when there is no catch in the voice—not artificially produced, but inevitable and irrepressible —of one who is overcome by the vision of something and Someone tremendous. Lloyd Douglas in his novel *The Robe* has a true insight when he makes the final precipitation of the long process of conversion of Marcellus the sight of Stephen being stoned. It is the expression in Stephen's eyes as he looks into the heavens and prays, "Lord Jesus, receive my spirit," that brings to Marcellus the overwhelming conviction, This man is looking at something real.

And in innumerable sermons, from that day till last Sunday morning, that same communication has occurred, that same undebatable conviction has formed: This man is looking at something real. Sometimes the words have been spoken in a poor lisping, stammering tongue—no matter. Sometimes the grammar has been defective. Paul, when he was trying most earnestly to convey his own vision of Christ, had a lot of trouble with grammar. But the thought breaks through language and escapes into the heart.

The pulpit which leaves out entirely this high poetry of the gospel— the communication of experience—leaves out a great power.

IX. IN THE BEGINNING WAS THE IDEA

A TYPE OF SERMON WHICH CANNOT BE SHARPLY HEDGED ABOUT WITH
precise boundaries is that which starts with an idea—some particular slant on a situation or human trait, some insight connected with a text or portion of Scripture. In some ways it is the preaching equivalent of what is called in story writing a "twist." It has enough distinguishing marks to deserve to be looked at separately. Inevitably this sort of "idea sermon" occupies much common ground with life-situation sermons. Yet it usually leads *into* the life situation rather than starting *from* it. Indeed, if it does not lead directly into life and its concrete problems, it is more often than not just an assemblage of idle words.

This sermon might be called biblical, for the idea is often rooted in a Bible passage. Yet the core of interest is in the idea rather than in scriptural exposition. This type of sermon often begins with the preacher's seeing what seems to him a new and valid idea in a text or passage. The text comes to mind and joins something already in the mind (the process is frequently not consciously directed), and a new creation comes into being. Emerson comes close to giving a picture of the process when he says that the art of writing consists in joining together two things which are unlike but which belong together, like a cart and a horse. Another illustration of it is found in the old-fashioned carbon electric light. It had one carbon coming up from below and another coming down from above. When the electric current was turned on, a flame leaped the space from one carbon to the other and light was produced. So an idea reaching up from the earth meets a truth reaching down, as it were, from heaven; and light emerges. It is not too fantastic to say that a true sermon is preached when a flame leaps the gap between earth and heaven.

To help make this more concrete, here are the basic ideas of some sermons which fall into this general class:

A sermon preached many years ago by Dr. Henry Sloane Coffin started with the opening picture of a sign on the electric light plant in New York, visible from the railroad just before it crosses the Harlem bridge—a sign with three words, "Light, Heat, and Power." That is what the electric power plant gives to a city; that is what, the preacher said, the Christian gospel gives to a person and to the world—light, the interpretation of our puzzling existence; heat, the love which warms men's hearts with the sense of a friendly universe; power, conferring mastery over fear and selfishness.

A sermon of Dr. Albert W. Palmer's, in his volume *The New Christian Epic,* also begins with a picture, that of the hero of Ernest Poole's novel *The Harbor,* who as a boy lived on Brooklyn Heights. He would wander out to the edge of the heights overlooking the harbor, and "could see the stars above the freight trains." The sermon goes on to ask arrestingly and in several relationships, "Can you see the stars above the freight trains?"

A third example is the famous sermon of Dr. Charles E. Jefferson on the unpromising text "And Noah was drunk." The sermon was preached in 1919, at the conclusion of the first World War, when the world was confronted with a great opportunity and responsibility. He pointed out that in the story in Genesis there had been a world catastrophe and Noah was faced with the opportunity of reconstruction of a world after disaster. But in the presence of so great a responsibility "Noah was drunk." So, the preacher said, men at that hour, confronted with the task of reconstructing society after the disaster of the World War, might also fail to meet it, through various kinds of intoxication. It is possible today to look back twenty-five years to that sermon and see what a truly prophetic message it was. The dangers that Dr. Jefferson pointed out have come to pass—hence World War II.

In these sermons we see clearly that in the beginning was the idea. There are many advantages to this style of approach, when it is mixed in with other kinds of sermons. One great advantage is that it makes for variety, without which the message of the pulpit becomes blunted by repetition. There is a dulling quality about the repetition of form as well as of substance. The form of the preaching may be shrunk to the constricted range of Tom the piper's son:

> All the tune that he could play
> Was "Over the hills and far away."

A famous modern description of a similar lack of variety is the sarcastic tribute to a Hollywood film star, who "stretched the whole octave from A to B."

This danger is pictured, with a close relationship to preaching, and to anyone who speaks continuously to the same audience, in a phrase frequently used of a pitcher in a baseball game, "He had nothing on the ball." That means that he had no curves; it was all straight pitching. No matter what the speed or control, if a pitcher has no baffling variety of ball, no change of pace, if there are no inshoots or outshoots or drops, if the ball never breaks over the plate in a beautiful curve, the batters soon get his measure and begin to hit him all over the field. Many a preacher, in that sense, has "nothing on the ball." It is all straight stuff, honest, earnest, and sincere. But his sermons never break over the mind in any kind of a beautiful curve; there is no unexpected relationship or turn which compels attention to find out how it is coming out, no creeping up to capture the interest by a flank attack.

The surprise element in preaching is one real asset of sermons which begin with an idea in the preacher's mind. Of course, if this degenerates into a strained striving for the fantastic, it is not only a bore to the hearer but a formidable obstacle to the gospel. Nevertheless, a sermon with relationship to life, with freshness and point, with the relationship unforeseen but such as all recognize to be valid, has real power of mental disturbance. It brings both awakening and refreshment. One of the highest of intellectual pleasures is to be "stung by the splendor of a sudden thought." Large multitudes of churchgoers who are not in an intellectual profession and are not wide readers but have active and able minds depend on their preacher for all they ever get of this "splendor" of the quickening stimulation of the mind. If the preacher fails them in this, they are shut out from a real source of spiritual energy.

This failure is often aggravated by the preacher's traveling over a pitifully limited range in his scripture reading, trampling down familiar passages until they lose freshness and leaving untouched vast ranges of the Bible which have unmatched splendor, imagination, drama, poetry.

Jesus' listeners experienced much of the glad disturbance of sudden surprise. He frequently stood a familiar idea on its head. "Ye have heard that it was said, . . . but I say unto you." Quibbling ecclesiastical lawyers who came to him confident of impaling him on one horn of a dilemma soon found themselves on the defensive against the swift thrust of a new idea.

This element of surprise is not captured and put to fruitful service when it becomes a hunting expedition for the bizarre. The most productive service is found in bringing fresh wonder to the much-traveled roads near to home. Keats has a final word here, as applicable to preaching as to poetry: "I think Poetry should surprise by a fine excess and not by Singularity—it should strike the Reader as a wording of his own highest thoughts, and appear almost a remembrance!"

The arousing of interest is a related asset of the "idea" sermon here under consideration. Very often the real effectiveness of the sermon turns on a question which does not appear either in the choice of theme or in the logical development of it—the question "Is it interesting?" Does it have any grappling hooks for the attention? Does it induce involuntary attention? Does it have any strong hand of interest to be laid on people in the congregation which, like the strong hand of a policeman on a shoulder, conveys the firm command, "You might as well come along quietly"?

These are important questions. For interest is an essential pathway of truth to the mind. Often it is the only drawbridge over a moat of indifference into the citadel of Mansoul. Dean Willard L. Sperry of Harvard says that preaching in a college chapel where attendance is compulsory is a modern form of being thrown to the lions. Perhaps that is a reason for not having compulsory chapel. At any rate, it does express the necessity of the preacher's seizing the attention and interest, and of doing it speedily. But college chapels are not the only habitat of lions; they roam in churches as well, and the demand for the compelling of interest is great there.

Some may object that all this is giving preaching a very low standard. It may be. It need not be. It need not be a futile appeasement of minds "itching for some new thing," resulting in the debasing and dilution of the message. It may be a genuine ministry, as productive to the spiritual life as spring plowing—overturning hard, encrusted surfaces of the soil, opening them up to commerce with the sky in the form of rain and sunlight—is to the fields. Here again the discourses of the greatest preacher are instructive. Go over the discourses of Jesus in the Synoptic Gospels from the standpoint of sheer interest-compelling qualities in relation to the groups to which he spoke. The common people heard him gladly, for many reasons. Among them, surely, was this: he had a surprising and unfailing interest. The disciple is not above his Master.

Of course, there are great dangers strewn along the way, as there are scattered along any road in human life which leaps to a destination worth reaching. Interest in ideas may tempt one into the dreary, sterile realm of the fantastic; it may lead off into the pursuit of "pretty" sermons, or clever ones; it may draw the preacher into the tangles of merely verbal distinctions, not much, if at all, above the level of labored puns, mere sound and fury—or, rather, sound without the alleviating excitement of fury.

More than that, facility in ideas may lead a preacher into laziness. E. F. Benson has a sharp observation on this point concerning Oscar Browning, the historian: "His facility and his exuberance in ideas made him indolent: he could not bother to work any of them out, because it was so much easier to think of fresh ones."[1] A good picture of poverty from abundance. A preacher may spawn ideas like a herring, or like a Micawber, and bring none or few to fruition, disguising from himself his own laziness.

Such are the dangers of "idea sermons." But never let us forget the greater danger of dullness involved in neglecting them.

Some procedures by which the mind may be helped to keep alert are discussed later in chapters on the harvest of the eye and the imagination. There are mental habits, which can be strengthened, leading into greater resourcefulness in setting the truth in fresh ways, so capturing and holding interest. One inclusive word is that of Tom Masson, editor of *Life* before it became a picture magazine. He once gave the advice to would-be contributors: "If you have an idea look at it steadily until you see in it something fresh and true. Then it will be your own, and it will be something I want."

97

IN THE MINISTER'S WORKSHOP

Perhaps as practically helpful as anything will be to describe very briefly a number of sermons which seem to come under this general classification. They are sermons given by many different preachers over a number of years, reported by several different hearers and readers. They are widely different in many ways, but they are alike in two respects at least: each has stuck fast in some memory, a sure evidence of the arresting interest at the time of hearing; and each is emphatically an "idea sermon," the unfolding of a special aspect or relationship of religious truth. It is hoped that they will give clearer definition to the theme of this chapter. They are given simply as examples of a type of sermon. No attempt is made to anticipate the Judgment Day by assessing them as great or otherwise. Some may strike the reader as genuinely effective. Others may seem much less than momentous. No matter; the sole aim is to illustrate a type.

Reference has been made to Jesus' turning an idea around, standing it on its head. "Ye have heard, . . . but I say." There have been many arresting idea sermons of this sort. One was on the familiar text that for every idle word we shall be called into judgment. "True," the sermon declared, "it is a sobering word; but it is also true that we shall have to face judgment for every 'busy silence,' the very opposite of idle words. We betray our Master by silence as well as by idle words, when we are too busy to speak the word of help, too cowardly to speak the word of witness," and so forth.

"The Art of Getting into Trouble" was one preacher's sermon topic—a common idea, that of the desirability of staying out of trouble, stood on its head. The Bible and church history are full of instances of people who practiced with great skill the high art of getting into trouble for the sake of the Kingdom of God.

The title of Vardis Fisher's novel Forgive Us Our Virtues furnished the starting point for a California preacher's searching sermon on which of our so-called virtues at times become sins needing forgiveness.

From the text "Lord, increase our faith" a sermon was preached several years ago with emphasis on the reverse petition, "Lord, increase our doubt." The first part of the sermon was devoted to the desperate need for faith; the second to the need for clear-eyed, courageous doubt about the worth and validity of some dominant conceptions in the world's life, a plea for the overcoming of a vicious gullibility in social and economic affairs.

Often a picturesque frame into which the core of the sermon can be legitimately put serves as an effective first aid to the imagination. A good example is Washington Gladden's famous sermon "Where Does the Sky Begin?" The idea was exceedingly simple, and the sermon powerful. The common answer to that question is, of course, "Up there"—and we point to the heavens. Dr. Gladden easily

98

demonstrated that, with the earth a ball sailing through the sky, every part of it is equally in the sky, the depth of a coal mine as truly as a cloud high in the heavens. The sky begins right where we are. From there he went on, with the persuasive picture clear in the mind, to show that eternal life begins, where the sky begins, right here today. The idea in the framework gave the sermon its memorable quality.

James Black, of Edinburgh, Scotland, preached a sermon at one of the "May Meetings" in London some years ago on the text, "I am come that they might have life." The "idea" was to take four definitions of "life," given by scientist, psychologist, philosopher, and man on the street. The scientist described it as the constant adjustment of an organism to its environment. The psychologist described it as progress toward a full self-consciousness; the philosopher, as an attempt to assert reality and to form values of things most worth while. The man on the street described it as the chance of catching happiness. Taking each of these definitions, the preacher showed how they were completely met by the life that Jesus offered.

Professor John C. Schroeder once preached an arresting sermon which crept up on the congregation on the line of least expectation. It was on the Gadarene demoniac, its text being, "And they . . . found the man, . . . clothed and in his right mind, at the feet of Jesus: and they were afraid." The sermon turned on the startling succession of events when the people of Gadara, upon seeing the demented man in his right mind, were afraid. That is what terrifies many of the ruling powers of this world—sanity. As long as men are "demented" with the approved delusions, such as a system of profit making which leaves human devastation in its train, or racial antagonism, or an acceptance of war as a law of nature, all is well. But when a man begins to "go sane," they are afraid. They are afraid, also, of a man at Jesus' feet.

L. P. Jacks once wrote a well-remembered sermon on the resurrection. His point or "twist" was this: The resurrection followed the crucifixion; too many people in the church today want to have resurrection without crucifixion.

A British preacher listened to a lecture by Philip Guedalla on the art of biography. In discussing his problem when writing his life of the Duke of Wellington, Mr. Guedalla said that the hardest matter was not in finding out what Wellington did—that was easy—but in discovering what sort of a man he really was. The most dependable evidence he found was Wellington's checkbooks covering several years. Here was trustworthy testimony on what the man cared most about. The preacher wrote a sermon on "The Stump of an Old Checkbook." What does your checkbook tell about the inmost you? What does it show about what you care for most, about the relative place you give to the cause of Christ? The man who reported the sermon said that it "got under the skin." If so, it was partly the picturesque framework which carried it well on its way past the guarded portals of the conscience.

Dr. J. H. Jowett was certainly the last man to be accused of "sensationalism" in the pulpit. He once preached a sermon set in the framework of an experience he had in going into a little church in a strange place on a weekday and wondering what kind of people belonged to that church. The only thing he found which might be regarded as evidence on that point was the hymnbook they used. So he raised the question: On just the evidence of the hymns they habitually sing, what sort of people must they be? On that basis he concluded they were people with a deep sense of the majesty of God, with a passionate devotion to Christ ("Jesus, the very thought of thee . . ."), and an unswerving feeling of human brotherhood. "How true was that picture?" he asked. The sermon was on "Living Up to Our Hymns," and anyone who remembers Jowett will have no trouble imagining how close and searching the sermon must have been.

A simple sermon, taking an opportunity, which deserves so eagerly to be searched for, of stating old and familiar truths in a new setting, was preached in a village church on a bit of detail told by Van Wyck Brooks in *The Flowering of New England* about Oliver Wendell Holmes in his last years. He was a great lover of trees and took many long walks. He always carried with him a compass and a measuring tape. That was the preacher's text. That is what the gospel of Christ gives us, among other things—a compass with which to find true direction in life, and a measuring tape with which to measure relative values.

A large section of Sholem Asch's novel *The Nazarene* contains what is described as the reminiscences of Judas Iscariot. This section might be called "The Gospel According to Judas." On this arresting phrase a preacher delivered a Lenten sermon. The question was: What would the Gospel According to Judas be—this man who was once a loyal disciple, who evidently wanted to force Jesus into his way? How would it differ from the Gospel According to You?

Another example of a fresh starting point for an old message was the use made by a preacher of the phrase descriptive of Silver Bow Mountain in Butte, Montana—"the richest hill on earth." The copper mines in that mountain had greater financial value than that of any hill on earth. The subject of the sermon was Calvary, "The Richest Hill on Earth." Why and in what respects was that so? What riches from that hill are available for the world today?

A striking sermon made use of the old Greek myth of Prometheus, the man who made himself independent of God and in consequence was chained to a rock. It is by no means a farfetched analogy to think of the late-nineteenth- and twentieth-century Prometheus—man in his own thought making himself independent of God, and brought by his own pride to the rock on which mankind is at present impaled.

Lines from the hymnbook, so often read and sung with little attention, frequently give wings to a message. Such a sermon sometimes has a cumulative value from memory; the sermon is associated with the lines of the hymn, and some of its point comes back when the hymn is sung.

Professor Millar Burrows once gave an illuminating sermon on Whittier's lines:

100

IN THE BEGINNING WAS THE IDEA

> Where Jesus knelt to share with thee
> The silence of eternity,
> Interpreted by love!

So frequently the words are passed over without any thought of the range of their meaning. So much in the world is silence. Some of our deepest questions meet only silence shrouded in mystery. Jesus interpreted the silence, the unknown, by the best that he did know—love. We can interpret the universe by the worst that we have feared, or by the best that we have known.

Take the line from the hymn "God of the Prophets," so often used at ordination services: "Each age its solemn task may claim but once." It does seem to be historically true that to certain ages have been given great opportunities which could be met then and not later. Illustrations will flock to mind. The lines suggest a sermon of broad social and international implication: What is the solemn task given by God "but once" into the hands of our age?

Or take that stinging phrase from Chesterton's great hymn "O God of Earth and Altar,"

> . . . the easy speeches
> That comfort cruel men.

What are some of the "easy speeches" today, the popular slogans, the accepted stupidities, whose thoughtless repetition comforts cruel men in the field of economics and race relations?

Another example for imaginative pondering is the line from the hymn,

> The changes that are sure to come
> I do not fear to see.

So easy to sing; so hard to make true. Confine it to the change from time to eternity, and many can sing it with deep sincerity. But let the words mean also the changes that are tied up with anything to be called "a just and durable peace" or "a more Christian industrial order," and can we say lightly that we do not fear to see them? On the contrary, they wear a face of sheer terror to multitudes. How may we acquire a faith that will enable us to live up to that hymn?

Often a quotation will provide a picturesque image as a starting point and frame for the sermon, giving it power of impression not only on the interest but also on the memory. Sometimes this serves as a subsidiary text, either coming after and reinforcing a text from the Bible or leading into it. Such use has been made of a lovely sentence in which Dr. Cairns of Aberdeen described the Scottish Highlands: "It is a land where the great mists lie; but it is the land where the great streams rise." Mists and streams—a theme with both individual and social implications! A beautiful description of the Christian religion! It is a land of mists; there is more in it than the clear hard sunlight of common sense and

101

reason. But out of that land of mist, what great streams of noble living have risen! And out of it what streams of redemptive social action have flowed, rolling mightily like the stream of righteousness pictured by Amos!

Here are two sentences from Phillips Brooks which almost get up from the page and march as sermons (one man has remembered for more than thirty years hearing a sermon preached on the first of them): "Be more afraid of the littleness of life than of its bigness"; "Attach yourself to the center of your ministry and not to some point on its circumference."

Some fruitful sermons have been preached on these lines from Swinburne (of all people!):

> For tender minds
> He served up half a Christ.

If that phrase "half a Christ" does not suggest anything vital and exciting to the minister as he looks about him, both at the church and at the world, he had better ask for a retired relationship.

A New York newspaper a few years ago reported a few sentences of a sermon evidently based on a saying of Albert Einstein's, or at least supported by it as by a flying buttress. Asked how he came to discover relativity, he answered, "I challenged an axiom." Whether apocryphal or not, the answer is suggestive. How desperately the world needs many unscrutinized axioms to be challenged. How much of Jesus' time was spent going up and down Palestine challenging the axioms of his time and world—the axiom that suffering was the result of sin, that ritualistic orthodoxy was the important thing in religion, and a score of others. What are some of the axioms of our day to be challenged in the name of Christ?

An imaginative framework, useful if employed sparingly and with restraint, is the "if" construction: what would have happened if—what might happen if—certain conditions were to obtain? Two magic words for a preacher are "if" and "suppose." That word "suppose" has something of the magic of the storyteller's "Once upon a time." It makes a legitimate, purposeful use of an anachronism.

This device is seen in W. T. Stead's flamboyant but disturbing book, published in 1893, *If Christ Came to Chicago;* in C. M. Sheldon's *In His Steps Today;* in Jerome K. Jerome's *The Passing of the Third Floor Back;* in Charles Rann Kennedy's *The Servant in the House;* in the Grand Inquisitor section of Dostoevski's *The Brothers Karamazov;* and in the epilogue to Bernard Shaw's *Saint Joan,* where Shaw turns his imagination loose, with devastating effect, on the idea of what would happen if Joan of Arc should return.

Thus Dean Inge approaches the question of the unchristian character of much of our social and political life by means of an hypothesis: Suppose Christ came back to earth. "Where would he live?" he asks. "Possibly in the United States. And what would he be? Possibly, as has been suggested, a schoolmaster." By this time the imagination of the hearer is off for a brisk ride. The ride is exciting; but the preacher—and this is the chief point of this whole type of sermon—is not interested in merely toying with an interesting situation. He is making an ethical and religious criticism of our civilzation and issuing a call for repentance. He goes on:

It is not likely that He would say the same things in the twentieth century that He said in the first. He came into a world of Syrian peasants, utterly unlike our modern industrial civilization. And yet we are all convinced that if He came again, He would have much to say to us about problems which never came within His purview. What He would say we can only infer from the New Testament; for the Church is not infallible, and has sometimes wandered far from the spirit of the Master. It is certain that He attached very little value to the accessories of civilization. He disliked luxury, which diverts the mind from higher things, multiplying cares and complicating life to no purpose. He would have been quite uninterested in automobiles and aeroplanes. But anythiLg which makes human nature intrinsically better would have His warm approval. It is not unfair to conclude from His often repeated sayings about the tree which is known by its fruits, and the impossibility of gathering grapes from thorns or figs from thistles that He would have heartily approved of eugenics. And in spite of the austerity of His outlook upon life, He tells us that men and women will be judged—rewarded with eternal life or condemned to enternal punishment (the word is the same in the two cases)—according as they have, or have not, ministered to their brethren in sickness, want, or other bodily troubles.

A line of thought which has often been raised with productive results opens out from the question: "Suppose the church after Pentecost had shown the same spirit and followed the same conduct as many churches today. What would have happened?" That is, suppose complacency had prevailed instead of an outgoing missionary passion. Suppose the members had said: "We're sitting pretty. We have the most eloquent preacher in the city and three thousand conversions. Not bad; not bad at all! All we need is to put the finances on a firm basis. Forget this extravagant nonsense about Judea, Samaria, and the uttermost parts of the earth." What would have happened? We do not need to guess. We know. The church at Jerusalem did exactly that a generation later. It died. The Christian church was saved by its outgoing evangelistic and missionary passion. As it was in the beginning, it is now.

A final warning, to be taken in the fear of God. The most arresting introduction, the most striking idea or framework, is worth nothing at all if the sermon does not have a core of clear Christian preaching which can stand on its own feet without any aid whatever.

X. THE HARVEST OF THE EYE

THE THEME OF THIS CHAPTER CAN BE SIMPLY STATED IN A PHRASE OF Christopher Morley's, "the promotion of the diligent capacity of the eye." For the eye is basic and central in all persuasion that reaches, by means of the imagination, the secret places of the heart where the springs of life are coiled. What one reveals depends in large measure on what one actually sees and what the seeing suggests to him. Effective writing never begins with the hand, with the whittling of sentences, the building of paragraphs, the choice of words—indispensable skills though they be—but with the eye, with what one sees. We speak of a poet's ear; it is entirely secondary to the eye. Here is Keats, for instance, whose serene valuation of his work, "I think I shall be among the English poets when I die," has found abundant justification. Here is a typical harvest of Keats's eye, as described by a biographer:

Even to the artist trained to use his eyes Keats's power of observation was an abiding marvel. The song of a bird, the rustle of small creatures in the hedges, the changing light and shadow with their shifting colours, the swaying of a leaf, a branch, the shivering of tall grasses, the slow pageant of the clouds; nothing escaped him. He was aware, too, of the human beings they met; the creeping animalism of many tramps in that starving, workless age, a woman's bright hair, the smile of a rosy child. The sea was never far from his mind. When a wind arose and went, as he said, "billowing through a tree" or he heard it springing up from afar across the dark-hued woodland, he would shout "The tide, the tide!" and leap up on to a stile or a low bough and await its coming, listening with breath held and cheeks a-glow, "like a young fawn waiting for some cry from the forest-depths." [1]

104

That man could see and, seeing, could make others see. In many preachers the one great defect is not in the voice or religious experience or mental ability or sympathy or fidelity to duty. It is "eye trouble"—they do not see enough or clearly enough and do not hand over to their imagination enough things seen in sharp detail as fine grist for its productive mill. The realm of experience suggested in the title of Aldous Huxley's book *The Art of Seeing* is one worth most serious thought and endeavor.[2] Eyes which have stared vacantly at too many things can be re-educated so that not only one's written words but his whole manner of thinking may capture more of the power of discourse which draws richly on sensuous experience.

But, of course, the preacher is not primarily in training to be a naturalist. His harvest of the eye to be placed at the service of God and man is the fruit of a "double eye," that is, the ability to see a thing not only clearly in itself but also in its possible relationship to something else which does not register on the physical retina. This double eye sees the object and the symbol, the object and the parallel in some other realm. In a reverent sense we can say, for example, that Jesus saw with a double eye. He considered the lilies with the physical eye, seeing them, no doubt, with an optical alertness beyond that of his disciples. But with the other eye he saw the lilies as symbols of the care of a Heavenly Father: "Be not therefore anxious."[3] The preacher can add to the statement of Jesus, "If . . . thine eye be single, thy whole body shall be full of light,"[4] this additional word for his own guidance: If thine eye be double, thy whole message shall be full of light.

This mental and visual double life can be cultivated, without degenerating into that distressing preacher's myopic vision which thinks continuously in terms of sermons. For, verily, the preacher's mind shall not live by sermonic bread alone, but by everything that proceedeth out of the creative mind of God. Yet the alertness which can see a true analogy, a fruitful use of observation, is a beautiful instrument of service and one which can be developed.

William Blake, who had, no doubt, too much "double eye" in his cosmos, makes the matter clear:

> For double the vision my Eyes do see,
> And a double vision is always with me.
> With my inward Eye 'tis an old Man grey;
> With my outward, a Thistle across my way.[5]

Again Blake writes: "What, it will be questioned, when the sun rises, do you not see a round disk of fire, somewhat like a guinea? O, no, no, I see an innumerable company of the heavenly host crying, 'Holy, holy, holy is the Lord God Almighty.'"[6] It is not strange that this man, so uniquely double-visioned, could see and convey in moving poetry Jesus' walking not merely in Palestine but also "in England's green and pleasant land."

With the same gift another poet, Francis Thompson, saw Jacob's ladder reaching from Heaven to Charing Cross and saw

> . . . Christ walking on the water,
> Not of Gennesaret, but Thames!

The classic description of this process so near to the center of a preacher's power is found in Shakespeare's oft-quoted words:

> The poet's eye, in a fine frenzy rolling,
> Doth glance from heaven to earth, from earth to heaven;
> And as imagination bodies forth
> The forms of things unknown, the poet's pen
> Turns them to shapes and gives to airy nothing
> A local habitation and a name.[7]

That is the highway which the preacher's as well as the poet's mind should travel, from heaven to earth and from earth to heaven, from things seen on earth to their divine meaning, a two-way traffic as on Jacob's ladder.

This habit gives what Logan Pearsall Smith calls "imaginative domain over experience." It is very close to the preacher's daily thinking and working. Such "imaginative domain" does not require world-wide travel if one can really travel with his eyes, mind, and heart, across a courthouse square, or down a country lane. Extension of movement has nothing to do with it; intensity of seeing and experiencing, everything. Another poet, Walter de la Mare, has stated the whole case for the harvest of the eye, and the double eye:

Any mere "Sweet Stay-at-Home" will, however, be astonished at the little which even the wide and practised traveller may appear to have brought back with him. Or is it that the wallet of his mind is packed to bursting, yet words wherewith to share it are wanting? On the other hand, a twilight expedition even to the nearest pillarbox may present another order of traveller with an evening star that seems in its serene and solitary beauty to have been awaiting the assignation until that very moment; with a common bird, the meaning of whose cadences his ear had never really caught before; or with a wild flower until that moment never seen; and—perhaps, even with an Idea! It is not distance that counts, or hope, or even longing; but the mind's looking-glass, which not only reflects but transmutes to its own purposes all that it receives. Whatever, then, the journey may be, the wayfarer must bring to it at least as much as it offers.[8]

That is the heart of it—"transmutes to its own purposes all that it receives." Jesus looked at a persistent woman pestering a judge to death, and transmuted it into a picture of the soul at prayer. He comes to a barren fig tree, sees it, and transmutes it to his own purposes.

This, of course, is part of the familiar use of figures of speech and of what are known as "illustrations." The chief trouble with sermonic illustrations, which are indispensable to preaching that etches into the mind, is that they are too often falsely considered as a sort of thing apart by themselves rather than a quality of writing and thinking. They are hung on the body of the sermon as bright ornaments are hung on a Christmas tree. They did not grow there. The wire which ties them on is all too often visible. They are decorative rather than in any sense structural like an arch or a keystone. Then all too often the illustrations are treated as Pharaoh treated the Egyptian slaves—they are expected to make bricks without straw, to make sermons without coherent, consecutive thought.

There are dangers, of course, as in all good things, in promoting this diligent capacity of the eye to see relationships and analogies. In its intemperate pursuit a man can become a leech, or a Shylock demanding of each person and thing he sees his pound of sermonic flesh. He

107

becomes a conversational Black Death. The marvelous pageant of life is missed while he muckrakes his way along looking for sermon illustrations. But one can avoid the dangers while realizing the outstanding values. There are dangers in air; germs infest it. But the remedy is not to stop breathing.

There are some specific ways in which the harvest of the eye may be increased. To be born with a strong fund of curiosity and interest would be a good first step, if one could manage it. Willa Cather, in her novel *Sapphira and the Slave Girl,* says of a little mountain woman that she was "born interested." That is a heritage far better than all the subterranean gold at Fort Knox. But, even if the natural endowment for seeing is not exceptional, it may be enhanced.

One help is an increased use of the eye. This will be conscious at first; later it will become more unconscious. John Burroughs once said, writing of the observation of nature, that some people had buttons instead of eyes. We have all known them. When the minister has a pair of shiny black buttons set firmly in his head instead of eyes, his congregation is out of luck. Buttonlike insensitiveness can be reduced by deliberate practice. In a later chapter means of increasing the eye's harvest in reading the Bible are discussed. In seeing the world and people, the process is essentially a religious one, that of diminishing preoccupation with self. A mind at leisure from itself is the only one that has time to see. Only he that loseth his life shall find it. We never really hear other people if our ears are deafened by the clamor of our insistent desires and self-affirmation. We never really see the world or other people if our own figure is always in front of us blocking the view. A genuine humility is the beginning of all observation and insight.

A good field for practice is in what is called the "tail of the eye." In an eye specialist's office will be found an instrument called a perimeter, which is used for testing the range of the eye. It is formed by some metal arcs making a hollow hemisphere. The eyes of the patient are focused at the spot in the center where the arcs intersect and then a light is moved from the left and from the right, from below and from above. The patient gives a signal as soon as the moving light comes within his range of vision. People differ greatly in the range of the eye. The machine really asks this question: "At what angles can you see a thing when you are not really looking at it?" It is an important question. Progress in preaching is partially measured by the widening of the tail of the eye, increasing the distance at which we can become aware of things. As this goes on, a person increases his capacity to discover significant relationships, significances, symbolisms.

A continual play of the mind on relationships is not only a mental stimulation, expelling the evil spirit of sluggishness, but it also enables one to see farther into whatever he looks at. Life becomes sacramental in the sense that it becomes a mediator of grace. The Rev. Peter Bell comes to see more in a yellow primrose than a yellow primrose.

Christopher Morley has a remarkable facility for this kind of double vision. Here are two fancies selected at random:

VOICES IN THE DARK

There are echoes and shoutings in the dark of the mind,
As menacing, reiterative, calamitous-sounding,
As extras indistinguishably bawled
In uptown streets at night.

And then the next morning
You learn they meant nothing.[9]

THE POWER-HOUSE

Out for my evening stroll
I discovered on 84th street
A power-house, quietly humming to itself,
And though I lived near-by
I had never known it was there.

Some people are like that.[10]

How many people we know are brought to mind in those six lines, quiet powerhouses going steadily on whether they are ever noticed or not! Aldous Huxley's idea of sight, set forth in the book referred to above, includes something of this grasp of possible relationship between the thing seen and something else. Seeing, he says, is made up of sensing by the eyes and nervous system, plus selection, plus that faculty of perceiving what is related to the individual's accumulated experiences.

Another help is that of increasing the range of one's observation. The preacher may become a veritable one-eyed Cyclops, gazing exclusively on a circumscribed ecclesiastical field. Actual experience can be widened by getting off a person's familiar beat; it can be supplemented by the extension of vicarious experience by personal contacts and reading. Reference has been made to a "sermonic Shylock." There is another sense in which a minister may resemble Shylock: he may be completely unaware of experiences common to others until they happen to him personally. Recall Shylock's fervent exclamation: "The curse never fell upon our nation till now." The curse, of course, had been on the tribe for much over a thousand years; it had been under his very eyes; but it had to hit him before he had any realization of it. He had employed no means of vicarious experience. So a minister may have no awareness of what does not push its way into his own parsonage if the vicarious enlargement of experience and suffering is neglected.

I conclude with a sample or two of the use of the double eye in finding sermon themes. It is all so familiar that the very subject may strike some readers as a discovery of the obvious, the thrilling announcement that two and two make four. Yet much preaching is unnecessarily pedestrian, repetitive, and no more explosive than a load of damp cement because the lines between experiences and ideas, between objects and symbols, are invisible.

First of all, here is a noble plea made by Donald Slesinger for eyes that can see people through a page of statistics:

When you interpret the curves of the elasticity of demand for cotton, never forget the aching muscles and sweating backs that produce it. When you make spot maps of delinquency in metropolitan areas, remember the boys and girls, with the marrow scarce formed in their bones, who spin the cotton sweated from the fields. Your sciences are human sciences, not the juggling of figures, and the neat fitting in of proposition to doctrine. That, too, has to be done, but with men and women, boys and girls in mind, not symbols.

110

A student's sermon—and a searching one, too—came from a sentence in a novel he had read: "Their marriage, after fifteen years, had become a sort of tired friendship." The student saw "double" on that, one eye on marriage degenerating into merely a tired friendship and the other on the fact that our relation to Christ can dwindle down to a tired friendship—very tired in many cases. The sermon was on how to prevent that.

G. B. Stern, the novelist, was thinking and writing as an effective preacher in her book *Another Part of the Forest* when she took a text from a London workman who was watching some railings around exclusive private parks in London being torn down to make armament. The workman said, "The damned things will never come back." Her sermon was a plea against setting up again the old railings of exclusiveness which have separated nations, races, classes. They must never come back. It was a simple but effective "double-eye vision," seeing a thing in itself and, by a quick play of imagination, allowing it to picture a spiritual truth.

XI. "IMAGINATION BODIES FORTH"

P RACTICALLY ALL OF THE PRECEDING CHAPTER COULD HAVE BEEN LOGI-
cally included under the head of the preacher's use of the imagination. So much that is penetrating and helpful has been written on that
theme, it is so large a part of the rich tradition of preaching, that
nothing to be said here can have any remote claim to freshness. A
few practical words of reminder are set down to give the theme a
setting in the whole.

Using the image-making faculty in preaching is a means of helping
people to see. And that is a primary purpose of sermons. At the beginning we may boldly transfer from fiction to preaching the classic
words of Joseph Conrad: "The novelist's purpose is by the power of
the written word to make you hear, to make you feel, . . . before all,
to make you see." "Before all, to make you see"—that is a preacher's
purpose, too. There is no way of accomplishing it unless the preacher's
mind thinks in visual images and on occasion paints pictures.

Out of hundreds of suggestive definitions of imagination take
Wordsworth's as something to work on:

It is the faculty of brooding upon some conception until it begins to
take shape and color, to spring up and to dilate, to put forth signs of life
and to dilate, and so to clothe itself in words and images and trains of
thought, which are as truly expressive of its real nature as the human face
and body are expressive of the human personality which informs them.

In those words the poet has described an incarnation. The idea becomes flesh and dwells among us—"begins to take shape and color,
. . . and so to cloth itself." Unless there is some real incarnation of
ideas into pictures there is no full salvation of preaching. For the purpose of preaching is not to make people see reasons, but visions. To

112

say this is not to join the Nazis (or the extreme Barthians, for that matter) in their disparagement of reason, but merely to put first things first in preaching. It was not the conclusion of a syllogism which arrested Paul on the Damascus Road and turned his life in a new direction, but a vision: "Suddenly there shone from heaven a great light round about me."[1] Where there is no vision in the pulpit, the people perish.

Imagination plays a vital part in a preacher's life in two senses: first, in helping him to project himself into the experience of others and, second, in helping him to put the truth into images, which people can see and hence feel.

The first sense is not our immediate theme and need only be mentioned. Nothing is more central to a genuine ministry than the faculty of feeling one's way into the lives of others—what General "Chinese" Gordon called "creeping under the other man's skin." It is more than sympathy; it is *empathy,* the imaginative projection of one's consciousness into another's being, the ability to see with his eyes, to feel with his nerves. Walt Whitman, writing of his days as a volunteer nurse in Washington hospitals during the Civil War, expressed it, with characteristic grandiloquence but with truth, no doubt, "I *become* the wounded man." Keats had empathy to a remarkable degree. That was one reason he gave up the study of medicine. He was too physically affected by illness. He wrote of himself, "If a sparrow come before my window, I take part in its experience and pick about the gravel."

It is the other sense of imagination, that of putting the truth into images, which concerns us here.

One of the most helpful of all the rules of thumb which can be given is this: Turn the ear into an eye. No rule can be universal in its application to a profession, and that one certainly is not. There are many occasions when the habit of writing and speaking in pictures is a cheap and easy escape from the discipline and duty of hard, straight thinking. A beautiful illustration is a vain thing for safety when there is need for an argument to be carried home in clear, direct words. This must be granted. Yet the rule of thumb has real wisdom for many occasions; for when the truth is put in pictures and images which make one see as well as hear, not only is the immediate impression greater, but the memory lasts longer. This is particularly true in what can be called an eye-minded generation. People in our mechanized world take in so much of all they get through the eye. The heyday of the picture magazine makes one wonder whether the next generation may not find that reading anything longer than a picture caption brings on prostration and a splitting headache. Indeed, until the advent of the radio the ear was rapidly disappearing as one of the organs of sense. Recently, also, the craze for jazz and swing has been an aid to the ear in its rivalry with the eye, aided by the amazing spread of interest in the best in music. And of course the advent of the sound-track moving picture played a timely part in saving the ear. In the days of the silent movies, multitudes became so accustomed to seeing that they became very poor listeners. Complaints that they could not hear from a pulpit or platform were common, and very often they were merely an excuse to cover a sense of hearing that was growing atrophied from disuse.

Yet for all the rescue-party work of the radio, the increased interest in music, the sound motion picture, ours is still so largely an eye-minded world. No one who seeks to arouse conviction by means of words should ever forget it. This is often forgotten by those who gather at the wailing wall and lament the trend of the crowds away from church, as though it were only religious services which were having a hard time today. The hard fact is that anything which depends entirely or largely on the ear for its attendance and acceptance is having a hard time. The lecture platform, the political speech (without benefit of radio), are hardly hot spots in the present scene. Even the radio tries, often feverishly, to "turn the ear into an eye." The sports broadcasts, descriptions of current events, radio dramas, and operas—"horse," "soap," and Metropolitan, all three—bring as much of visual sensation as can be brought with words. (Even the prayers, particularly at broadcast outdoor services, sometimes tell the Lord, and the distant listeners, how the scene looks, who is there, and what they are doing.)

Some implications of all this stand out rather clearly. One is aside from our present interest, but well worthy the attention it is receiving from leaders and thinkers in the field of worship. It is in the question:

What can be done to deepen and enhance the effect of worship by acts of worship ministering through the eye, particularly in churches roughly grouped as nonliturgical? That deserves continued exploration and reverent experiment. (Incidentally, the candlelight service, while along this fruitful line, is surely not to be the sum total of our visual aid to worship.)

But here we are concerned with the word from the pulpit. Simply stated, turning the ear into an eye means bringing to the presentations of truth the aid of sense perception in all the ways possible, by images, pictures, narrative, thus breaching two gaps, eye and ear, into the walls of man's soul. For most people, general statements, with which we must deal if we are preaching the Christian gospel, must not only be stated clearly but pictured. Pictures were man's first language, in the caves of the Cro-Magnon man, in the tombs of Egypt, and in the buried palaces of Crete. In every age man's most impressive language has been that which visualizes and makes the reader see. The Elizabethan power of the visualization of abstract ideas was a wonderful achievement worth a lifetime's effort by the preacher. Not only Shakespeare but many of his contemporaries could personify conceptions and platitudes that were centuries old and make them walk on the stage as concrete things. Thus the dramatists took phrases and ideas that were almost in the sleep of death and infused them with emotion and touched them into life.[2]

A minor but real service of thinking in images and visual pictures is that it stimulates a liveliness of mind and speech which a man needs desperately if he is not to be an itinerant performer, setting off the same set of fireworks in a different place each week, but is to preach to the same congregation for five or ten years. A habit of earnest, solemn exhortation may rob the mind of its last trace of sprightliness and agility. Mark Twain once gave good counsel to a friend: "Take your mind out and dance on it; it's getting all caked up." The imagination is a dance of the mind. It helps to dispel the miasma of dull solemnity which hangs over too much preaching. It is no wonder that the minds of the congregation get all "caked up" if the preacher's mind has hardened and solidified. Christopher Morley speaks to the same point with an attractive visual imagery when he says: "It was

115

a fine day for flying kites; I had no kite to fly, so I flew my mind instead."[3]

Another real asset of the mind flown as a kite is that it embodies the sound military strategy of creeping up on an enemy on the line of least expectation. It may seem strange to call a congregation an enemy, but in a real sense it is—an enemy to be captured as well as a friend to be loved. When a preacher ceases entirely to think of an audience as a speaker's natural enemy, to be engaged with all the strategy and resources he can summon, and with whom the struggle is always in doubt, he loses a saving fear and sinks back into a dangerous complacency. The frontal, direct attack on a congregation, even though employing the loud guns of command and dogmatic assertion, is often far less effective than an indirect approach through the imagination, in which the enjoyment of the picture opens the mind to the entrance of the truth. The guards of the mind are lowered and sometimes disarmed.

One way in which the powers of imagination may be increased is by reading in books of imagination. A preacher's mind needs much travel in that realm of gold. To employ De Quincey's distinction, he needs more of the literature of power to balance the large amount of the literature of knowledge which he must study. He needs books with color and fire and music in them so that his mind and his speech do not become strangers to what it is in language which has given it lasting power over men; otherwise he will begin to speak in an alien jargon and think in unfamiliar terms. The tragedy often is that the more a man studies, the worse he gets; his mind becomes subdued to what he works in, and the textbook style of language hardens on him like a shell. He becomes a literary and vocal crustacean. The preacher who is too busy to read poetry, fiction, drama, and the naturalists is too busy. While he is busy here and there with Kant or John Dewey or Karl Barth or Karl Marx or other Olympians, the opportunity of speaking for God to people in their native tongue is gone.

A word on the training in theological seminaries naturally follows from this. Few men with ten years experience in parish preaching week after week would disagree with the statement that seminary

116

courses fail much more on the side of art than on the side of theological and biblical and sociological content. The seminaries give four fifths of their attention to training men to preach to one fifth of their audience, that is, to the one fifth of the congregation which can follow an abstract train of reasoning. In most congregations, the estimate of one fifth is a gross overestimate. The theological and biblical loading, of course, must not be left undone. But to it should be added more attention to the power to carry truth to people through the development of imagination. It is a great mistake in aeronautics to build transport planes to carry a load greater than the wing power. The average student leaves the seminary with more load than wing power to carry it.

XII. STRUCTURE AND OUTLINE

MUCH THAT HAS BEEN SAID AND WRITTEN ON "STRUCTURE" IN THE SER-mon might be put into one sentence: The power of a sermon lies in its structure, not in its decoration. This is equally true of beauty, in spite of a common tendency to find beauty in ornament rather than in form.

In this respect the relationships between architecture and sermons are many and significant. In buildings, all the way from a Greek temple with plain Doric columns or a Gothic cathedral in its sublimity of mass and shape to the simple beauty of proportion in a rectangular Georgian Colonial house, beauty comes from structure. This is still true even when decoration is added to structure and form. Doric columns may give way to elaborate Corinthian capitals, the cathedral may be enriched with exquisite sculpture, the Georgian house acquire a notable doorway with fluted sides and rounded top. The great beauty and power of the building lies still in its form.

Aristotle expressed this truth, applying equally to building with words, in his dictum that "beauty depends on order and a certain magnitude." That is basic foundation for all forms of expository, argumentative, and persuasive writing and speaking—including, emphatically, preaching. To get it well in mind will help to keep in remembrance the truth so important to a maker of sermons, that ornament often blurs what should be the clear, hard beauty of structure. Where an essential rightness of order and outline are not present, even a frieze rivaling those of the Parthenon will not make up the deficiency. Dean Meeks of the Yale School of Fine Arts once made the remark about that architectural monstrosity, Grant's Tomb, in New York City, that no conceivable change could be made without improving the proportions. That remark would apply equally to many

118

sermons, especially those by men cursed with a facility for extemporaneous oratory.

Edna St. Vincent Millay has put this primacy of structure in a noble sonnet, the first line of which is, "Euclid alone has looked on Beauty bare." Bare beauty, the beginning of all grace, is structure. Euclid has never been canonized as a saint in any list. Students of high-school age have usually been sure that he was one of the evil princes of darkness. But he deserves a place in the preacher's gallery of saints, a niche in his private pantheon.

A striking picture of the power of line in architecture applied to builder with words is to be found quite unexpectedly in the experience and words of the actor and theater manager Henry Miller. Once, just after the completion of St. Thomas's Church, New York, designed by Ralph Adams Cram, while the stone was still white, he passed it on a moonlit night and looked up spellbound at the Gothic structure piling up to the pale sky. Then he said: "The clean lines reaching up, the detail all in place and emphasizing them, the planned effect of spontaneous unity, and the whole thing beautiful! That's the way a play should be!"[1]

Those are lyric words, and true ones. We can add to the craftsman's exclamation and say, "That's the way a sermon should be!" For notice the priority of his words, "the clean lines reaching up," and the detail merely emphasizing them. That is the charter of preaching.

Granted that this emphasis on the basic importance of structure is elementary. It has been enforced both with eloquence and with convincing detail in all the rich library on preaching which has been produced in the past century. Yet there is constantly recurring occasion for its repetition. For there is a contemptuous disdain, endowed with the persistence of a hardy perennial, on the part of many preachers for a serious and painful concern with sermon outlines, as a sort of pedantic technicality unworthy of the attention of a truly prophetic mind. Such do not see that it is not only vitally related to the effectiveness of preaching but also inseparable from a man's inner integrity, from the honesty of his soul, like the professional integrity of an architect, who scorns to throw timbers and stones and cement together in a formless sprawl. Such a thing, in architect or preacher, is not merely

119

inartistic; it is unethical. In all the creative arts, the two words "art" and "ethics" cover much common territory.

Changing the figure, the preacher must not be merely the intrepid leader of a verbal Charge of the Light Brigade; he must be a Carnot, "Organizer of Victory." Evangelistic victory rests heavily on organization of the words of the message. Look briefly at some of the utterly indispensable advantages which a clear-cut outline in a sermon— simple, logical, readily visible, with movement and goal—gives both to the congregation and to the preacher himself.

For one thing, it gives to the hearers continuous clues to what it is all about. That is an eminently reasonable service. A sermon is not a species of detective story, inducing a maze of baffled speculation about whether it is this or that. It is more like a highroad well posted with legible signs indicating, "This is where we are now; the next place will be so and so." A panorama without pattern is a distraction to the mind, no matter how bright the occasional vistas. Evident structure and a consecrated devotion to clarity, which sets the preacher free from a self-regarding fear of letting the outline appear point by point, give the hearer a necessary map of the journey. Stages of movement, definitely announced, clarify the mental trip as helpfully as do the announcements of the railroad conductor when he calls out, "This station is Utica; the next stop is Syracuse." That may be stooping to a lowly service, but it does serve the traveler in a way that no eloquence alone could match.

A word frequently heard on the radio is well worth a preacher's remembrance: "There will be a brief pause for station identification." A good idea! Then the hearer knows exactly where he is on the radio map. When the preacher makes clear the point at which his sermon has arrived, he too gives a needed pause for station identification. He says in effect: "This is where we are. Let's keep that in mind, pull ourselves together, and go on to the next step."

In all this it should be remembered that there is no one kind of outline to be reverenced as the tables of the law. The three-point sermon, despite a long deference to it and its manifest utility as a frame in which suggestive implications of a proposition may be stressed in a short time period, is by no means a holy trinity. God fulfills himself in many ways, in the pulpit as well as in nature. Nature has many forms: ground pine and tall sentinel pine, gnat and giraffe, humming-bird and eagle—many forms, but all have definite structure, order, and outline. So there are many varieties of effective sermons. New ones must be created and will continue to be created for new generations, new wineskins of form into which to pour new experience of God.

Among some familiar forms, Frederick W. Robertson held a loyal devotion through his life, all too short, to a two-point sermon. As inevitably as dawn follows night, his roman numerals I and II follow the introduction. They are the watermark of a Robertson sermon. Looking at it from the outside, one might well exclaim, "What a terribly cramping scheme in which to confine everything!" Yet what a large place, with illimitable ranges, he made it! Many men have done wonders with a short one-point sermon, Hugh Black among others. Dr. Charles E. Jefferson, in sharp contrast to his usual organiza-tion of a sermon, once preached a Thanksgiving sermon with nine points on the text, "Where are the nine?" He gave nine possible rea-sons which might have kept the nine lepers from returning to give thanks, and showed how those same reasons may kill the spirit of gratitude in any time. It was a sermon which went home to many hearers. And all done with an unorthodox sort of "centipede outline."

Julian Huxley, in an address given in the United States a few years ago, gave a striking picture of a sermon without bony structure. He said that a sea animal essaying motion on land without a skeleton would collapse gelatinously. A good word that, "gelatinously"—hard to pronounce yet a fine addition to a preacher's familiar vocabulary. Who has not seen a sermon collapse gelatinously all over the church auditorium because there was no hard skeleton? The fear of the Lord is the beginning of wisdom in preaching, but the fear of gelatin also helps.

Before this discussion goes any further, it may be of some help to a few readers to give an example or two in specific detail of just what is meant by the simple, very evident outline. Here are two examples, chosen entirely at random:

121

The first is by Dr. A. H. Boyd of England. It was on the Rich Fool and his three mistakes (based on a comment made by Professor Alexander Hislop: "This man's folly lay in his three mistakes"). Here is the outline:

1. He mistook his body for his soul.
2. He mistook man for God.
3. He mistook time for eternity.

The second example is much more recent, taken from a newspaper report of a sermon by that master of clarity, Dr. William P. Merrill. The text was timely, "Art thou he that should come, or look we for another?" The sermon dealt with a widespread mood, the question whether in this world with so much awry the wisdom of Jesus is really true. Here is the report of three points, based on the Gospel record of Jesus' answer to John's question. Dr. Merrill asked, "Is Christianity What the World Needs?"

John the Baptist put this question to Jesus nineteen hundred years ago: "Art thou he that should come? or look we for another?" Jesus gave a threefold answer, which still holds good:

1. First Jesus says, "Ask those who have tried it?" Find the best Christian you know and ask him to tell you what and why he believes.

2. Then Jesus says, "Look at the fruits." Does not that still hold? Would you like to live in a world from which all that Christianity has brought was swept away? No churches, no hospitals, no rights for women, no modern science, no freedom of thought? Ask the leaders of the heroic struggle in China what they think of Christianity. Watch the splendid stand of Christians in Norway and elsewhere.

3. But the climax of Jesus' answer is a direct challenge to faith. How does one prove that marriage or patriotism is worth while? Only by a venture of faith. So it is with religion. There is just one thing that can ultimately make you sure that Christianity is worth while, and that is "betting your life on God."

Both simple and big, that sermon was.

One advantage of a definite structure, planned and clearly foreseen to the end, is that it helps the preacher enormously in keeping a grasp on his subject itself. For a sermon subject is like a greased pig. It can slip through the hands with incredibly elusive wriggles. While he is busy here and there, it is gone—and, worst of all, often the preacher wists not that it has departed from him. In following a beckoning aside, in some detour which seems to demand attention, he gets off the center of his exact theme or proposition. Often when a man complains that in the writing of a sermon he has lost his way, what he has really lost is his subject. Grasping a definite, sharply limited subject is often like trying to pick up a drop of mercury: it runs all over the place. In this demanding and often baffling task nothing helps more than stout fences and clearly marked progression points definitely accepted. They compel the question: "Just exactly what am I talking about, and what, specifically, am I trying to enforce?" When this question is answered, one can thank God and take courage; for, as Gaius Glenn Atkins says, when the organization is structurally right, the next point becomes clear to the maker of the sermon.

Movement is another indispensable advantage of sharp, clear outline. Any discourse designed to win and hold human attention must have movement. The eye and the mind are so designed that they follow movement involuntarily; and the public speaker had better remember it. People's attention will follow a thing as long as it is moving; when it stops they relax, as though the plot had sagged. A young preacher in a country church, one summer Sunday when the windows and doors were open, was greatly disturbed by the rivalry of a bird flying around the sanctuary. He felt rather bitterly the trivial-mindedness of the congregation in watching the bird instead of listening to him. There was no "trivial-mindedness." The people were merely exhibiting a law of attention. The bird was moving, and perhaps the preacher's sermon was not. The sermon should move along straight lines rather than revolve in circles around the same spot. Even when one is purposely speaking on one point, there must be certain aspects of it progressively brought under the focus of the mind if one is to respect the powers and limits of attention. This is true in optics. The eye cannot remain focused on one black dot; its very nervous mobility compels it to travel to other dots in the same area. It is oriented to movement, and so is the attention of the mind.

One of the most helpful of all the large, sweeping divisions which can be applied to sermons, as well as other kinds of discourse, is the twofold division of predicament and cure. This can be stated in the barest terms, with too great a simplification; but nevertheless they will serve: First, what is the matter? Second, what can be done about it? A member of a notable group in Great Britain which studied together social and economic questions after the first World War, the Conference on Politics, Economics, and Christianity (popularly known as C.O.P.E.C.), has given a suggestive account of their general procedure in research and preparing their findings. The two general divisions were the "Mess" and the "Cure." The "Mess," of course, was the existing conditions, the forces at work and their results, the obstacles to social and religious welfare. The "Cure" included all the positive and constructive action possible in improving the conditions, and the social and moral and religious resources available. Those two grand divisions of "Mess" and "Cure" are immensely valuable in dealing with almost any vital sermon subject. This does not mean that every sermon should have these two points. That would be intolerable monotony. But the two realms of diagnosis and treatment should have a permanent place in one's thinking.

About this simple major division there are two important cautions to be stressed.

The first is, *Do not omit presentation of some actual means of cure.* That is one of the commonest weaknesses of sermons. The problem is presented, some interesting aspects of it discussed, and then follows either some harmless, and useless, generality—such as recommending the spirit of Christ—or else the benediction. The analogy of medicine is close and pertinent. Thus, Professor Crane Brinton uses it in criticizing a book of Ferrero's because of its substituting eloquent diagnosis for concrete suggestions of remedy: "It is as though the doctor had made a confident and sharp diagnosis of a disease, indicated that without therapeutic measures the prognosis was a lingering and horrible death, and then announced that all he could offer as a therapy was a sermon on the necessity of getting well."

There are many natural reasons for this tendency. For one thing, it is much easier to describe than it is to prescribe. It is easier to describe arthritis than it is to outline a course of treatment that will relieve it, to say nothing of curing it. So in a sermon it is far easier to describe the evil effects of fear, or worry, or envy, or lust, than to present clearly and persuasively the resources and disciplines which might overcome the evil. Another reason is that naturally the presentation of the evil, of one sort or another, comes first, and unless the preacher has a sure view of his destination and rightly divides his time, he will waste all his substance in riotous living in describing the disease, and be in want when it comes to suggesting a cure. Even so simple a matter as the careless and inaccurate estimate of time may prevent a man from reaching the real point of his sermon with opportunity to enforce it. Many a man has preached for thirty years without ever having come within gunshot of having any correct idea of how many words can go into twenty-five minutes of time. So the preacher cuts at the place where cutting can be least afforded, in the positive remedies offered.

A word from the Gospel is the best prescription for this common calamity, "The last shall be first." Back into it. Give the first attention to where you are coming out rather than to where you are going in. We can do a great deal worse than follow the professional song writer who frequently in his composition jumps from the title to the last line. A sermon is much more like a drama than it is like a novel. Many a novel has been begun with the author having his characters and main situations in mind but without final decision in detail about how it is going to come out. Some novelists call it allowing the characters to take charge and go their own way. Some have even altered the ending because of the pleas of readers while the novel was appearing in serial form. But with a drama the author must know the end from the beginning. He knows that Hamlet gets killed in the last act and does not ascend triumphantly to his villainous uncle's throne; he knows that Othello does not uncover Iago's villainy in the nick of time and live happily ever after with Desdemona. A very able writer in other fields, with large and successful experience, James Thurber, thus recounts whimsically his first experience in writing a drama:

It is very hard for a man who has never had anywhere to go to begin going somewhere. That is, it is very hard for a man who has always just sort of started to write pieces and begun to make scrawls on paper, wondering what they were going to turn into, to encounter what is known as the three-act play. The three-act play has sharp, concrete edges, rigid spacings, a complete dependence on time and more than eleven hundred rules, all basic.

Even so the preacher should know the end, the positive affirmations and remedies which are to be offered to meet the situation. He must be

125

sure of his landing field when the journey starts, like a good aviator; else he, too, will be left "up in the air" looking vainly for a place to come down. How many times have congregations listened to a preacher circling around his theme, not knowing how to quit, all because he has not selected his landing field in advance. On this, Gaius Glenn Atkins has formulated one of the most helpful, simple directions that can be given on preaching: "Spend two thirds of your time on the last third of your sermon." That is, emphatically, "rightly dividing the word of truth." Such a practice will save a preacher from making what may well be called "the elephant sermon." That comes from the natural-history lore of Hilaire Belloc:

> When people call this beast to mind
> They marvel more and more
> At such a little tail behind
> So large a trunk before.[2]

The "elephant sermon," whose habitat is all over Christendom, has a large trunk before, of introduction, description, illustration, or diagnosis, with such a little tail behind, of positive remedy or word of salvation.

The second caution is really a division of the first: *Work with the truth always in mind that it is so much easier to discuss symptoms than to suggest therapeutics.* Remembering this, we can watch and pray against the deceptions of our own minds, the clever rationalizations we make to ourselves of our failure to meet head-on the issues that have been raised, and to bring light and power. Thus we can catch ourselves when we start to follow that line of least resistance of Peer Gynt and "go roundabout."

An effective sermon is marked by progress, and progress is impossible without structure. Progress includes movement, but it is more and other than movement. It is strategic and cumulative movement toward an assigned goal. The grand old Duke of York, when he went up the hill and down again, had movement but little progress. A sermon should gather strength as it goes along, reaching a climax or a series of climaxes. That can be achieved only under a planned strategy of operation, with the successive objectives to be taken well mapped.

126

Otherwise, even when the idea is good, there will be a tendency for the sermon to run down hill after the central idea has been unfolded. Unless there is an outline that compels progress, the sermon will trickle like a thin stream running down from a spring. That is the reason why one of the commonest questions in the theatrical world is, "How's your second act?" Does it gather strength and go on, or does it trickle out? A critic has made an acute comment on the later novels of H. G. Wells, that after they get a good start, they sit down like a baked apple. Sermons "sit down" too. Sometimes they sit down lumpily for as much as five or ten minutes at a time, giving the whole thing a static quality.

But structure and outline in sermons are not all a matter of logical sequence and order and progress in relation to a subject. There is also what might be called a psychological outline that must be kept in mind, one that takes account of the emotional rhythm of an audience. A sermon is not a chapter in a textbook, where ideas can be unfolded in a near vacuum. It is a co-operative achievement with an audience, and the audience must be kept in mind at all costs. Thus, material which is immensely valuable in getting into contact with an audience and holding that human contact may often seem a wasteful detour from the point of view of strict logic. But it justifies its place in the structure by the indispensable service it renders. Frequently very unfair and unskilled criticisms of preaching have been made by amateurs, often theological students, who have never grappled much with the difficult and mysterious task of holding an audience. Such critics often complain that the preacher was not doing very much with his subject; they do not notice that he may have been doing remarkable things with his audience, and often by the use of material at which they looked with pedantic disdain. That is one of the most evident differences between an amateur and professional speaker, in the best sense of professional. For the competent professional knows that there is not much use in holding to your subject if you lose your audience. There must be an emotional outline, so to speak, a chart of keeping in touch with the audience, as well as the orderly outline in developing the subject. Sir John Adams, the British educator, author of many books on teaching, has written suggestively on this point:

In listening to the sermon there is a sort of rhythm of attention, a more or less regular rise and fall of attention. There is an alternation of two beats—an intensive beat and a diffused one. Now the attention is concentrated on a narrow area, and again it is scattered over a wide one. When this is pointed out to people, they are inclined to agree, but are apt to come to the erroneous conclusion that the intensive beat is the important one, and the diffused beat more or less negligible. They watch a painter, for example, working close to his easel, using his smallest brush. "Ah," they say. "Good man! He is working for his living." By and by he steps back from his easel and takes a general look at the picture, maybe scratching his nose the while with the butt of his brush, and the watcher thinks, "Now he is loafing," but is kind enough to add, to himself, "After all, the man cannot be working all the time; he needs a rest now and again."

In truth the painter is doing as good work at the distant range as at the close. When he stands back he is at his diffused beat, but this is as important for the picture as is the intensive beat when he is working out some of the delicate details.[3]

So in any outline which is to operate in the realm of human contacts; there should be place for some things which do nothing except win the possibility of success for the whole enterprise by establishing and holding close interest and contact. A man preparing a sermon can well hold in mind a sort of invisible structure paralleling the development of his theme. He can ask himself: "Where in all this are any mental grappling hooks which may hold me close to the minds with which I am engaged? Where are the places at which I can come to some kind of an emotional climax, figuratively getting up on my tiptoes and with intensity and directness packing my chief appeal in a few words?"

That word "climax" suggests one weakness of many sermons, perhaps the commonest weakness in sermons of beginning preachers. The sermon may have almost everything of value and yet be constructed in a manner which quite fails to take into account the attention limits of the human mind. The preachers seem to proceed on the theory that they can move along a horizontal line, like a string drawn tautly, which never has any peaks or valleys but moves with severity of thought and earnestness of appeal from start to finish. The true graph of attention is never a straight line; it is more like a graph of the fluctuations of the market—a level plateau, then up and down, plateau again, up and down.

Recognition of this will lead to two things to be done deliberately:

One is to "rest" an audience occasionally, to give it a breathing spell, so that it can come back to move along with the preacher with renewed vigor. This does not mean trivial interludes of any sort. It does call for change of pace, for vocal variety, for variation of intensity and different types of material. For instance, in the midst of a close-knit argument some narrative will come like an oasis, at which the traveler can break the steady march and find renewal. This strategy in sermons marks out places where the endeavor is to win the audience. The concern is for the moment not theological but psychological. Sometimes it is nothing more than the inducing of a feeling of good will, or heightening the appreciation by a homely illustration from a well-known realm of life, about which at least some in the audience can inwardly agree and say, "That is true."

The other thing is the provision of a series of climaxes, places where the preacher can "break through." Not necessarily in a noisy bombardment at all, but with emotional peaks which break the pattern of the level plateau, or the tightly drawn string, where the feeling is definitely intensified, or the presentation or argument reaches a culmination of a particular stage. In this way one follows the "grain" of the mind and attention. A study of many sermons will reveal an emotional outline as well as a logical one—places where there is a "break through," with a stepped-up animation and intensity, climaxes arising like peaks from a plain, after which, with a change of tempo and volume, the sermon goes on to reach, after a stage of the journey, another climax.

One critical point in any kind of outline is that at which the central idea or proposition is "broken up" into significant and relevant aspects, divisions, and relationships. Unless this is done, the sermon is liable to stop in its tracks and go into circular repetition. Or else the value of the initial idea is lost by not being carried through to practical implications. The analogy to the task of the diamond cutter is close and instructive. The skill required in splitting up a diamond by striking it at the right spot so that it will fall apart in regular fragments and

129

not lose its value by being ground to mere chips and dust, is a very great one. Expert diamond cutters have looked at a large diamond for weeks, studying to find the place to strike the careful blow which will break it up into unmarred fragments. Needless to say, the moment of striking the blow is a tense one. So much depends on finding the natural grain of the diamond and aiming the stroke of the hammer so that it will fall into natural divisions.

The preacher, too, must split his diamond carefully. The critical point of the sermon is the breaking point, where, after clearly revealing the central idea, it is "cracked open" so that it may fall into significant divisions.

Take some simple illustrations of this "breaking point," where a general idea is split up into sections which move close to various realms of experience. Here is a sermon of Dr. Herbert H. Farmer of Cambridge, England, on the theme "The Called of God." He starts with the contrast between the frequent use of the word "called" in the New Testament and the degree to which it has so largely dropped out of our thinking and living today. The sermon is a plea for the renewed sense of God's calling as a force to counteract our practical secularism. Then the diamond, the idea, is broken up into significant divisions, showing what such a renewed sense of God's calling would do for our lives. Here are the results of the hammer blow:

1. In the first place, the recovery of a keener sense of the activities of God would give a new basis for faith as we look out across the troubled world.
2. In the second place, a renewed sense of the activity of God would quicken and deepen our earnestness in relation to the issues of good and evil in the soul.
3. Finally, a renewed sense of God's active interest in and dealing with us would give us the secret of that strange power to endure tribulation with patience and victory which is so characteristic of the New Testament.[4]

That is preaching which creeps well into the mind and heart. Much of its force comes from the importance and relevance to life of the divisions which result from the breaking up of the central idea. Much of what is loosely called a "genius" for preaching resides somewhere about this point. The development of the capacity to find natural and relevant aspects of a central theme, which carry the truth into vital areas of experience, is worth long labor.

Another illustration of this particular stage in sermon making is found in Dr. Ralph W. Sockman's sermon "The Unemployed Carpenter." It caught interest from the timeliness of mood in that it was preached at a low point of the depression, when unemployment was a national specter. The main point was that Jesus, the carpenter of Nazareth, is also among the unemployed. We do not give him the job to do in our lives which he can do so well. The idea is "cracked open" with the hammer, and natural divisions result: We do not employ the carpenter sufficiently (1) in our homes, or (2) in our business, or (3) in our international relations.

Now move the camera up closer to the beginnings of the process rather than to the results. Imagine a sermon being contemplated on a familiar phrase of Stevenson's. (This was an actual experience of a theological student a few years ago.) The phrase is from a familiar story of Stevenson's last days. A missionary wrote him that he would be glad to come to see him and to talk to him "as to one in danger of dying." Stevenson wrote back gaily that he didn't want him if he were going to talk to him as to one "in danger of dying," but that he would be glad to see him if he would talk to him "as to one in danger of living." All right, the preacher spears that phrase as a fish might be speared in a mountain stream. Here is a possible theme worth saving —the dangers of living. It has a strange sound; but there are dangers of living, are there not? What are some real dangers of living to which all people are exposed?

Remember that the point here is not at all what the final outcome of the sermon may be. That is aside from the issue. The effort is simply to try to glimpse the process of exploration of trial and error, of deciding whether this or that line of advance, or aspect of the subject, seems to be most important and helpful. It is just at this point, rather than on any later "polishing" of the result, that the expenditure of time is most rewarding. Frequently it is of very great help to a preacher to explore his theme in terms of questions which he asks himself. If one can really ask pertinent questions, he is well on the way toward helpful answers.

To get back, then, to the turning over in the mind this question: What are some common and real dangers of living? Many will come

131

to mind; those which come most readily should be viewed with suspicion; many should be rejected. Thus, one risk of life is the danger of "going sour." That happens. Then the mind bounces off to the opposite danger of "going sweet," so sweet that one never gets a real view of his world, so sweet that he never becomes an active combatant against evil. That also happens. But are either of these things important enough? Are those lines the best use that can be made of the theme. Evidently not, so they are rejected, or at least set aside. The process is not unlike that of trying a lock with several keys, persisting until the right one is found. Hurry is fatal here; a slap-dash, make-it-go selection, anything as long as it seems to have some connection with the theme and will last twenty minutes, does not unlock the door. All right, then; back to the bunch of keys. Start on another effort: Do the words of Jesus throw any light on the question? Did Jesus ever point out any risks of living? Now we are striking ore; there is a gleam of gold in it. People flash through the mind. The Rich Young Ruler, what was his great danger in life? The Rich Fool, the Pharisees; perhaps Judas? Possibilities come faster than one can evaluate them. They must be reserved for final choice. Where else in the Bible are there conspicuous examples of people who succumbed to the dangers of living? Let another gallery of pictures pass through the mind. What actual people has one known who have either failed to master the dangers of living or, more positively, who have surmounted the inevitable risks? Now there is plenty to work on, and the working can be done in an atmosphere of stimulation, even of quickened excitement, the real joy of a maker. What the outcome of this particular sermon might be is not important at all here. It might include a portrayal of the risk of living in a meaningless world—a world well upholstered, with bright flashes of color here and there, but no high meaning to it all—or the risk of missing the joy of being caught up in a great cause and so finding life by losing it.

One general observation applies to most sermons. The most helpful sermon is usually one which teaches in detail in a limited area rather than one which travels, no matter how eloquently, over a wide stretch of territory. There is a "catch" in this; it is that the sermon which concentrates on bringing specific teaching and help at a particular point cannot be as "showy" as a sermon that includes the heavens above and most of what is beneath. To do such preaching, a man must care more about bringing help to people than about his prestige as an orator. Like his Master, he must make himself "of no reputation." That is often the last full measure of devotion, to a man whose career is made up so largely of public speaking.

It is for this reason that regular parish preaching offers so much greater opportunity for lasting results in the lives of people than the occasional sermons of a wandering minstrel of any sort, be he bishop, board secretary, or a mere professor. The congregation knows its pastor's general positions. He preached last Sunday; he will preach next Sunday. So today he does not have to give his whole last will and testament; he can confine himself to a limited theme and do something with it by intensive examination. If he is preaching on ways of praying, he can give himself to the theme with a united mind, free from the fear, which is liable to beset a preacher in the college chapel, that the congregation may think he has no views on the international situation or the economic order.

In the early days of the participation by the United States in the second World War, there was much discussion, which often grew acrimonious, over the best method of extinguishing incendiary bombs. The method of turning a jet stream against a bomb had its partisans; so did the method of spraying. At an official test by officers of the Army and the New York City Fire Department it was determined that the jet was mightier than the spray. A three-eighths-inch stream of water through a jet doused a four-pound magnesium bomb in fifteen seconds, whereas it took sixty-five seconds to extinguish a similar bomb by the spray method. Also, the spray method took twice as much water. The jet is better than the spray. The "jet sermon," which concentrates a stream of thought on a limited area, is better than the "spray sermon." But make no mistake about it—it is harder.

XIII. SOME TYPES OF OUTLINE

CERTAIN SPECIFIC PATTERNS OF OUTLINE WHICH HAVE BEEN USED WITH more or less frequency may be worth looking at in some detail. They are offered without any undue solemnity, or any pride of parentage, for they are not the creations or inventions of the author. They are just a few reports of observation, coming from hearing sermons or reading them, or from second-hand reports of other hearers. They are presented in the tentative spirit in which most clinical reports are given in a medical journal. They do not say, Here is a sure cure for anything. They simply report: Here is the way in which one practitioner has approached a common medical problem, with mixed results, which seem to warrant continued experiment.

Every preacher must find his own most natural ways of doing his work, the methods that work "with the grain" of his nature, mind, and personality. The thing to avoid at all costs is any outward compulsion which pontificates, in a ludicrous imitation of the thunder of Sinai, "This is the way, walk ye in it." It may not be the way for a particular person at all. Brooks and Spurgeon, to mention only two out of ten thousand—and those two are as unlike as possible—did not come off a mass-production assembly line. The one caution worth paying continued attention to is that against the danger of settling prematurely into one method, before others, which might have given greater range and power and which certainly would add to a preacher's variety of resource, have been explored and tried.

Here, then, are a few types of outline:

1. The first might be called the "ladder sermon." It takes one from point to point like the rungs of a ladder. It is a type of structure well adapted to argument, persuasion, and the appeal to reason. There is always a place for reasoned argument in the practice of preaching.

This is particularly worth stress and remembrance because in some quarters of the religious world it is definitely "out of season" today. Under the strong influence of the theological trend, variously known as neo-orthodoxy, Continental theology, Barthianism, in violent reaction against the liberalism of the nineteenth and early twentieth centuries, there has been a disparagement of reason and a slighting of the whole approach to the mind which has gone under the now discarded heading of apologetics. The tendency manifested by many exponents of this theology has been simply and dogmatically to announce revelation—"This is the word of the Lord"—and to regard as unnecessary and even beneath the dignity of a herald of revelation the matter of any attempt to commend the truth to reason.

Any discussion of the effect of the Barthian theology on the presentation of Christian truth is beyond the limits of our present interest. It is emphatically beyond the competence of the present writer. Anyone interested in the subject will find a penetrating discussion of it by one of the most distinguished theologians of our time, Professor John Baillie, in his *Invitation to Pilgrimage*. His main defense of the appeal to reason can be indicated by quoting a few sentences, but the whole chapter should be read by those interested:

I am convinced that some of the Christian thinkers of our time have allowed themselves to be too much caught in the current of the present reaction. Just as the theology of the eighteenth century tended to be too much affected by the rationalism then current, and the theology of the nineteenth by the characteristic contemporary blend of rationalism and romanticism, so the theology of our twentieth century tends to be too much affected by the current distrust and denial of reason. It is obviously no accident that the appearance of certain extreme anti-liberal movements in theology has closely synchronized with the appearance of the extreme anti-liberal movements in politics. The two are plainly parallel products of the same spirit of the age . . . In that day [the eighteenth century] the abstract rationalism of unbelief was met by an equally abstract Christian rationalism; in our day the new unbelieving authoritarianisms are met by an equally uncompromising Christian authoritarianism . . .

Much as I have learned from many of the theologians of the Barthian school, the straitest sect of them both puzzle and distress me by the way they speak of what they call "human reason." They distress me because

135

their language bears too suspicious a resemblance to the language of the totalitarian propagandists, whom nevertheless many of them most stanchly and gallantly oppose.[1]

The "ladder sermon" is a form naturally adaptable to the presentation to the mind and reason of the claims of Christian belief and discipleship. It follows somewhat the pattern of William James's well-known "ladder of faith":

On the first rung of the ladder we say of a momentous view of life, or of the world, or of religion, that it is a possible view, it is not self-contradictory, it is not absurd; on the second round we may say it *might* well be true as far as the actual facts are concerned; on the third we may say, it *may* be true now for all that anybody knows; on the fourth we add, it is *fit* to be true; on the fifth, it *ought* to be true; and on the sixth we affirm it *must* be true. Well, then, we say at the top of the ladder, it *shall* be true, at any rate for me, because I am going to adopt it as my truth and live by it henceforth.[2]

Professor D. C. Macintosh has made effective use of the "ladder of faith" progress in presenting the "reasonableness" of Christian faith. It proceeds from a minimum as a first step, then goes on to a more inclusive proposition; often the next proposition is one which, in the opinion of the speaker at least, is involved in the first. In accepting a readily-agreed-to first step, you are committed to a second.

Paul follows this method shrewdly in his address to Agrippa. "King Agrippa," he asks, "believest thou the prophets?" He does not wait for an answer; he need not. That much common ground between the two can be assumed. In effect Paul says, "All right, then, Agrippa, a belief in the prophets logically commits you to a belief in the Messiah foretold by the prophets"; for, as Paul explicitly claims, he has been "saying none other things than those which the prophets and Moses did say should come."[3]

Here is the shape and movement of a ladder sermon outline, proceeding from a minimum that is undebatable to affirmations running farther, a sermon by Dean Emeritus Charles R. Brown, facing with characteristic clarity and forthrightness the question, "Does Prayer Change Anything?" There are three steps:
1. It changes me.

2. It changes the atmosphere of a home in such a way as to affect the lives of the entire family.

3. It opens doors into the unseen order which enfolds us all.

The final affirmation represents the preacher's full faith; the chances of its acceptance by the hearer are greatly enhanced by the gradual steps by which it is reached.

This moving from common ground to outlying territory is adaptable to almost any theme where persuasion is the object. Here, merely for illustration, might be some possible steps in a plea for a larger measure of social control of economic life:

1. We can't go on as we are going.
2. We all depend on one another, groups as well as individuals.
3. Individual desires must be disciplined.
4. We cannot depend entirely on voluntary control.
5. There must be, for the welfare of all, more social control.

2. Another type of outline might be called the "jewel sermon." Its development consists in turning one idea around as one might turn a jewel in his fingers, allowing different facets to catch the light and throw it into different realms of experience. Its usefulness consists in unity of theme, with diversity of relationship and application.

Thus take one idea, "Be not overcome of evil, but overcome evil with good"— one jewel, but the different facets might include such widely different applications as the personal fight for moral character and the means of reducing juvenile delinquency. Do not struggle against evil temptation chiefly by will power, which keeps the mind focused on the evil; but crowd it out by the positive establishment of good habits. So the evil of juvenile crime cannot be remedied by policeman and reform schools; the evil must be overcome by good, by provision of recreation and other means of channeling the energies and impulses of youth to constructive ends.

Leslie Weatherhead has written many sermons, biblical sermons which jump quickly into current life, with this general form. One is on the familiar theme of the return of the shepherds after the visit to the Bethelehem stable. There is only one idea—going back from a great experience to the common round of life. He pictures the return of the shepherds, and our return, to take up old familiar tasks in a new spirit—the family, our work, our religious life. Another sermon in similar form is "The Disturbing Christ." Christ disturbed people. There are many Gospel instances that this is part of his redeeming work. He ought to disturb us—here, and there, and there.

3. The classification sermon—based on dividing people and things into different classes or types—is literally as old as the hills, and may partake of the strength and beauty of the hills. A typical form is that which points out different ways in which an issue can be met. How to meet trouble, for instance? Well, men have met it in three ways: Some have grown bitter. Others have "thrown up the sponge." Others have kept on going, upheld by a great faith. Here, for instance, is the way in which one man met great trouble: "We are troubled on every side, yet not distressed; we are perplexed, but not in despair; persecuted, but not forsaken; cast down, yet not destroyed." [4]

The same scheme offers a means of treating timely contemporary problems. There is everyone's problem in a world engulfed in disaster: what attitude to take? Many seem to think that there are only two alternatives—a bleak defeatism or a blind, sentimental romanticism. There is a third alternative, a realism which sees evil but which also sees God and good—phrased in whatever way the preacher wishes to present the Christian alternative to these two inadequate moods.

This process of classification has a sure interest because it has deep roots in the nature of the mind, as developed throughout all history. When a speaker says anything like, "There are four ways of acting in this situation," he can depend on the same unfailing interest which Jesus met when he said, "Behold, a sower went forth to sow"—and found four kinds of soil. Folk lore, fairy tales, the first stories to which the child listens, rest heavily on a sort of innate pleasure in classification. The baby begins with it, long before he understands language. His first intellectual joy is the classification of toes—

> This little pig went to market;
> This little pig stayed home;

on to the thrilling climax of "Wee, wee, all the way home." Some of the best-loved fairy tales are exercises in dividing things and people into classes. Baffled parents for many generations have wondered why "Goldilocks and the Three Bears" is greeted with joy on what seems to be the thousandth telling, with its recurring rhythm: the first porridge was too hot, the second too cold, the third just right; the first

138

bed too hard, the second too soft, the third just right. So it is with many others.

Many of Jesus' parables turn on some kind of classification: the talents, the sower, the good Samaritan, or those many twofold classifications which draw on the powerful effect of contrast—the prodigal and his brother, Pharisee and publican, wise and foolish virgins, sand and rock foundations.

Samples of effective sermons employing this device are on every hand. Take John Haynes Holmes's sermon on the three kinds of people among the Israelites in their march through the desert:

One group wanted to go back to Egypt. They preferred slavery to the uncertainty of the wilderness. At least they would have plenty of food and the protection of the Egyptian government. The second group was satisfied wherever they might be at night. They were content to gather the manna as it came. This is the group that built the golden calf and worshiped it as an idol. The third group, the smallest, wanted to go forward. Moses was among this number. He heard God say to him, "Speak unto the children of Israel, that they go forward." In our own tongue, these are respectively the spiritual, moral and social reactionaries, conservatives and progressives. They are the people of yesterday, today and tomorrow.

Look at the following piece of highly patterned prose, and note the cumulative interest in the description of three ministers. It is by Dr. John Snape of Los Angeles:

I know personally three ministers. They have been successively the pastors of one church, a strong church of more than twelve hundred members.

The platform of the first could have been expressed in these words, "Here am I; let me do all I can for you." And they let him. He was big-bodied, big-hearted, sympathetic, industrious—and he worked for them. He was the bond slave of his congregation.

The platform of the second man could have been set forth in these words, "Here am I; do all you can for me." And, strange to say, they did! They praised him to his face, bragged about him to others, sent him to Europe, and read with unrestrained delight the reports about him and his

139

work—which he sent regularly to the papers. He was the private chaplain of his congregation.

The third minister came and he said, "Here is Jesus Christ; let us together do all we can for him." And, strange to say, they did! Immediately their vision was enlarged, their evangelistic activities quickened, their gifts to missions doubled. He was the ambassador of God to his congregation.

4. The "skyrocket sermon" is a fantastic name which might identify an order in a sermon, usually a life-situation sermon. This name is given not because it goes with a fizz and a bang and is a sensational affair. It is nothing of the sort. The name is given because its movement follows that of a skyrocket in that it begins on the ground, rises to a height, then breaks into pieces and comes down to earth again, often in red, white, and blue stars. So the sermon begins on the ground, in life; it travels up to a spiritual truth which has meaning for that situation on earth; and then the sermon comes down, as it were, in separate divisions to that situation. For example, a theme comes to a preacher from pastoral contact—say, people in whom the zest of life is almost, or completely, gone. What shall we do when life loses its zest? The Bible suggests many answers. People who have kept a zest for life in various situations suggest others. The sermon will move up to a spiritual truth and then, like the skyrocket, break into separate observations, pointing out reliances or suggesting action.

5. Another rather specific form of treatment of a theme might be called the "twin sermon" in that it has two divisions—twins, as it were—setting forth opposing or contrasting aspects of one truth or one word of scripture. It is particularly useful where clarification of common misapprehensions is needed. It may follow this form: (1) This statement is not true in one sense; but (2) it is true in another sense, usually a deeper or a broader one. It is useful in the necessary work of pointing out pitfalls which lie in a superficial or too easy interpretation of some great words of the Christian revelation. The negative first section helps to sharpen the understanding and appreciation of the second section.

Suppose the theme were God's gift of peace and the text, "My peace I give unto you." The progress might be along this line: (1) This is not true in a way commonly accepted and in a wrong idea of peaceful life—that of a placid, unruffled existence. If that is what you want, stay as far away from Christ as you can. He is the great upsetter; he brings "a sword"; he sets "at variance"; he breaks up the complacent self-satisfaction; etc.; etc. But (2) it is true that Christ does bring a deep peace to the mind that is stayed on God. No matter what storms may sweep the surface, etc.

Or imagine an exploration of the text, "When thou prayest, enter into thy closet, and . . . shut thy door." The first point might be that shutting the door on the world is a terrible thing the way many people do it. A whole world of Christ's brothers and sisters may be in cruel suffering, yet when they pray they shut the door of the world and concentrate on their own little aches and pains. This is a vicious travesty of prayer. True prayer keeps the door to a world of need open: "Thy kingdom come"; "Send forth labourers." With this wrong conception dealt with as forcibly as possible, the way is open for a stress on a truly Christian way of shutting the door—as Jesus did, for instance—a much-needed art in a day when the multiplying intrusions of the world—radio, telephone, and so forth—have almost robbed us of doors.

Or take such a theme as living a day at a time. There are two very evident sides to this. (1) Living a day at a time may be a thoroughly bad thing. It may be, and often is, living at random, with no great design or meaning running through the days; it may be the eat-drink-and-be-merry philosophy of existence. But (2) living a day at a time, in the midst of long-range concern, may be a life of trust.

6. The Roman candle may serve as an identifying clue to a sermon which consists of a succession of statements or observations which follow without any other particular design except that they are all related to the subject. A Roman candle throws out sparks for a few seconds, then discharges a ball, then more sparks and another ball. So a sermon on this general form may consist of an affirmation or a point or suggestion, followed by discussion of that, as the sparks come after the ball in a Roman candle, and then another point, and so on. As an example of a theme particularly suited to this sort of "planless" treatment, Dr. James L. Gordon, of San Francisco, once preached a sermon packed full of helpful suggestions on "If I Were Twenty-One Again." The form was just a succession of statements: If I were twenty-one again and could use the experience of a lifetime, I think I would do this, that, or the other, on up to nine or ten separate observations. Dr. J. Edgar Park, of Wheaton College, gave a few years ago a chapel talk, in which much shrewd wisdom was presented with wit and im-

agination, on "How to Hit the Nail on the Thumb." The outline was a succession of directions for doing things in a manner sure to miss their value entirely.

This form has been of great value in meeting a widespread mood in these days, that of the helplessness of the individual in a day when vast mass forces are in destructive action. Some have phrased the question, "What can you do when you can't do anything?" In spite of its paradoxical form, that question expresses the perplexity of millions of people. It is not a mood to be lightly dealt with. The process of gathering the genuine elements of hope and direction has often been a means of fortification and encouragement. It begins with "At least one can do this; and, more, one can do that; and, still more, do the other thing"—so that when all the light in a dark place is gathered, there are steady gleams.

7. The analogy sermon is so familiar that no comment is necessary. It represents the effort to impress the truth by means of analogy, talking about one thing in terms of another. The discourses of Jesus as reported in the Fourth Gospel make large use of it. "I am the door"; "I am the good shepherd"; "I am the vine." Dean Willard L. Sperry is an expert with impressive analogy. No one who has read his *Reality in Worship* will ever forget the analogy of the ship in the first chapter. Dean Charles W. Gilkey has used it effectively as a favorite form in preaching—life as bridgebuilding, the sermon on a moraine, and others. There is a "catch" in this form, however, a trap for the lazy preacher. Superficially, it is so easy to do that, unless it is handled with skill and costly effort, it readily becomes commonplace and tiresome, a succession of juvenile and wooden didacticisms—"life is like this" or "life is like that"—till most of the congregation set out on their own mental travels.

8. The surprise-package sermon is naturally one to be used sparingly; yet its occasional employment does sound an alarm, "Awake thou that sleepest." This is the sermon which, after it gets started and the ending, or at least the general direction, seems predictable, makes a surprise turning into unexpected territory. A preacher may start, for instance, with the text, "It is more blessed to give than to receive"; and, after a recognition of that truth, the audience discovers that the

point of the sermon is that it is also good to receive, the sermon being on the grace or art of receiving—on which there are pertinent things to be said.

Dr. Walter Russell Bowie preached a notable sermon on the well-known text, "Isaac digged again the wells which they had digged in the days of Abraham his father." He began with a tribute to the high values of tradition and the needed service of the conservative, who preserves the things of proven worth. But that was soon finished. The stress was on the often forgotten factor in this redigging of the traditional wells, the pioneering of Abraham who dug the wells in the first place. So, instead of being merely a tribute to those who walk in the old paths, (a theme which the average congregation can always take with wonderful fortitude), it was a plea for the innovator, the initiator, like Abraham, without whose daring the Isaacs of this world would have nothing to redig. This was carried into such contemporary fields as civil liberties and social legislation and world-mindedness.

This form can be something like the military strategy of "defense in depth," that of allowing an army to advance into a given territory and then giving it some unexpected treatment.

In different form, there was a surprise element in Rabbi Stephen S. Wise's sermon on the words of Jesus, "Father, forgive them; for they know not what they do." He asked his hearers to face the problem which is a real one, involved in the prayer, "Father, forgive them; for they know what they do."

9. Among the special techniques listed by Professor H. A. Overstreet, in his very useful and suggestive book *Influencing Human Behavior,* as having value for making contact with an audience is what he calls "the chase technique." This is, in essence, getting an audience to explore a problem and pursue a solution rather than merely announcing the result to them. The latter course leaves them, while the process is going on, with little to do but accept or reject the conclusion. This form of outline is useful, not so much for specific sermons, though on occasion that has its value, as for a manner and method of thinking with an audience which can be employed in all kinds of speaking and in many types of sermon outline. When a speaker is telling an audience, instead of seeking to lure them into thinking with him, there is a static quality about the address or sermon. A joint enterprise, with a speaker who says, "Let's go together and try to find the solution of this," has power to win close and continuous attention, for it has a mutual quality about it. This approach, if it really arrives

143

at some spiritual truth, does not detract from the authority of revelation; it is a method of persuading people to accept for themselves the authority of revelation. Jesus did often proclaim dogmatically, as recorded in the Synoptic Gospels—for instance, "Your heavenly Father knoweth that ye have need of all these things." But recall how he often asked, "How does it seem to you?" This was an invitation to a spiritual pilgrimage: "Let's look at this together—which of you that is a father . . . ?"

The form of the "chase sermon," reduced to its baldest terms, is something like the familiar parlor game:

"Is it this?"

"No."

"Is it this?"

"No."

"Is it this other thing?"

"Yes."

We get a glimpse of it in the familiar twenty-eighth chapter of Job: "Where shall wisdom be found?" That is a definite invitation to go out on the chase, a mental exploration to discover the real source of wisdom. So the results are examined: "The depth saith, It is not in me: and the sea saith, It is not with me." "It cannot be gotten for gold" or silver or jewels. Finally, here is the end of the search: "The fear of the Lord, that is wisdom." [5]

In a volume of sermons already referred to, *The New Christian Epic,* by Albert W. Palmer, there is a sermon quite specifically in the "chase" form. Its occasion was the dedication of an inscription over the entrance to the church in Honolulu of which Dr. Palmer was the pastor. The sermon outlined the process of choosing the inscription; it had to be of a certain length and from the Bible. The sermon moved along the line of a search for a fitting sentence. It might have been this. It might have been that. It might fittingly have been this other quotation. But at the end this was chosen: "Love never faileth." The sermon dealt with this culmination of the search, the truth of this sentence in the Christian gospel.

Interest in a mutual exploration of many topics can be stimulated by this form. Take patriotism, for instance. "What is Christian patriotism?" Is it this—flag waving, and so forth? Obviously not. Is patriotism that selfish interest covered by loud, swelling words which Samuel Johnson called the "last refuge of a scoundrel"? Certainly not. Is there any light on the matter from the devotion to his people of the one who cried, "O Jerusalem, . . . how often would I have gathered . . ."

The road is traveled together with the congregation.

10. There may be occasional use, if the occasion is chosen wisely, for a type of sermon that might be called "the rebuttal sermon." It consists, in the main, of something which is an answer, as spirited and conclusive as the preacher can manage, to something he considers emphatically false and dangerously misleading. Some view accepted by many or some striking statement is presented; and the preacher asks, "Is that so?" and goes on to convince that it is definitely not so.

Jesus did that when he presented and faced a view of sin and punishment widely accepted in his time: "Suppose ye that these Galilaeans [killed by Pilate] were sinners above all the Galilaeans . . . ? I tell you, Nay." The nay is a forthright rebuttal. "Or those eighteen, upon whom the tower in Siloam fell, and slew them, think ye that they were sinners above all men that dwelt in Jerusalem?" The fact is, of course, that many in Jesus' time and place—some, perhaps, in his immediate audience—thought exactly that; so the vigorous denial comes again, "I tell you, Nay: but, except ye repent, ye shall all likewise perish." [6]

A present-day example is to be found in the many effective sermons that have been preached on the text from Karl Marx, "Religion is the opiate of the people." Millions of people have accepted it uncritically. The preacher asks the question, "Is that so?" and then goes on to say with feeling, as Jesus did, "I tell you, Nay." Sometimes this sermon goes on to give historical evidence of religion. So far from being an escape from life, religion has laid upon men and women a strong compulsion to toil terribly, to give up all they held dear, to hazard and give up their lives. Strange opium! So Jesus, when he went to his death, was just taking "dope" to get away from reality. Luther was just an opium eater, etc., etc.

Another example is found in the sermons, and there have been many, finding their object of denial in the statement attributed to Thomas Carlyle, looking up at a crucifix on the outside of a Paris church and saying, with a shake of his head: "Its all very well, old fellow, but you've had your day." That preposterous judgment is the spark that sets off the explosion. So, Jesus has had his day? Imagine saying that in a world which has collapsed because it received him not! There has never been a day in history so emphatically Jesus' day as the time of war and its tragic aftermaths, in which it has been so clearly proved that no other foundation can be laid for international security and human welfare than that which is laid in Christ Jesus.

This does not take back at all the stress previously given to the superior power, in general, of the positive and repeated affirmation of the truth over the negative dealing with objections to that truth or denials of it. A herald's chief business is not to refute the claims of his opponent. That gives the opponent a psychological advantage: it puts him in the center of the stage, under the spotlight. His chief business is to present positively his own case.

Nevertheless, on occasion, great service can be rendered by a spirited and pertinent refutation of a lie. There is a quickening of mind which comes in conflict with an idea or affirmation which we do *not* believe, as Paul was stirred by the idols he saw. Anger at untruth and evil can act as adrenalin pumped into the blood for an approaching conflict. One reason why some preaching is so tame that it is almost a species of blasphemy against the Holy Ghost is that the preacher never gets deeply stirred by arrogant falsehood, so that he never sallies forth like young David going across the valley whirling a slingshot. A veritable gift of tongues often descends on a person when he is deeply moved by something he recognizes as an authentic child of the father of lies. Sometimes this stirring calls forth a genuine eloquence.

Often a congregation is moved by the spectacle of a preacher not cowed in a corner—overawed by some contemporary contempt for religion, or merely teasing people to be good, like an incompetent mother wheedling her child—but advancing to the center of the ring with a joyous lust for battle in his eye and in his words. G. K. Chesterton did exactly that service for the Christian religion in his generation, and a tremendous service it was. In like spirit a preacher might take such a statement as that of a fairly prominent man that "this talk of brotherhood is all very well in the pulpit, but in the world we must be realistic." What crimes are committed in that name "realism." So he is off to a sermon on the realism of Jesus—a truly terrible realism beside which that of the "hard-boiled" who think, or pretend to think, that an enduring national or international order can be built on greed and exploitation is softheaded romanticism.

On this a practical comment may have a bit of value. Some preachers never get the gift of tongues which often accompanies violent disagreement and fervent rebuttal because they do not have enough in

146

their reading diet with which they do disagree, which rudely attacks their accepted faith to the extent of stirring their minds. Their mental muscles get flabby, their blood gets anemic, by continually saying "Amen" to the printed page rather than having often enough the redeeming disturbance of a violent "Is that so?" or an even more violent "That's a lie!"

About any sort of outline one truth should never be forgotten: it should be continually used as a means. The purpose of preaching is the same as that of a vegetable garden—always nutrition before display. Carry that figure of nutrition a bit further. Tuck away into the mind the profound wisdom of G. K. Chesterton's comment on the sparkling wit of Bernard Shaw: "He had been wondered at as something brilliant and barren, like a meteor; but no one would accept him as a sun, for the test of a sun is that it can make something grow." [7] A sermon, rightly, is not a meteor but a sun. Its true test is, Can it make something grow?

XIV. THE BIBLE AS A SOURCE OF PREACHING

B EGIN WITH THE SHEER WONDER OF THE BIBLE, ITS ENDURING QUALITIES
as a source of wisdom about life, inspiration, awakening of the
conscience, stirring of the imagination. It has been subjected to a scrutiny and study and use, for over seventeen centuries, unmatched in
intensity and continuity by that given to any other body of writing in
the world. Things new and old have been unfailingly brought out of
its treasure. It has been the burning bush that was not consumed; or,
to change the figure, it has been an inexhaustible well of water springing up unto everlasting life. Anne Morrow Lindbergh has put the
ever-renewed service of the Bible into a beautiful figure of speech:
"Bible stories so simple that they are like empty cups for people to fill
with their own experience and drink for their own need over and over
again through the years."

This will all be granted by the preacher. His own experience has
been that of the church .hrough the centuries. Why, then, vex the eye
and ear by enlarging on the obvious? It is a natural question. The
preacher lives and moves in the Scriptures. There is as much need for
recommending the Bible for the preacher's study and use as there is
for counseling people to take a breath once in a while. There is, however, danger of underestimating the obvious, of taking it for granted
and allowing it to go into low visibility. That danger is glimpsed in
Jesus' words, "Ye know these things, happy are ye if ye do them."
Among the many kinds of courage a preacher needs is the courage of
the obvious, the courage to consider the truth that has become an
axiom and thus grown befogged. He needs to remember that, if a road
is beaten down with much traveling, it is so because it leads to a de-
sirable destination. Remembering this, he will be fortified against
spending his days on alluring detours of novelty which end up in a

148

desert. Another reason for emphasis on the Bible as a source of preaching is that we may easily overlook its amazing relevance to contemporary life and need. It would be hard to find a better picture of this close relevance of the Bible than is found in the description of history given by a great American historian, Carl Becker. He says that the use of history is "to enlist the experience of mankind in the service of its destiny." Lift those words up to their largest possible meaning, and we have the Bible, the highest and deepest experience of mankind, to be enlisted by the devotion, the imagination, and the skill of the preacher in the service of man's destiny.

"A great deal of the Bible," writes Bernard Shaw, with understatement, "is much more alive than this morning's paper."[1] As John Jay Chapman puts this amazing relevance, "The Bible is a luminous congregation of vapors, a cloud by day and a pillar of fire by night, and the darker the skies grow, whether above an epoch, or an individual, the more light it emits."[2]

It is probably true to say that the Bible rates much higher as a source of preaching today than it did a generation ago, particularly than it did among many young ministers. A number of men who graduated from theological seminaries around 1910, of whom the present writer is the chief of sinners, have a special qualification for speaking a warning word about extra biblical preaching. It is the same qualification which the prodigal son had for speaking about the pigpen, where he landed after wasting his substance in riotous living. They know something at first hand of the homiletical poverty of a preacher who has thrown the Bible out of the study window. In those days quite a number of young Apolloses, on graduating, having become men, put away such childish things as texts and Bible stories. In the pulpit they lived amid the immensities and starry galaxies. But after a while, when the little long-suffering congregation had heard their sermon on "The March of Progress" (for progress was marching in those days) and the one on "Science and Religion" and the one "Pragmatism" (for pragmatism was going big then), like the prodigal son, they began to be in want. Then they came to themselves and said, "In my father's Book are texts enough and to spare." And they said, "I will arise and go to the Bible."

149

They found out, as many have, that when they put aside the Bible as the chief source of preaching, they have thrown away the most dramatic material possible; they have sold a great birthright for a mess of generalities; they have put away what, in Markham's words, has

> The color of the ground was in him, the red earth;
> The smack and tang of elemental things.[3]

Two negative observations may well be made at the outset:

One is that the great and real values of preaching rooted in the Bible are not to be realized by an uncritical and line-of-least-resistance reversion to "expository preaching." Whenever contemporary problems of the pulpit and church are discussed, someone always bobs up with the nostalgic sigh, "Ah, if we could only have more expository preaching. Those were the days!" Such a backward glance fails to note some things about the decline of expository preaching, or, rather, much that passed under that name without being the real thing. Much of it died for very good reasons. It had paralysis and a weak heart and a clot on the brain and finally succumbed to senile decay. It failed to grasp the truth imbedded or pictured in a biblical passage and then to set it down in the soil of modern life. Biblical drama is very hard to write effectively, for the reason that it tends to become a weak paraphrase of the original. That was the danger, and always will be, in the sort of biblical preaching which is a lazy man's delight. He gives a weak paraphrase of the scriptural passage, probably adding a moralistic P.S.—it is as easy as that, and as feeble. Scripture used in that way actually comes between the preacher and his congregation as a barrier to the passage of vital thought rather than as a bridge over which it may cross.

There has been far too much reliance on the delusion that there is something magical in knowing the contents of the Bible. Someone has well said that there is no more religious or moral value in reading about the pugilistic exploits of Samson than there is in reading about those of Joe Louis. Knowledge of the Bible, the whole Bible, and not very much but the Bible has not often done much to produce Christians. Some people have been greatly worried because their children have never heard of the ax that floated or the bears which ate up the

150

disrespectful children, but they have never been greatly worried about the Kingdom of God.

A second negative observation has to do with that perverted use of the Bible which treats it as a silk hat out of which the pulpit prestidigitator conjures little rabbits. We get a glimpse of that legerdemain in the title of a book of sermons published more than a generation ago, *Quick Truths in Quaint Texts*. In the very "cute" alliteration we can almost see the pulpit magician at work. "Now, you see this text, folks? Nothing in it. Look on both sides. Nothing up my sleeves, see! Now watch carefully; the hand is quicker than the eye. Presto change! See the little rabbit jump out of the text!"

That sort of thing, often called "Bible preaching," may have some of the dexterity but not the single-minded devotion of the juggler in the old legend who performed his tricks before the statue of the Virgin Mary as a religious offering. Dr. Robertson Nicoll wrote in tribute to S. A. Tipple, of Norwood, England, "Mr. Tipple is like a conjurer— the text, the hat, the sermon, egg, birds and flowers." [4] The figure of the conjurer is unfortunate, even in honor to a workman of the fine integrity of Mr. Tipple; for it suggests cutting capers with the Word rather than rightly dividing it. And very often the spectator—that is the right word for him—must explain, "Such a small rabbit to come out of such a big hat!"

The best name for this sort of trick is that given by stout old John Byng, whom we meet in the *Torrington Diaries,* who calls the subservient chaplain of the Duke of Marlborough, in the 1780's, "Dr. Tickle-Text." Biblical preaching, in the true sense of the word, is not the finagling of quaint allegories out of isolated texts but preaching that makes the faith that is in the Bible real to people.

On the positive side of the theme, some large things are true of preaching which finds a chief source in the Bible.

1. For one thing, such preaching speaks in the common language, the native tongue of the Christian church. Lord Eustace Perry has written with sure insight on this:

The Bible is the language of the Christian faith, and the only language that the church has ever used. A message can be delivered only in a living language. A confusion of tongues has fallen on the church, and its members speak in loose phrases which might fit a dozen meanings in terms that are indeterminate. We no longer preach "Christ crucified" so much as the "principle of the Cross"; regeneration and redemption are swallowed up in "a process of spiritual development"; the gospel itself is converted into "the New Testament ethic." . . . We must learn again the free speech that our fathers used.[5]

Those words can be dangerous, of course, if illegitimately used as a justification for merely repeating traditional phrases. But there is real salvation for preaching in them.

2. The Bible contains the most vivid, dramatic, and arresting material the preacher or any public speaker can use. What an irony if, in the very days when the novelists, such as Sholem Asch and Thomas Mann, and dramatists are demonstrating the inexhaustible power of the Bible narrative, the preacher should meekly hand over his heritage and wander off into the waste land of abstract generalities.

In John Masefield's recent volume of reminiscences, *In the Mill,* the author shows the grip of the dramatic when he records that the workers in a carpet mill in Yonkers, New York, had no interest in the carpets they worked on unless they showed a dramatic design, such as, for instance, a fox carrying off a bird. They cared nothing, he writes, "for festoons of blue roses in yellow baskets or big, expensive kaleidoscopes." The preacher had better note, for these words record a primary fact about mental attention. Audiences care little for verbal "festoons of blue roses." Bible stories give the saving grace of the concrete to the preacher's words. We may take a word of wisdom from Lewis Carroll and say that at eleven o'clock Sunday morning in the pulpit the time has come

> To talk of many things:
> Of shoes—and ships—and sealing wax—
> Of cabbages—and kings.

That is what people respond to, the concrete, the specific—shoes and ships and sealing wax.

Many readers today find it difficult to understand the immense vogue of Hall Caine in the 1880's and 1890's. The literary critics greeted him with groanings which scarce could be uttered. But the preacher had better try to understand the popularity of Hall Caine, for it has more than somewhat to do with his own work. His best sellers did rock the pulpit and press. In a literary sense,

> His sins were scarlet
> But his books were read.

This was so largely because the themes came from the Bible treasury of stories, and Caine made an effort, successful with multitudes of people, to show how the old truths continued to be true under the varied and strange conditions of the modern world. That is an essential task of biblical preaching. Look at one very notable and moving description of the effect on a young man of a sermon on a Bible narrative, a sermon that became a lasting force in his life. It is Dr. L. P. Jacks's report of a sermon by Stopford Brooke:

This, thought I, is not going to be dull nor dry nor stupid nor hollow nor feeble, like so many sermons I have tasted. It wasn't. There was meat on that bone; nay, a banquet for the hungry. The sermon was about Abraham and Lot, how when they had to choose between the good land and the bad, Abraham, like a great and generous soul, gave Lot the first choice, and when Lot chose the best for himself, as your greedy ones always do, Abraham with a magnificent gesture (magnificently reproduced in the pulpit) bade him take it and go to the devil (the preacher didn't say that but he meant it by his gesture). While Abraham went forth by faith into the barren mountains, not knowing whither he went, Lot taking the low road—he the high, the pioneer of humanity through all the ages. Talking of tasting a sermon! I swallowed it in great draughts and was intoxicated.[6]

3. Preaching from the Bible saves us from the futile strain of trying to preach a "great" sermon every Sunday. That has been a curse of the pulpit. The oratorical sermon has slain tens of thousands of preachers. They have been prevented from doing a vital service to the needs of people that they might otherwise have rendered. If we are living with the Bible, we are able to forget the thunder of Niagara and the music of the spheres and speak in the vernacular of our home town. Jesus was the model for helpful preaching devoid of straining ambition

153

when he "took a towel, and girded himself" and stooped down to a bit of lowly service. If there is any future for preaching, it is in the human equivalent of that act. To lay aside our flowing robes, the rhetorical sins that do so easily beset us—and so easily trip us up—and to bring some Christian truth in detail to a point of need—that is a service in which the Scripture helps us as nothing else can.

The snare of the consciously "great" sermon, depending for its effect on the noise of its detonation rather than on its aim or content, has never been more vividly put than by John A. Rice, writing in *Harper's Magazine* of the preaching of his uncle. a Methodist bishop:

To listen to him was like quietly getting drunk. He led his hearers by easy stages into an unreal world of effortless peace, drugging them gradually into unconsciousness by the melody that was himself. They went home to eat their Sunday dinners in dazed silence, and remained befuddled until Monday morning, when they woke up and went about their business.

"But what good came of it at last?" quoth little Peterkin. We may with some truth paraphrase familiar words and say of such a picture: "There, but for the grace of Jesus, Peter, Paul, Judas, Amos, Daniel, Moses, and Jacob, go I!"

The sharpening and limiting of focus which comes from faithful dealing with a Bible narrative and truth, delivers the preacher from the false lure of what might be called "the Magellan sermon." Magellan, as we all know, sailed around the world. The Magellan sermon is one which tries to do the same thing every Sunday morning. It circumnavigates all the issues in this issue-full world. And the passengers, after such globe-girdling voyages starting every seven days, get to listening eagerly for any cry which sounds like "Land ahead!" They welcome a solid, specific area of experience where their minds and hearts can "land."

4. One chief value, of course, of preaching which has its source in the Bible, lies in the parallels which it affords to present experience. Let no one embark on the suggestive and fruitful task of drawing parallels between another historical era and our own without realizing he is engaged in a hazardous undertaking. Professor Henry J. Cadbury has stressed one aspect of this hazard with warning detail in his

154

book *The Peril Of Modernizing Jesus*. Philip Guedalla has put this warning in painfully clear words. "Historical parallels," he writes, "may be a display of impressive information by a faint similarity of two widely separated events, and a common result is the distortion of two sets of facts, and the substitution of a common denominator of falsehood in the minds of a bewildered public." That is enough to scare anyone! Drawing parallels does run the risk of pushing back forcibly into another day ideas and conditions quite foreign to it. But if the preacher is going to be afraid of danger, he might as well retire. The ground on which parallels are drawn is holy ground wherever records of man's experience of God, and the judgments of God in human life and history, are made to walk our common streets. A great New Testament scholar, C. Harold Dodd, of Cambridge University, has urged the preacher on to the drawing of parallels in New Testament study in spite of the visible risks. "The present task," he said in his inaugural address in the New Testament chair, "is to grasp the whole first-century gospel in its temporary, historical, and actual reality, and then make the bold and even perilous attempt to translate the whole into contemporary terms." As an illustration of how an able and conscientious scholar and preacher tried to do that very thing, here are the words of Canon F. R. Barry, of Westminster Abbey, drawing a parallel between the first Christian century and our own: "The world into which the gospel first came was haunted by the disastrous suspicion that somehow man was played out. Moral standards were all tumbling down. Philosophy was bankrupt and the universe seemed to defy interpretation. The weight of life lay heavily on men's hearts." Unduly simplified? Perhaps. But nevertheless valid in its broad outlines—a tremendous parallel to a common mood of our own day and a starting point to the conviction that the Christ who met that despairing mood of the first century has resources for this, another day when the weight of life lies heavily on men's hearts.

One crux of the matter is a conscientious moving of the truth in a narrative or word of other centuries and other places into the midst of present experience. It is the absence of the engaged "clutch" of the present-day parallel which meshes in with the machinery of the mind and heart that has made so much alleged expository preaching irrele-

155

vant and obsolete. A strange incident in recent American history throws a great deal of light on this art. That was the broadcast made by Orson Welles out of H. G. Wells's scientific romance *The War of the Worlds,* a story of an imagined invasion from Mars. Orson Welles broadcast it as though it were actually happening at the moment over in New Jersey and up in Westchester, just a few miles from the studio. Neither he nor the officials of the Columbia Broadcasting Company ever dreamed that anyone would accept it as present fact. But the realism and the near location of the imaginary invasion from Mars were too great for tender and jumpy minds. The actor described the attack of weird creatures from Mars armed with "heat rays" as they descended upon a section of the state of New Jersey. The spectacular radio broadcast was interspersed with hair-raising "news flashes" that threw into a panic a large number of men and women, who had not heard the preliminary radio introduction and explanations. They thought that the Martians were really attacking the world and that its end had come. They fled to the streets, tried to buy newspapers, called up studios and the police, and otherwise behaved as delirious grasshoppers.

At the time many thought, "What a tribute to H. G. Wells!" But later H. G. Wells gave a disgruntled interview denouncing the effrontery of Orson Welles. He said that all the trouble came from Orson Welles's taking liberties with the story by moving its location. If he had left it in Brighton and London, no one would have been excited. But "by moving it to a close location, he got a nervous reaction."

Those are words for a preacher to ponder well. When we leave the Bible stories in Palestine, all is well; the congregation can sleep safely and murmur, "Never touched me." It is when we move the good Samaritan from the Jericho Road to Main Street, just around the corner, or move the rich fool from Judea to our own neighborhood in Nebraska or Texas, or move Judas into our own congregation, that the trouble begins; and that is when real preaching begins.

"No story is older than its applicability to life." So wrote Sidney Howard, the dramatist. The use of the Bible in preaching, from the days of Chrysostom until now, is full of scores of examples of stories shiningly new in their application to new life. The characters of the

THE BIBLE AS A SOURCE OF PREACHING

Old Testament and the New walk our streets; their temperaments and
problems are ours; and the way they met them, for good or evil, comes
close to us when brought close by the preacher. Sara Henderson Hay
looks at the city with the eye of a preacher as well as that of a poet:

> Stone crumbles, but more staunchly fares
> A dust incredibly translated:
> Judas still haggles at his wares,
> Cain is forever new-created.
> Delilah, in a Paris frock,
> Goes out to tea at five o'clock;
> Salome climbs the subway stairs,
> Potiphar takes the elevated.[7]

The people of the Bible are all about us in modern clothes; they are
the most effective instruments on which the preacher can lay his hand.

Suggestive visual aids to this high art of moving the truth embodied
in a tale and in a character are to be found in the multiplying books
representing Bible history in modern dress and situations and in unfamiliar settings. A deeply moving series of woodcuts is that of Alfred
Wagg in his illustrated book *The Psalms in Modern Life,* in which
great words from the Psalms are illustrated by drawings, some beautiful and tender, some terrible in their power. Somewhat similar in idea
is Owen Washburn's *Book of Psalms.* The English artist Thomas
Derrick has illustrated some parables of Jesus, including the good Samaritan and the prodigal son, in vivid and often amusing cartoon
drawings in his *Prodigal Son and Other Parables Shown in Pictures.*
In America, Lauren Ford, in the *Ageless Story,* has illustrated the text
of the Nativity stories with drawings which put the events in a rural
present-day Connecticut setting. The wise men come to Bethlehem,
Connecticut, by sleigh across the snow-covered New England hills.
It is essentially the same divinely inspired "anachronism" which is
found in the many notable paintings which clothe the disciples of
Jesus and Jesus himself in the garments of European peasants and set
them against a contemporary European background. This artistic
anachronism catches and represents in a striking way the universality
of the Gospel stories. The brush of the painter proclaims that:

157

Faith has still its Olivet,
And love its Galilee.

Some of Rembrandt's memorable paintings portray the Gospel stories in contemporary settings, such as "Pilate Washing His Hands"
and "The Supper at Emmaus." Murillo's painting of "Christ Supported by St. Francis" portrays St. Francis in the garb of a European
monk embracing and supporting Jesus, still nailed to the cross, showing in its strictly "incorrect" jumbling of costumes profound truth
about both St. Francis and Jesus. Giotto's "The Betrayal of Christ"
shows his arrest by a mob of Italian soldiers in the garb of the artist's
time. In Fra Angelico's "The Annunciation" the angel is dressed in
an embroidered gown which any Italian princess would have envied.
Karel Capek records his discovery of "a fine old picture in which John
the Baptist christens our Lord in a cold Norwegian fjord." [8]

The present years are witnessing the uncovering of a new wealth of
art in which the stories of the Bible are pictured in the indigenous
settings of the Orient. Many have become familiar with the Christmas
cards reproducing paintings of Chinese artists. "The Nativity in a
Cave" presents the holy family with a charming little angel in Chinese
costume standing by with his lantern. In the cave flowers are in bloom;
outside the cave little shepherds are standing in the snow. "The Holy
Family in Winter" reflects the Chinese delight in showing different
seasons of the year in a series of paintings. Joseph is shown as a typical Chinese carpenter trudging through the snow; Mary, with the
child in her arms, stands at the gate of a rustic house such as one sees
in central and southern China.

Many of these have been gathered in Professor Daniel J. Fleming's
book *Each with His Own Brush*.

All of this is a visual representation of the preacher's opportunity
and responsibility, in dealing with the Bible, of bringing near to life
that which in time and space is far away.

5. The Bible is an unrivaled spring of variety and freshness. In fact,
it is the only sure reliance for a man who speaks to substantially the
same group of people Sunday after Sunday, year after year. A character in Walter D. Edmonds' novel *Rome Haul,* a preacher who had
given up preaching and become a dentist, speaks a word of profound

wisdom in homely form. Some one asked him, "Why don't you go back to preaching?" "Trouble is," he replied, "people don't leave you to give one sermon. They want you to stay in town and give five or six. I've got one or two that are wizards, but when it comes to five or six, I just run out of Gospel." Thousands of preachers can testify to how easy it is to "run out of Gospel." If one is to "stay in town," not for five or six sermons, but for five or six years, or for twenty years, there is no substitute for the inexhaustible wealth of life that is found in the Bible.

The longer a preacher stays in a parish, the higher he comes to rate variety in sermons, in subject and approach. For the man who lets himself go along the line of least resistance will find usually that his own personal tastes (or whims or hobbies) are determing too largely his sermon themes. He will have just about one sermon, or, to be generous, call it two or three. Of course they will have different titles and texts; but the difference between them will be somewhat like the difference between macaroni and spaghetti; some will be longer and thicker than others. The Bible presents a saving source of variety. A noble tribute to this was paid in words spoken by Dr. Charles H. Spurgeon at the twenty-fifth anniversary of his pastorate at the Metropolitan Tabernacle in London. He said: "If anybody had been standing in this place and preaching politics and temperance for twenty-five years, I wonder if he could have kept a congregation. All other subjects become exhausted; but give me the Bible and the Holy Ghost, and I can go on preaching forever."

6. What prescriptions can be made for making this wealth of life continuously available for the needs of present life? There is no bag of tricks that can do it. The need is deeper than can be met by any repertoire of devices. Nothing less than lifelong habits will avail.

Basic to all is the preacher's lifelong habit of reading the Bible. To announce that commonplace may seem as much of a letdown as Elisha's telling Naaman to bathe in the Jordan. It is literally the same prescription: Bathe in the Bible; swim in it; live in it. That continuous immersion in the Bible is a vastly different thing from the last-resort use of the Bible which is the mechanical, standard practice of many preachers. This habit of reading the Bible, completely dissociated from whatever sermon or problem we are working on, sticking to it weekly though the heavens fall, is a vastly different thing from turning to it as a last resort—"when other helpers fail, and comforts flee."

Most of us know, alas! that last-ditch use of the Bible. Too often the Saturday night revels in the parsonage, as the zero hour for Sunday looms like the Day of Judgment (which it is), have followed the model in the 107th Psalm: "Their soul is melted because of trouble. They reel to and fro, and stagger like a drunken man, and are at their wit's end. Then they cry unto the Lord in their trouble."

In other words, then the preacher reaches for the Bible!

As opposed to this, the fruitful reading of the Bible, is a sort of brooding, not frantic reading; rather it is watching the narrative pass before one's mind, holding the mind loose, with no tension or tautness at all, not worrying whether one finds anything or not. The key point is that one is not working for a particular end. The mind broods over the page like a hawk over a chicken yard; then, from a leisurely wheel in the air, it swoops down on what looks like an idea. You don't always get a live chicken. Sometimes it turns out to be merely a hole in the ground. Don't fret about that. The chief thing is the habit, the procedure.

A better figure of speech is that of the process of using a hazel branch to find water. Rudyard Kipling is willing to go on the witness stand for this traditional way of finding water. He writes in his autobiography: "When we wished to sink a well opposite some cottages, he [a journeyman bricklayer] said he had the gift of water-finding, and I testify that, when he held one fork of the hazel Y and I the other, the thing bowed itself against all the grip of my hand over an unfailing supply." [9] The mind bends down at places. That is the fascinating mystery of the Bible—we come across things at places which are the beaten path of centuries, across words that are as familiar as our own names, and yet we see some truth and relationship we have never seen before, and which, perhaps, no one has ever seen before in that particular way.

If we look at a passage or a text long enough, thoughtfully considering it from all sides, asking what its vital relationship to life might be, it sometimes becomes a sort of Mexican jumping bean in our hand.

160

It seems to move of its own volition. Try an experiment. Here is a theme one young minister shaped as a possibility for a sermon:

"He cannot be my disciple." There were some disciples Jesus rejected. Who were they, besides the rich young ruler? Why did he reject them? What light do these rejections throw on the question that comes close to us: what are the sort of disciples Jesus does not want today? Those of divided allegiances, for one. Those who postpone active following, for another, perhaps. What else?

The Mexican bean begins to jump in the hand.

Two practical counsels may be worth giving. First, work at long range. The most helpful sermons come, as a rule, not when one is looking for "something for next Sunday" (that very strain and urgency freezes the genial currents of the mind), but when one is just reading the Bible, on the alert and mental tiptoe but giving himself up to it without regard to any particular occasion, as part of a continuing habit of life. It is one of the perversities of the human mind that you can usually do a thing better when you don't have to do it at all. Emerson recognized this perversity and made it an ally. In his journal for 14th of October, 1834, he wrote: "I will say at public lectures and the like, those things which I have meditated for their own sake, and not for the first time with a view to that occasion." It is not from that which is meditated for a particular occasion that the richest harvest comes. The core of the Christmas sermon that meets the occasion may come from the brooding over the Scripture that was done in May. Many ministers have found it productive to keep the study of two books of the Bible going together for a period, one in the Old Testament and one in the New—First Samuel, for instance, and the Gospel of Luke, and then when these are finished, say, Jeremiah and Romans. A good commentary is an invaluable companion for the journey; but the study should not become a critical or technical one. That can come in as another part of a preacher's study. The process in mind here is rather a "double eye" reading, with one eye on the story and the ideas, whether in Egypt or Samaria or Jerusalem or Corinth, and the other on Chicago or Jersey City or Fargo—wherever one lives. One eye on 1000 B.C. or A.D. 30 and the other on the twentieth century. It is as though we were reading in double columns—as indeed we will be.

This kind of Bible reading is not a passive affair. It means plowing

161

work. A youth once wrote in a "confessional" magazine, "My father was a farmer, but he loved nature so much he wouldn't ruin her with a plow, so we were always poor." If the preacher loves the Bible so much he won't ruin it with a plow, he, too, will always be poor, in the study, pulpit, and parish. Phyllis Bentley, the novelist, writing of fiction, describes the intensely active process of looking at a scene, which is much like the way of a preacher with a scene in Scripture: "For scenic background I visit a setting perhaps a half a dozen times and simply sit and look at it, letting my mind range over its possibilities. Under this process the setting changes; it becomes something of my own." This kind of meditating, whether for novel or sermon, is as active a process as that represented in Rodin's statue "The Thinker," where the tense muscles proclaim that an activity of the whole man is going on.

This lifelong work of the preacher on the Book finds an unforgettable expression in the classic passage of noble prose in which the Russian novelist and mystic Dmitri Merejkowski described the New Testament which had been in his possession for thirty years.

I read it daily, and shall continue to read it so long as my eyes can see, and by every kind of light, by rays coming from the sun or from the heart, on brightest days and in blackest nights, happy or unhappy, sick or well, full of faith or of doubt, full of feeling or devoid of feeling. And it seems to me that there is always something new in what I read, something unfathomed, and that I shall never plumb its depths or reach its end. . . . The gilt edges of the leaves are tarnished, the paper is yellow, the leather binding is coming to pieces, and the back has come unstuck. Some of the pages are loose. . . . It ought to be rebound, but I cannot find it in my heart to send it away; indeed, the thought of being separated from it for even a few days frightens me. . . . What shall be buried with me in my coffin? The Book. With what shall I rise from the grave? With the Book. What did I do on earth? I read the Book.[10]

Of course, it follows that some record must be kept of this reading and study. A notebook in which are put down the ideas and interpretations and comments which are the fruit of the labor will be of enormous value. If only as much as one tenth of what one writes down in the notebook, as possibilities for future sermon use, is ever used, that proportion is a high one and will abundantly reward the practice. Sometimes an entry which is made will flower five years later into a sermon. As one goes over the book, this idea or that, by some strange process never wholly clear, will proclaim itself ready. It is the continuing mystery of the seedtime and harvest in the mental life.

There is no more impressive demonstration of all this than in the ideas written down by Phillips Brooks in his seminary days, ideas which grew throughout the years into the great and moving sermons of some twenty years later.

XV. GETTING STARTED

O UT OF THE MOUTHS OF SCHOOL CHILDREN THERE HAS FREQUENTLY
been ordained strength, and wisdom. For the preacher at the outset of his task of getting started on a sermon, there is some painful
truth of observation in the comment of a high-school boy on the adventures of his soul among the masterpieces of Euclid. He said that the
hardest thing, when a proposition in geometry was being demonstrated
on the blackboard, was to have the teacher pounce on him with the
words of doom—"Jones, you proceed." "Proceeding," the boy added
feelingly, "is tough."

It *is* tough. "Proceeding" often seems like the ascending of a sheer,
forbidding cliff. Finley Peter Dunne, "Mr. Dooley," has given his own
experience in words that will strike a painful echo in the preacher's
mind. He is describing the writing of those humorous pieces which
seem, to the uninitiated, things to be tossed off lightly:

> The actual writing is not hard, but the beginning is painful to the point
> of tragedy—the attempt to produce the state in which work of an imagina-
> tive nature can be done, that terrible dislocation of mind, in which he is
> capable of reaching what is called "inspiration." This apparently outside
> force is not his to command at will, and there is always the terrifying fear
> that it will fail him.[1]

Getting started is often the crux of sermon making. The preacher is
in his study. He has a theme, and probably a text, and a general idea
of the objective to be taken. But where is the path from here to there?
The explorations for that path will determine whether the sermon will
follow the order of nature as described in the Ninetieth Psalm: "In
the morning it flourisheth, and groweth up; in the evening it is cut
down, and withereth." Will the idea which flourished so hopefully

164

at nine o'clock in the morning wither by noon, or by the next day?

Any attempt at giving specific directions for an uncountable variety of minds and temperaments would be an impertinence. The most that may be risked is to say, "Here is a procedure or two that has been of some help to some men at some times. They may be worth looking at." Every man must find his own way to creating a finished work from his own individual material. It is like the conception of the musician feeling its way into notes of music. There are no rules. Counterpoint will help in the final score or orchestration; it will not create. All that one can do, in preaching or any other art dealing with words, is to help another avoid the danger of having one method crystallize prematurely, before alternatives and additional resources, which might widen the range, have been tried.

Here, then, is the workman at his desk, ready to proceed. What then? Here follow three main suggestions for practice, all of them obvious, all of them from the adventures of many preachers:

1. The first suggestion is to wait, to delay the building by taking off time enough to engage in the process which balks at hurry, that of imaginative creation. The first task is not to manipulate anything, texts, ideas, or illustrations. It is to stop and look and if possible see, to see both the truth as it is set in life and the people whom it is designed to help. Just to sit and look and ask, What is it all about? and to feel one's way with the truth and theme into the lives of people—that is the best kind of acceleration in getting on. Then the kindling pictured in the Psalms takes place, "While I was musing the fire burned." [2]

Unless one does that, tactics, to use a military figure of speech, displaces strategy; the means of working out an idea or theme gets a false priority over the purpose and goal of the undertaking. This pause for the effort of imaginative creation, before any details cloud up the picture, is a stage all too frequently skipped or slurred; it cannot be omitted without loss to the warm human quality of the preaching, or its closeness to experience. Storm Jameson, writing of the novelist's problem, turns to the Greek myth of Proteus and says that it is the novelist's first job to "hold the beast in his hands till it turns into proper shape." That, too, is the preacher's job. It takes time, and humility, but it is the delay which makes ultimate speed possible.

165

A number of years ago a series of cartoons ran for a long time in many newspapers, with the general theme, "Wonder what a traffic cop thinks about," or "Wonder what a trapeze artist thinks about," and so on. The purpose was humorous entertainment, of course; but it did picture the high task of trying to enter, by imaginative projection, the mind of one whose situation and job is quite alien to our own. That, of course, is the heart of the minister's profession. What does life feel like to this person or that; what does it add up to? The classic description of this kind of creation which comes from patient, humble, imaginative projection is in the much-quoted words of Arnold Bennett picturing the beginning of his truly great novel *The Old Wives' Tale*. In the autumn of 1903 he was in a restaurant in the Rue de Clichy, Paris, and saw an old woman come in to dine.

She was fat, shapeless, ugly and grotesque. She had a ridiculous voice and ridiculous gestures. It was easy to see that she lived alone, and that in the long lapse of years she had developed the kind of peculiarity which induces guffaws among the thoughtless. . . . I reflected, concerning the grotesque diner: This woman was once young, slim, perhaps beautiful. . . . One ought to be able to make a heartrending novel out of the history of a woman such as she. Every stout, ageing woman is not grotesque—far from it!—but there is an extreme pathos in the mere fact that every stout, ageing woman was once a young girl with the unique charm of youth in her form and movements and in her mind. And the fact that the change from the young girl to the stout, ageing woman is made up of an infinite number of infinitesimal changes, each unperceived by her, only intensifies the pathos. . . . At that instant . . . I was visited by the idea of writing the book which ultimately became "The Old Wives' Tale." [3]

In these words Bennett exemplifies his own dictum that "the first qualification of a novelist is an 'all-embracing, Christlike sympathy.'" That quiet, unhurried wonder about the life of another person is truly creative. It came first with Bennett. All the remarkable detail of life in the pottery towns, and the turmoil of the Paris commune, came later. It depended on the original creation of the vision which saw and mused. The preacher is not writing fiction, but he must enter into other lives through the same doorway. So we reach the paradox that often the first step is to stand still: the people to whom one speaks must be looked at with consecrated wonder so that the sermon can mean something real and close.

2. A second method of proceeding which has been useful to many men is to make sure there is enough material in front of the eye and mind, so that they can act on it selectively. In practice this often reduces itself to a very simple process, and one which may seem to be distracting and even trivial. But it need not be either. This method, is, after the theme has been chosen, with some idea of its general development in mind, to put down on paper, without any worry about logical order or continuity, anything that comes to mind that has any real connection with the subject. Much of what one puts down will not be used at all. Do not fret about that. If this seems to involve a lot of lost motion, remember that the purpose is to get the mind out of neutral into an active engagement with the subject. That in itself is an accomplishment of major importance. So just let the mind run along, with what the psychologists call "free association." Put down things which you know, even as you put them down, you won't use. Even that helps to get the machinery oiled and running. The thing which is not used in the sermon as it takes shape may be a sort of mental billiard shot which sends the mind bumping into another idea which seems to belong unmistakably in the sermon. Thus the stone which the builders reject does become, by a roundabout bouncing, the head of the corner. At least, you wouldn't have found the head of the corner without the intervening step of the rejected stone.

Experiment with a sample of this getting sufficient material in front of the mind, discussed in very crude fashion. Take a theme on which you might never make a sermon. This topic on a church bulletin board caught the eye of a passer-by: "Living in an Overcrowded World." What the minister had in mind, or whether it was worth preaching about or not, is entirely aside from the present experiment. It does at least suggest a clear idea; possibly there might be something of worth in it. Very well, what happens? Here are some random entries for later weighing, rejection, or development.

It is an overcrowded world in some places. Standing room only on trains. Long lines at ticket offices and stores. Workers living in trailers, even in tents. But is the world really overcrowded? Surely it could easily support its two billion inhabitants. What, then, is the matter? Overcrowding at certain points. Any reasons? One thing—recognize the overcrowding, adjust to it, don't set up a wail over every wait or inconvenience. Don't cry like a baby; be an adult.

Respect the burden that others carry; carry your own—we are members one of another. Here's something else—is your own personal life overcrowded? Need it be? What junk can be cleared out so that life may be simplified?

Attack the causes of the overcrowding of the world. What are they? War certainly is one. Diminishing food supplies, transportation, gathering people into bottlenecks. Greed, which looks on people as chattels which can be turned into profits, is another. That was the cause of slum tenements, etc. Did Jesus ever meet crowds? Any suggestion there?

At least, the mind is in motion. There is something present for it to work on, which it can discard, reject, change, or at length accept.

This method of beginning work is a dangerous thing unless there is rigid discipline. When the time for shaping the sermon out of the material comes, nothing will save a man except a ferocious brutality toward his own mental offspring. The savage question must continually be asked, "Does this idea or line of thought or illustration really advance the thought in a coherent fashion; or does it, in the phrase of John Oman, merely 'maul it around'?" The standard of significance and relevance of the material actually used must be set very high—or the result will be a plate of hash, a lazy preacher's delight but an abomination to a congregation. If a preacher is so tenderhearted toward his mental progeny, or so obsessed with pride of parenthood, that he cannot drown them ruthlessly, he had better not set pen to paper at all.

With this solemn caution kept in mind and conscience, there are some positive advantages in this method of beginning work.

One of the most practically helpful descriptions of this is to be found in a book on preaching published twenty years ago or more, a book of enduring worth, James Black's *The Mystery of Preaching*. In one chapter he likens the process of assembling material indiscriminately for possible use to the process of making cider. The first step, he says, is to gather all the apples there are, even those which are obviously no good; gather the windfalls under the tree and those to be picked off. Some will be rotten. Never mind. Get all the apples. Then discard the bad ones and put the good ones into a cider press. In his analogy the cider press is the form of the sermon into which the good apples will go.

168

One real advantage of thus getting a sum of related material visually before the mind is that it frees the mind from the paralyzing inhibition which, for many people, comes from a completely blank sheet of paper. This is such a common experience that there ought to be a name for it in the bright lexicon of psychology, just as for other phobias, such as "agoraphobia" and "claustrophobia." Most students know this feeling well. At the top of a page of gleaming white paper they write down the title of the term paper. And then the mind goes into a coma. The preacher knows it when he tries to begin the writing of the sermon too soon. The blank page becomes a definite mental hazard, inducing the blank mind. Covering the page with ideas of some relevance says reassuringly to the congealed author: "Cheer up. This isn't going to be impossible. Drop the strain and relax. See, we are on our way already." It is a bit like the miracle of the feeding of the five thousand; five loaves and two fishes are small enough, but at least they are something to work with.

Van Wyck Brooks, discussing his own methods of writing, said: "There is nothing more discouraging than to face a blank sheet of paper at the start of a day's work." [4] So each morning he rewrites the work of the day before and thus has a warm-up start, and a confidence based on fairly easy accomplishment; that carries him on into another day's work. It is no small matter, establishing a confidence by which the mind is girded to go on. Another positive value is in helping to avoid the danger of trying to arrive at an outline too soon. This is one of the commonest causes of mediocre and commonplace sermons. An outline, or general conception of a sermon, arrived at prematurely, before one has walked around the subject and seen it from various points of the compass, is nearly always a wooden outline. There are exceptions, of course; there are bound to be in a realm as unpredictable and mysterious as the mind. Men do occasionally get into that shadowland called inspiration. Sometimes there comes, with the suddenness of a revelation from outside, like a flash of lightning, a way of developing or impressing a truth that seems to have the inevitable quality of something ordained from the foundation of the world. But such occasions, even for the genius, are rare. For the large majority of preachers, counsel in the words of Habakkuk applies: "Though it [the vision]

169

tarry, wait for it; because it will surely come" [5]—the vision in this case being the plan or line of march of the sermon. And—make no mistake about it—it will usually tarry. So wait, not somnolently, but actively, engaged meanwhile on the rewarding process of trial and error.

The old Greek myth of the birth of Athena, springing fully armed out of the forehead of Zeus, has been an evil influence on many preachers. They expect sermons to be born that way, to leap in full panoply, with introduction, points, and conclusion, out of the mind. They forget that the miraculous birth of Athena was just mythology. Sermons are not born that way in the course of nature. They come from a long succession of slow unfoldings, of following promising leads which turn out to be mare's-nests, of grim hanging on to an elusive idea, of mental labor pangs.

Often what is found to be the most productive lead for a sermon is not the thing which is put down first, second, or third but the thing which is put down as the seventeenth possibility. The preacher looks at this idea, come lately, sitting at a lowly place at the bottom of the table and says, "Friend, go up higher." For often the last shall be first.

From time to time, as this is going on, the sermon maker will watch to see if an outline is ready to emerge. This, ordinarily, will not all come at once; it will grow. Some one proposition will demand a place irresistibly, to be followed by others. One caution, already made, is not to try to force a final form on the material until it is "ready." When the outline does appear, then it can be imposed on the material. Certain parts of it will fall into the appropriate places; other parts will be discarded. Of course, certain illustrations and considerations will already have been attached to the affirmations they support or enforce at the time when they were put down just as raw material, of possible usefulness. The process of the material's falling into shape under the influence of an outline is much like an experiment frequently made in physics classes. Metal filings are scattered on a thin metal plate. Then a violin is played near the plate, and the filings form themselves into regular and changing patterns. The outline, sometimes at least, is like the melody played on the violin. It causes the material—the facts,

170

ideas, narratives, questions—to move, almost of themselves, under the various aspects or divisions of the theme.

3. A third suggestion in beginning work is to ask oneself certain questions, to be applied as keys to see whether they will not open doors into the meanings of the truth or theme. The provocative value of this cross-examination of the theme, and of the preacher, is very great in the way in which it starts the mind on new trails. Here are a few sample questions to ask oneself in getting started:

1. What is the particular truth or statement that comes out of this Bible passage? How can it be shaped as an affirmation?

2. To what possible situation or realms of experience does it apply?

3. How can it be made vivid and easy to remember, either in (a) describing the need or situation or (b) describing the solution or cure.

4. What are some causes of the condition or situation discussed?

5. What might be some effects of the solution proposed if it were really adopted?

6. Has this solution or remedy ever really been tried or demonstrated by anyone? If so, give examples.

7. Does the sermon tie a knot in the memory?

8. What are some objections to the solution proposed, or the affirmations made; or what may be some real difficulties? This is done to be fair with an audience, or to anticipate the unvoiced queries or skepticism in an audience. In church, hearers do not heckle the speaker; hence he must do it himself on occasion if he wishes his persuasion to have the utmost carrying power. St. Paul does exactly this in the great fifteenth chapter of I Corinthians. He heckles himself, thus making a dialogue instead of a monologue: "But some man will say, How are the dead raised up? and with what body do they come?"

It would be hopelessly mechanical to think of asking all of these questions, or a list of similar ones, of any theme. But the use of some of them may act as a self-starter for the mind.

XVI. COLLECTING AND ASSIMILATING
MATERIAL

EVERY PREACHER MUST FIND HIS OWN WAY OF SEEING AND NOTING AND remembering suggestive material for the mind to work on—ideas, notable passages, and arresting facts and statements in books, periodicals, and newspapers, and from his own observation of life and events. Beyond the alertness of seeing and noting is the necessity of doing something about it so that it does not pass completely from mind. Otherwise, he will have to report on his mental operations, "We have toiled all the night, and have taken nothing." No "catch" has been drawn into the boat; it has merely been seen swimming by. But what that "doing something about it" may mean in terms of specific actions varies so greatly and inevitably with different individuals that it is doubtful if anything of very general helpfulness can be said. One man's salvation may be another man's mental damnation.

It must not be forgotten that the very process of what is called "saving" material is so fraught with danger to one's original creative processes that there is a real question whether the best thing might not be to post a solemn warning against the dangers of the habit-forming drug of depending on "collected" material, and let the matter rest there. This much certainly needs to be said as clearly and positively as possible: Sooner than become a bond slave to any collection of sermonic treasure, be it in files, notebooks, card indexes, or any other form of safety deposit vaults, throw them all away and proceed with no more cluttering paraphernalia than Plato had in his olive grove or Robinson Crusoe on his island.

It is the old danger of the means' becoming an end, or at least defeating the end, so that what is called in to aid and stimulate one's

172

thinking ends up by smothering it. These dangers are not fantastic and remote, but real. Many a minister's mind has been buried in a filing cabinet, the promising capacity of original thinking imprisoned behind the stout bars of a card index.

There is, first of all, the danger of forming what may be called the "confetti mind"—that is, the mind made up of small, bright-colored pieces with no coherence, pattern, or consecutiveness. Such a mind can never be what an adult mind ought to be, a kit of keen-cutting tools. A child reading some vital statistics once noticed that more people died from "miscellaneous" than from any other cause, and he concluded that "miscellaneous" must be a very dangerous disease. It *is* a dangerous disease—for preachers! When the eye is intent, mainly or only, on collecting variegated "bits," the sermon dies of "miscellaneous."

Another danger of the collecting preoccupation, even though the items collected seem at the time to shine like precious gems, is that the mind loses its range and capacity of appreciation and gives itself up to thinking always of how a thing may be used in a sermon. Dr. L. P. Jacks has given a picture of a man who, born for the universe, narrowed his mind until it became a mere sermon machine—a picture that has a grim warning:

Now Smith was a man whose vocation required of him the making of a vast number of speeches, and I had often observed in the course of our travels that his interest in a topic of conversation waxed and waned in proportion to what he could get out of it for platform use. If it promised nothing in that line it was "bosh." There are preachers, even great ones, whose interest in the universe is similarly conditioned; they have the eagle's vision for everything that promises a sermon and the bat's for everything else.[1]

The bat's vision for anything but a sermon may be brought on by a collecting habit which gets out of hand and becomes a master instead of a servant. On this Dr. George A. Buttrick speaks with withering scorn:

Reading for "homiletic bits" is the abomination of desolation. A brother minister told recently that there was only one good illustration in Amy Lowell's *John Keats!* There is no need to search for some fit punishment

173

for such a man: he is his own castigation. Being "overtaken in one illustration, he flees unto another," and the breath of the pursuer is always hot upon him.[2]

Yet, surely, all these needed warnings are not the last word, even though they are a necessary first word. For when one scrutinizes a moving, effective sermon to which he has responded, he realizes that behind it there is some diligent care; not out of the air came the quotation that clinches the argument, the illustration that illuminates the discussion with sunlight, the bit of description that grips the attention and opens the way for the truth into the mind of the hearer.

The means by which that which passes before the mind may be made a permanent possession, so that hands can be laid upon it, are worth some exploration in the hope that the reader may be led to experiment until he find the method most natural and fruitful to him.

Before any specific methods are suggested, some things infinitely more valuable to mental resourcefulness than any "system," so called, claim mention. These are nothing more mysterious than close and sharp attention when one is reading, and the development of the power of memory by giving it continuous exercise. Men's memories were much better before they were strangled by so many aids to memory. Some reading ought to be done with a hammock frame of mind. But much reading must be done on mental tiptoe if reading itself is not to drug the mind and become a deceptive substitute for thinking. The extent to which a thing encountered in reading becomes a part of one's mental furniture depends, first of all, on the intensity and vividness with which it is realized at the time of meeting it. There is a kind of active pause which etches a thing on the mind.

But beyond these two reliances, the strong seizing by attention and the retention by a memory whose muscular grip is strengthened by exercise, there are useful ways of preserving ideas and facts and making it possible to bring them visually before the mind. For unless something active is done about them, unless they are speared as one would spear a fish in a mountain stream, far too many things of real value will swim by and be gone forever. The White Queen in *Through the Looking Glass* spoke real wisdom:

174

"The horror of that moment," the King went on, "I shall never, *never* forget!"

"You will though," the Queen said, "if you don't make a memorandum of it."

That is usually true. That phrase "make a memorandum," however, cannot be limited to one particular type of action. Every man must find the type of memorandum which yields him the greatest usefulness with the least distraction and the least liability to run into a waste of time.

A critic not long ago, indulging in the common sport of dividing the population into two classes, said that writers are either spiders or squirrels. The spider writers are those who spin their production out of their own insides; the squirrels, on the other hand, having no such power, must depend on finding nuts and burying them so that they can come back and use them. His general contention was that in the literary world the spider is a higher order of life than the squirrel. That would probably be granted in general.

But there are two things to be said about the contrasting classification. The first is that it overlooks the fact that the spider spins a web and thus becomes nature's most ingenious and persistent collector. So the spider, instead of being the example of the creator, *ex nihilo,* is a systematic trapper of raw material.

The other thing to be said is that not everyone has a vocation for being a mental spider. There are spiderlike minds which seem to produce their creations entirely from "their own insides," with no use of quotation or dependence on printed words of any sort. Phillips Brooks and Frederick William Robertson, two of the greatest of Christian preachers, were creators of that type, if judged by their written sermons. There is hardly a proper name mentioned or a quotation of any sort in the whole extent of their printed sermons. That is mental creation of a high order. Such work in its finished form, however, by no means indicates that there has not been great care in the noting and recording of material and annexing it to one's mental dominions. The carefully written notebooks of Phillips Brooks, particularly in the early years of his preaching, abundantly evidence this. The saving of material for possible use does not have to be manifested

175

by proper names and quotations and illustrations breaking out all over the page like a rash of measles. The harvests of the eye and mind can enrich the thinking and writing without making themselves obtrusive or even visible to the naked eye. The main thing is the habit of positive response to material felt to be suggestive and potentially valuable. This keeps the mind alert, develops the powers of observation, and prevents large amounts of a man's reading from becoming "frozen assets," mere inert knowledge out of reach.

Many varieties of habit and procedure have proved valuable to different men. Many preachers have been able to do remarkable things by reading with a pencil and jotting down on the back page of a book an index giving the subject and page number of passages which they wish to keep active in their minds. And with them it works out that way, at least to a degree which amply justifies and rewards the practice. When they are working on a kindred subject, they can remember the passage, go to the book, and find it. That is worth careful experiment and practice to see what value it has for a person. There are many, however, who must be content to regard this with wonder and awe, feeling it to be a greater miracle than feeding the five thousand or walking on the water. They can only say with a sigh, "Such things are too high for me; I cannot attain unto them."

Every preacher will keep two sorts of collections almost automatically. One is a book, the sort already mentioned, of possible sermon themes, texts, suggestions. This becomes a very part of himself. It is like a collection of things "on the fire" in the kitchen—dishes not ready for serving but on the way. A large number of the most fruitful sermons preached have first appeared in germ in such a book, have remained there for months, sometimes years, and then, in a manner and for reasons no one can describe in detail, become "ready."

J. B. Priestley, the novelist and dramatist, has described this practice:

I had a notebook that offered sufficient ideas for ten years' work, but not one of them clamoured to be attended to at once. I do not know how other people work, for oddly enough I do not remember ever discussing the subject with a fellow author, but my habit is to put down the ideas as they arrive in a little black notebook that goes everywhere with me, just an entry of a line or two for each possible play or novel; and then, unless the idea insists upon being worked on at once, as *Time and the Conways* did, I wait until I find myself thinking more and more about one particular idea, hear it knocking more and more urgently, before deciding to set to work on it. Much of this winnowing and choosing is of course an unconscious activity. Down there in the jungle the ideas struggle for precedence. The method is based on the assumption that there is a survival of the fittest. On the whole it works well.[3]

Put on the witness stand another contemporary writer, a man whose output is impressive both in quantity and quality. It is Van Wyck Brooks giving first-hand testimony on the way of a man with a notebook:

I copy all my notes out by hand, and it often takes me as long as to read the book. But I think this drudgery counts in the end; for every note represents a moment of excitement, and I hive away the excitement by copying the note. All the care I take in forcing myself to be accurate serves, I think, to drive the excitement in. Thus my notes are all deposits of feeling, and this feeling returns when I take up my notes in the course of my work. May heaven save me from typing notes and dictating to secretaries. It is this that produces the chalk-like style of most historical writers. Good writing is felt writing, and this effect is cheaply bought at any extravagant expenditure of time and effort.[4]

If only one entry out of ten ever matures into a complete sermon, don't fret over the nine but get down on your knees and thank heaven, fasting, for the one that came through. For that is a high average.

The other record, to be kept automatically, is a large file into which will readily go articles in periodicals, newspaper clippings, pamphlets, and so forth—subjects which are specific and continual concerns of the minister. These subjects, with a folder for each, may range from Christmas to Temperance, from Postwar Planning to Marriage. This is a good thing to do if one can do it with sufficient lack of attention and without coming to set any particular store by the collection in the file. It is useful, when one has occasion to deal in any way with the recurring subject, to turn to the file to see whether it has anything immediately valuable in it. Often it has. But a large filing cabinet is a snare and a delusion. The material goes stale very soon. Also, unless the keeper of the file can treat it with a sort of lordly disdain, it may come to occupy too much attention and take an amount of time, particularly if one is a methodical indexer, out of all proportion to any service it renders. Nevertheless, if the preacher can add material with his left hand, as it were, while his main attention is elsewhere, and if he does not try to save data on the universe but limits it to the few main subjects with which he has to deal either continuously or at intervals, it can be a valuable servant, even a present help in time of trouble.

Probably far fewer ministers keep notebooks today than in other years. The notebook was the private anthology, into which were copied things which the writer desired to make his own by a ceremony of adoption carried out by writing. With things copied were interspersed usually pieces, often mere bits, of original writing. A stiff bit of labor, no doubt, with the rewards remote and often problematical. Yet when one reflects on what the keeping of notebooks has meant in literary production, the conviction deepens that the habit has permanent values which survive all changes in custom. Emerson's voluminous *Journals* and notebooks, for instance, containing the mingled passages from his own reading and the expression of his own thinking were like the ruins of Carthage, out of which whole cities were quarried. The sixteen manuscript volumes of Hawthorne's notebooks are deeply impressive. They formed the literary warehouse in which he stored away the raw materials of his craft. Newton Arvin in his selections from these, entitled *The Heart of Hawthorne's Journals,* has presented seven entries, made over thirteen years, which trace the gradual unfolding of his greatest romance *The Scarlet Letter.* The list of authors who have made a notebook, kept over the years, into a sort of literary Aladdin's lamp could be extended indefinitely. It is a practice well worthy of experiment and exploration. One great value is that stressed by Robertson Nicoll: "The copying out of a fine passage is of itself an educative process." For often the effect of the effort is that of writing on the mind itself.

One obvious limitation of a notebook is its lack of mobility. The material in it cannot be moved; it cannot be rearranged and brought into ready visibility where it can catch the attention of the eye. Thus, frequently, the material in it drops from sight and remembrance and is, to all intent, buried. But, as many can testify, even so a resurrection day can be proclaimed by rereading.

Putting material on cards is a way of keeping a more mobile and flexible notebook. A card index is in fact an unbound notebook, whose entries may be lifted out and brought into any new combination. A collection of cards on which significant short quotations, references, and original writing is put down possesses varied and great values for the maker of sermons. These values are largely dependent on the preacher's being able always to remain its master and never to become its slave, on a stern refusal to write down anything that does not have real significance and possible value, and—let it be added dogmatically—the stern refusal to squander time making an index or classifying the cards by subject. The commonly expressed contempt for the card index is usually due to a failure to observe one or all of those three conditions. When one says of a sermon that it smells of the card index, it usually means that the index has run away with the man—that, instead of the card collection's furnishing dashes of seasoning to the banquet of his thought, the sermon is made by stirring a number of cards up into a sort of hash and dumping the product in public. But that is not a necessary result of a man's taking toll of the parade of ideas and narrative, of history and poetry which passes before his eyes. That just comes from a lack of discipline; and without discipline any good thing is dangerous—fire, water, or food.

There are two valid reasons for suggesting that material on cards be not classified or indexed. One is that the indexing takes time and attention that could far better be spent otherwise. The other is that, if the stuff is worth saving, it is almost impossible to classify or index it. Suppose, for instance, a young preacher comes across, for the first time, Kirsopp Lake's superb definition of faith: "Faith is not belief in spite of evidence; it is life in scorn of consequence." He thinks it worth writing down so that he will see it again. He could make a classification "Faith"; but other items would need other classifications, until the index weighed down the contents. Life is more

179

than meat, and the idea than its logical placement. A collection of cards is not a rival to a dictionary or encyclopedia; it is, or ought to be, a powder keg. Or take another remark that might be thought worth saving, Chesterton's observation that "there are lots of people who know the last word about everything and the first word about nothing." Index that! Or even a mere phrase—the oft-quoted description of Daniel Webster, "A steam engine in trousers." Will you index that under steam engine, or trousers, or Webster? The only index worth having is that in a man's own head. The mere active "doing something about it" by writing it down will help to make it a part of one's mental possessions. But someone may ask, "What if you can't find it when you want it?" Very well, lose it. It is just part of the natural loss of any worth-while enterprise. The main thing is not the collection of cards or the ideas and quotations and clippings on them; it is the habit of observation, of getting the mind out of the passive voice into the active.

Two practices will help to keep the idea on the card from being lost. One is to read over a number of the cards, with a prodigal and constant throwing away of those less likely to be of real, permanent value. This will do three valuable things—decrease the quantity, improve the quality, and help to keep the idea among current assets. Just as the grandfather and grandmother in the world beyond in Maeterlinck's *Blue Bird* came to life only when someone thought of them, so an idea, a quotation, a passage of prose or poetry, comes to life afresh in the mind when it comes into visibility. Another help is to keep the cards by years in which they were made. That will aid the memory to locate what one is looking for. It will also help to keep a person using fresh material rather than thrashing continuously in the harvests of earlier years.

One self-denying rule seems to be a good one for most preachers, even though it may appear a severe limitation. It is this: Do not use anything found in the sermons of other men. That will shut out much striking material, particularly in the form of illustrations and insights. But if rigidly applied, it will help greatly to prevent one's own original powers from being atrophied by leaning too heavily on other men's thinking. Let a man find his own illustrations! They may not be as striking as Dr. Chrysostom's. But they are all his own, and they hold open for him the possibility of growth. It doth not yet appear what he shall be if he does not allow his mental muscles and his sermonic nerves to become deadened by the use of crutches. There are, of course, inevitable exceptions to this Spartan law. But, in the main, it is a way of salvation.

In this whole matter of keeping material available there is one grand compensation for the preacher who lacks the money to buy many books. In a strange but real way that very financial limitation becomes a mental asset. When a man cannot afford to buy a book, so that he can always have it on hand, he will have to copy out or make some record of material that he judges eminently worth keeping if he is not to lose it altogether. That very necessity forces him into an activity which makes the treasure much more his own than it would be if it merely reposed in a forgotten book on his library shelf. It has been the experience of many ministers that the books which have meant most to them, whose power has stayed with them, have been books borrowed from libraries or other sources. This does not reduce at all the compulsion to the life-preserving habit of building one's own library. But it is a compensation, particularly during the lean years of financial famine with which the ministry of most men begins.

XVII. "WORDS ARE THE SOUL'S AMBASSADORS"

THE SENTENCE ABOVE, WRITTEN BY THE SEVENTEENTH-CENTURY OXFORD scholar and pamphleteer James Howell, expresses picturesquely and exactly the minister's interest in literary style for speaking and writing. The preacher, of all people, can belong to no "art for art's sake" school in regard to the use of words. He himself is an ambassador of God. His words, in turn, must be ambassadors of his own soul and hence functional in their importance rather than decorative. They must be the carriers of meaning, bearing the credentials of sincerity and force. The minister, as long as he is true to his calling, has no ambition to become a "stylist." He does not disdain art, he is committed to it by his allegiance as a bearer of the Word of God. But his literary creed is not art for art's sake but art for Christ's sake. He is concerned not with carving beautiful statues but with sending out living ambassadors, words which, in Kipling's expressive phrasing, "may become alive and walk up and down in the hearts of the hearers."

The theme of a minister's use of words is literally boundless. It deserves the lifelong diligence of every minister. The present writer has no presumptuous and swollen ambition to give here in a few words any ten tables of the law, or to commit a tabloid-sized book on English prose composition. The reason for this attack of common sense is not that such an attempt would run beyond the short limits of space; it is, rather, that such an undertaking would run far, far beyond the capacity of the author. More than that, there is no need of it. It is doubtful if any art or craft in the world has been more adequately supplied with able and dependable professional literature than has the craft of the writer. There are scores of books on rhetoric and composition, books new and old, written not only with knowledge but

182

with skill and vivacity. The preacher should give himself the treat of reading a new one every year or so. If he does, he need not be surprised when fresh wild flowers of spring begin to bloom all over his written pages! One book alone is mentioned here, the king of them all, H. W. Fowler's *Dictionary of Modern English Usage*. The very name sounds, to those who do not know the book, like the prospectus of a journey across the Sahara Desert. But the book itself is a Garden of Eden. It is full of fresh greenery, with all sorts of lively things bounding over the landscape. It is written with a lovely wit and with great learning worn lightly and even playfully.

The paragraphs which follow here are not concerned with correctness of language. They do not aim at keeping a man from doing damage *to* the English language; they merely try to suggest how he may do some damage *with* it.

A good text with which to begin the exploration is "The fear of the Lord is the beginning of wisdom." In order to make that fear productive, let the reader take out his pencil and do a little problem in elementary mathematics. How many words will a man speak in the course of a forty-year ministry? Do not guess; figure. Suppose he is not a seventeenth-century Puritan divine, to whom an hour's sermon was merely an abbreviated setting-up exercise. Suppose he is a modern minister who preaches once a Sunday a thirty-minute sermon. Call that 4500 words, allowing 150 words a minute. Give him a four-week vacation and two Sundays away. That makes 46 times 4500 words, or 207,000 words a year. Multiply by 40 years and you get a total of 8,280,000 words. But that is just a starter. Think of the endless other occasions when the minister speaks, as normal and expected a performance as that the sun rises. These will lift the total to well over ten million. Then think how truly terrible it would be, in the sight of God and man, to utter that many words, so many hundred times more than the number in the New Testament, without ever having undergone any arduous discipline to master the ways of words—as precision instruments of thought, as a richly filled palette of colors with which pictures can be painted on the mind, as dynamite! The man who never struggles with this angel till dawn has never deeply respected the tools he uses all his life, or learned to handle them with a craftsman's

183

conscience. Yet many a preacher has avoided the costly toil. Starting out with the terrible handicap of glibness (truly the devil's master-piece for sabotage of the church), he has gone on being glib for forty years. And the churchgoing of many of the faithful has been truly a sacrifice, in that they have been bored nigh unto death by the steady drizzle of the same words and the irreverent clothing of a King's proclamation in the tattered rags of outworn phrases. Surely there is a special meaning for preachers in the warning that for every idle word we shall stand in judgment. There are many kinds of idle words; one kind, surely, is that which comes from complacent idle-ness rather than from toil over language.

Here are considered just two aspects of this "many-splendored thing," the English language—clarity and force.

One of the most inspired misprints ever made (and truth often has an agile way of finding expression through printers' errors) was that of the compositor who, setting up the report of a sermon, began with the following text: "Though I speak with the tongues of men and of angels, and have not *clarity,* I am become as sounding brass, or tin-kling cymbal." In printers' language—STET! The high purpose of language is to communicate meaning. Whatever impedes that service, no matter how decorative, is an abomination. Clarity is the writer's and speaker's first commandment. It says with an august finality, "Thou shalt have no other gods before me."

It is rather amazing when we look in some detail at the extent to which the words of Jesus, about life and the Kingdom of God, are also guiding principles for effective prose composition. Take his great word, "He that loseth his life . . . shall find it." That is basic in living. It is basic in writing and speaking. It is when we lose our life, that is, when we put away thoughts of self-display, or pretensiousness, or self-consciousness, and speak with the one consuming desire to share conviction so clearly that the wayfaring man need not err therein, that we find life. It is true in reverse, as Jesus put it in reverse. When we find our life, our self-conscious gratification, in an exhibitionistic eloquence, in the deceptive ornamentation which focuses attention on ourselves rather than on Him we are appointed to serve, we lose life. Jesus said, "If thy hand offend thee, cut it off." That, too, is a first principle of style. If the skill of the hand in doing writing of "elegance" is so cunning that it offends the purpose of revealing the truth and makes it opaque, chop off that skill. "Seek ye first the kingdom of God," is a direction for writing as well as living. Let self and its reputation fade out of the picture; let the purpose of clear communication dominate—and the paradoxical miracle happens: other things are added; one writes and speaks effectively because he has put the purpose of service first. Bunyan's *Pilgrim's Progress* and the King James Version of the Bible are only two demonstrations of this paradox in the realm of writing.

Years ago there was much protest in Hartford, Connecticut, when the face of the clock on the Keeney Tower was completely obscured by the foliage which grew so luxuriantly over it. The richest foliage was a poor substitute for the primary purpose of a clock, to tell the time. A preacher's meaning may likewise be obscured by verbal foliage. His words may become a barricade rather than a medium. Here is a description of a "modern poet" by Alice Corbin, a picture which paints just as accurately the preacher who will not find his life by losing it:

> He weaves a wordy silk cocoon
> Of images, obscurely wrought,
> Then sinks into a dreamy swoon,
> Hoping some one may pierce the thought—
>
> Hoping some one may liberate
> A bright and brilliant butterfly!
> I'd rather leave him in his tomb,
> I would not wake the worm—not I! [3]

Be assured that the majority in the audience will not bother to "wake the worm."

There are many, many enemies of clarity; and they must all be fought. First of all, there must be the realization that it is the great treasure, something for which to sell all in the way of literary pretension. Paul put that high estimate on clearness as the supreme treasure of speech: "I had rather speak five words with my understanding, that I might instruct others also, than ten thousand words in a tongue."

How well worth framing as a motto to be set on the minister's desk!

Sometimes clarity is impeded simply by the speaker's failing to put himself in the place of the hearer and imagine how it must sound to him. That rare genius in simplicity of diction, A. E. Housman, wrote to his brother Laurence, who had asked him to criticize his poems:

What makes many of your poems more obscure than they need be is that you do not put yourself in the reader's place and consider how, and at what stage, that man of sorrows is to find out what it is all about. You see behind the scenes and know all the data; but he knows only what you tell him. It appears from the alternative titles "Heart's Bane" and "Little Death" that in writing that precious croon you had in your head some meaning of which you did not suffer a single drop to escape into what you wrote: you treat us as Nebuchadnezzar did the Chaldeans, and expect us to find out the dream as well as the interpretation.[2]

The vivid comparison in the last sentence is an earnest warning against becoming a pulpit Nebuchadnezzar. The one sure escape from cloudiness, in language as well as content, is to do what Ezekiel did: "I sat where they sat."

Sometimes, to mention a danger referred to a short distance back, the thought becomes obscure because it has been diluted with glibness. A gift for verbosity leaves a result well described by the notice sometimes printed on a bottle of medicine: "Active ingredients, 5 per cent; inert ingredients, 95 per cent."

Again, the sin against clarity is often committed by the preacher's involvement in a technical jargon, which winds itself around a man as the snakes wound themselves around Laocoön. The preacher may no longer be compelled to wrestle with beasts in the arena, but he must make a battle with the serpents of a specialized jargon. Here, for instance, is an earnest word from the Bishop of Hull in England, following observation of a special series of services for British troops in Yorkshire in 1942. He wrote:

Our ordinary church language is meaningless jargon [to those outside the church]. These men and women eager and anxious for deeper truth will not find their need met in Christ unless the leaders of the church are prepared to go to school and learn the language of thought and expression which will help ordinary men and women to understand what Christianity is. Much of what we are now doing might just as well be in Latin. The crucial need of our time is for a language of the gospel understanded of the people.[3]

One specific aid against these snakes is the careful observation, made at some pains, of just what a cross section of the human race can readily understand. Henry George used to read over his speeches to a laborer, of good mind and little formal education. What was muddy went out.

Deliberate efforts in the practice of condensation, of putting an idea into as few and simple words as possible, have been valuable exercises for many men. One minister gratefully recalls an offer made to him, in his early years as a preacher, by his father. The father offered to pay every Saturday night for a fifty-word night letter conveying the heart of the sermon to be preached the following day. The son says that the telegram was harder to do than the sermon but that the sermon gained in point from the telegram. This accords with the fact that the habit of sending stories by cable, where every word must literally be worth its weight in gold, has given to many war correspondents a greater economy and precision in the use of language and a more effective style.

There are other enemies of clarity. Two of them are sharply defined by W. Somerset Maugham:

There are two sorts of obscurity that you find in writers. One is due to negligence and the other to wilfulness. People often write obscurely because they have never taken the trouble to learn to write clearly. This sort of obscurity you find too often in modern philosophers, in men of science, and even in literary critics. . . . Another cause of obscurity is that the writer is himself not quite sure of his meaning. He has a vague impression of what he wants to say, but has not, either from lack of mental power or from laziness, exactly formulated it in his mind and it is natural enough that he should not find a precise expression for a confused idea. This is due largely to the fact that many writers think, not before, but as they write.[4]

The other word stressed by this chapter, in addition to clarity, is

187

force. That word, of course, has no precise meaning in relation to writing. It is like light in that respect; just as light can be broken up into a dozen colors, so force can be broken up into a score of elements contributing power to writing and speaking. Indeed, clarity itself is a great source of force. When one's speech is as clear and emphatic as a timetable, he gains power. Yet the stress on clarity may be very deceptive, lulling a person into the comforting but perilous illusion that clearness is all one needs. Beyond this there is a large and varied range of skills which must be mastered if one is to be that ideal of Paul's, "a workman that needeth not to be ashamed." We can have transparent clarity and still talk like a first-grade primer—"This is a cat"—or we can rise to the profundity of, "I think it will rain tomorrow." That is clear, but it is woefully noninflammable and nonexplosive. Fire and dynamite are needed in the assault on man's soul.

Jesus spoke clearly. But how much more there was to his style! The picturesqueness of the story of the prodigal and his brother; the white-hot fervor of his denunciations; the hammer strokes of the ending of the Sermon on the Mount; the two foundations, sand and rock!

In some places we can see Jesus using two types of language: the one a clear statement of his point, and the other a picturesque enforcement of it. Thus in Luke 18:1 we read: "And he spake a parable unto them to this end, that men ought always to pray, and not to faint." Then follows the story of the persistent widow and the unjust judge.

The chief inclusive suggestion that can be given regarding force in style is that one continually increase his familiarity with, and command of, the amazing varieties in the toolbox which is at his disposal as a maker of sermons in the devices of English style. Consider another kind of a maker, a carpenter. What a crippling limitation he would put upon himself if he knew how to use but one tool—a hammer. A useful tool, true. But think of trying to get along without the other available tools—the saw, the ax, the plane, the awl, gimlet, and adz. The constant user of words who is not master of his toolbox is in almost as bad a situation. The man who uses just one kind of sentence, when there are twenty kinds available, is like the carpenter trying to meet all needs with a hammer. In Proverbs are listed some mysteries which had moved the writer to wonder: "The way of an eagle in the air; the way of a serpent upon a rock; the way of a ship in the midst of the sea; and the way of a man with a maid." [5] To the preacher there should be a fifth marvel, the way of a man with a sentence. It is worth the wonder of a lifetime.

Just look at a few tools at the top of the box—lovely and powerful instruments. There is the deliberately framed short sentence, which can be like a spark, making an idea explode, or like the crack of a whip at the end of a paragraph. There is the periodic sentence, where the meaning is not completed until the end is reached (thus from Renan, "Whatever may be the surprises of the future, Jesus will never be surpassed"). It is a perennial source of variety and suspense; it compels a pause and vocal emphasis. Then there is the balanced sentence. This is dangerous, to be sure, in that overuse leads to stiltedness and affectation; but, like Edna St. Vincent Millay's candle, "it gives a lovely light." If you want to see how that light can glow, turn to one of the most beautiful and powerful successions of balanced sentences in all literature, in the Book of Ruth: "Whither thou goest, I will go; and where thou lodgest, I will lodge: thy people shall be my people, and thy God my God." [6] There are the keen-edged tools of contrast, parallel structure, parable, and climax. There is the sheer power of the apposite figure of speech.

Running all through one's writing, no matter what the subject or mood, there may be the "gritty concreteness" of the specific word and idea, instead of the vague general word. Such specific quality gives traction for the mind, as sand on a slippery pavement gives traction for feet or wheels.

Carlyle and Emerson both have paid tribute to the power of the specific. Carlyle does it in a sentence quoted in Harriet Martineau's *Retrospect of Western Travel,* published in 1842. He was urging her to write a second book on the United States in which she should put what was left out of her first book, those intimate personal experiences that make lively reading. He told her: "I would rather read of Webster's cavernous eyes, and arm under his coattails, than all the political speculation that a cut and dried system could suggest."

189

Emerson's tribute to the specific and salty is found in his familiar words in which the polished orator Edward Everett came in a poor second to the swearing teamsters of the Concord Square:

Everett and Bancroft should certainly have lived in Concord. They would never have poured out such floods of empty rhetoric if they had spent a few minutes in the square each morning listening to the drovers and teamsters. What rattling oaths, how beautiful and thrilling! They fell like a shower of bullets. What stinging phrases, and that fiery double negative! No pale academicians there, but a strong, salty speech, brisk and laconic, words so vascular and alive they would bleed if you cut them, words that walked and ran.

This is worth remembering by anyone who ever opens his mouth at all, or writes a letter. But it is particularly worth remembering by a preacher, for that is just the kind of language he is liable to leave out, if indeed he ever learns it, the strong, salty, vascular, and alive. He may be kidnapped and carried off into a cloudland of speculation and lose his native tongue of earthly speech, where "a word covers a thing."

Two specific words may suggest pictorially the danger of losing the power of concrete language. One of them is "silk." The other is "vanilla." Both have been used often in discussions of style. Thus Somerset Maugham comments on the style of George Moore:

He learnt to write sentences that fall away on the ear with a misty languor and it delighted him so much that he could never have enough of it. He did not escape monotony. It is like the sound of water lapping a shingly beach, so soothing that you presently cease to be sensible of it. It is so mellifluous that you hanker for some harshness, for an abrupt dissonance, that will interrupt *the silky concord*.[7]

The word "vanilla" in connection with style is the contribution of Dr. Oliver Wendell Holmes. He used it several times to describe sweet-flavored words, which he regarded as sheer poison. Thus he warned (without much avail) Thomas Bailey Aldrich against "verbal epicureanism and a liking for vanilla-flavored words, the end of which is rhythmical gout."

A final word about humor. There are so many pitfalls all around the subject that any generalization is bound to be open to successful rebuttal and any dogmatic statement seems an affront. Nevertheless, one or two tentative dogmatisms may be ventured. The only kind of humor which, in sermons, is more than, at its best, an interruption and, at its worst, an impertinence is that which is struck off incidentally while the preacher is moving directly on his way, just as sparks are struck off by the wheels of a railroad engine while it is going to a destination. There is no stopping the train for the purpose of showing off some sparks. The sparks do not impede the movement of the train or substitute a little show of fireworks for motion forward. They are an accompaniment of the motion, a product of the friction of the wheels on the track. Humor in the pulpit which is the incidental and occasional product of the friction between the mind and ideas may be of great and genuine service, a veritable means of grace. But humor which delays the train of thought or forces the train to stop on a siding till the humorous display is over is an obstacle to legitimate business. L. P. Jacks, describing James Martineau's lectures on theology uses a phrase that well portrays the useful function of humor in a sermon. He says that Martineau's lectures were "an orchestration of many instruments, imaginative as well as intellectual, with *an occasional drum tap of humor*." That just about says all that needs to be said, and says it vividly. Humor is a minor instrument among many; it is brought into play only occasionally; it is a tap and not a crash.

The dangers of humor in sermons are, or ought to be, well known and feared. Wooden humor is the most wooden thing in the world. The vast majority of "funny stories" in sermons are far more conspicuous for bad taste than they are for humor. More than that, the habit of telling supposedly humorous stories to illustrate a point grows on one like a drug habit. It is a sort of a drug habit—an escape from the hard labor of really advancing the thought. Once in a while a preacher does meet a humorous story that seems ordained from the foundation of the world to enforce or illuminate a serious truth. Then the only thing to do is to thank God and take courage and go ahead and use it. But such stories come only like the rare visits of Halley's comet. For a congregation to find that it has, as someone has well said, a Merry Andrew in the pulpit instead of a Saint Andrew, a man intent on jests instead of a man intent, as Saint Andrew was, on bringing disciples to Jesus, is a calamity grievous to be borne.

Yet, with all that due and doleful warning in mind, it must also be remembered that the occasional wit and humor which is incidental to the deep seriousness of the purpose, is a beautiful instrument in the service of truth. Such humor will usually be in the form of a phrase rather than in a story, in a characterization the accuracy of which is spontaneously recognized (For instance, "He could strut sitting down"). Its fitting response will be a smile which passes over a congregation as lightly as a ripple passes over a wheat field when a mild wind blows. Such humor renders many high services. It can weld an audience together into a unity. It can break down the stern guards of the minds and open the way for the passage of truth and appeal, if the truth is sent through immediately when the guards are down. Christopher Morley describes this succession: "After the mirthquake, the still, small voice." A touch of humor assures an audience that the preacher is a man of like passions with them and thus establishes a relationship over which the truth can freely pass. It may give an audience a pause, a rest, time to take a deep breath, as it were, so that it comes back revigorated, with enhanced energy for attention to another stage of the march. It will save both preacher and congregation from committing the monumental blunder (which must be hard for even God to forgive, in view of how much harm it has done) of confusing seriousness with solemnity.

XVIII. "OFT WHEN THE WORD IS ON ME TO DELIVER"

THIS CHAPTER ON THE ACTUAL DELIVERY OF THE SERMON IS A LITTLE exercise in *Hamlet* without Hamlet. Hence it can be brief. The real hero of the drama of delivery, the Hamlet of the occasion, is the voice. But vocal skills—the production and control of the voice, its placement and range—are left entirely out of view. The field is technical, and, even if one knew some of its laws and secrets rather definitely, it would be hard to convey much of practical value through print. Voice production is emphatically something to be learned under a competent instructor, and control must be developed through long and patient practice. The whole matter of voice production is of enormous importance and has been given far too little attention by a great host of preachers. A voice teacher of another generation used frequently to say to students: "You can put your mind into your sermon, and you can put your heart into it; but until you put your diaphragm into it, it won't amount to much." That was an exaggeration. Conceivably Paul's sermon on Mars Hill was not distinguished by any notable achievement in central breathing, and still amounted to a good deal. And yet the statement of the teacher has wisdom from experience.

The manner of communication of a preacher with his audience, however, is not covered by voice production and control. Delivery has a soul as well as necessary mechanics. The few suggestions which follow here are concerned with the realm beyond specialized skills of voice; they are concerned with the soul moving through the action of utterance, with the mood out of which moving preaching comes, with the eye as an organ of speech, with rhythm which harmonizes with

193

the rhythm of nature in the body—in a word, with many ways by which the breath of life is breathed into a manuscript, or into a sermon held in the mind and memory, and it becomes a living soul.

1. One factor beyond the realm of voice mechanics, always a tremendously impressive thing to watch and feel, is the absorption of the preacher, to the point of glowing fervor, in his message to people. It is not a matter of noise at all, or of motion. It is a matter of intensity, which may take many forms—a quiet whisper, a thought fittingly framed in a pause, a voice as natural and unstrained as in the conversation at the dinner table. The power comes from the impression conveyed by the speaker's being "all there," with his mind and heart and voice and eye focused on his theme and audience with all the intensity of a burning glass.

No better expression of this could be found than in the lines of poetry which follow the one which serves as a title for this chapter, taken from the familiar passage in F. W. H. Myers' poem *Saint Paul*. St. Paul is talking about his preaching:

> Then with a rush the intolerable craving
> Shivers throughout me like a trumpet-call,—
> "Oh, to save these! to perish for their saving,
> Die for their life, be offered for them all!"

This mood of deep feeling cannot fit every sermon; it cannot be all of any sermon. But if it never appears, or only rarely appears, preaching has lost a vital dimension.

A very different source, describing a very different hero, yet pictures a like value of selfless intensity. Gorky, describing Lenin's speaking, wrote: "His words always gave the impression of the physical pressure of an irresistible truth." That, certainly, is delivery that actually delivers.

Here is an engaging picture of Louis Agassiz, the naturalist, in full flight on a platform, very evidently "all there":

He came before one with such enthusiasm glowing on his countenance— such a persuasion radiating from his person that his projects were the sole things really fit to interest man as man—that he was absolutely irresistible.

"OFT WHEN THE WORD IS ON ME TO DELIVER"

He came, in Byron's words, with victory beaming from his breast, and every one went down before him.

Nothing is more worth a preacher's passionate gratitude to God than the retention of the capacity to pour himself out with a glow, a sort of spontaneous combustion, in his preaching. That will mean he has escaped the paralysis of ever regarding a sermon as just a routine performance, to be done with the casualness of putting another record on the phonograph. Stephen Vincent Benét, the poet— dead, like Lycidas, all too soon, when so much of his music seemed still to come—has an expressive phrase for this particular cause for thanksgiving. He gives thanks that "the metal heats." The whole poem from which this phrase is taken, "Thanks," touches closely a preacher's experience:

> For these my thanks, not that I eat or sleep,
> Sweat or survive, but that at seventeen
> I could so blind myself in writing verse
> That the wall shuddered and the cry came forth
> And the numb hand that wrote was not my hand
> But a wise animal's.
> Then the exhaustion and the utter sleep.
>
> O flagrant and unnecessary body,
> So hard beset, so clumsy in your skill!
> For these my thanks, not that I breathe and ache,
> Talk with my kind, swim in the naked sea,
> But that the tired monster keeps the road
> And even now, even at thirty-eight,
> The metal heats, the flesh grows numb again
> And I can still go muttering down the street
> Not seeing the interminable world
> Nor the ape-faces, only the live coal.[1]

The "metal heats": that is cause for preacher's thanks as well as poet's.

One obstacle to an effective delivery is the "too perfect voice." That sounds like sour grapes from someone poorly endowed in voice. But a little observation and listening will furnish evidence of its truth. The radio sounds out that truth day and night. Van Wyck Brooks thus records the verdict: "I well understand the desire to escape from the shocking flatness of most of our voices; but, to me, the synthetic voice is far worse. I prefer the worst voice in its native state to the mellifluous notes of the radio-announcers." [2] The orotund solemnity with which we are assured of the merits of cigarettes and soap powder is, of all instruments, the least effective in the pulpit. It is the kind of steady assault against which the mind puts up all its defenses. Eventually its soporific power rivals that of laudanum. The reason is that such a "perfect" voice loses its human qualities.

In one well-remembered passage in *The Divine Comedy* Dante, being led through the Inferno, met drab and dreary souls who had been damned because "they were deficient in human color." Vergil, his guide, said to him, "Let us think no more of such wretches but look, and pass on." It is not merely in the voice, of course, that one can be deficient in human color. He can be a mental albino in his writing and thinking. Vergil's counsel, however, "Let us pass on," is followed often when the voice gets so perfect that all human color has been bleached out of it. Radio hearers have frequently reached the point of feeling that raucous or even vulgar voices are successful because anything resembling real human speech is preferable to the empty elocution which so often follows that dread announcement, "And now a word from our sponsor."

A related hindrance to delivery that really delivers the sermon to the mind of the hearer, is the reading voice. This is by no means the same as that of the clearly enunciated "boom-boom" of the synthetic voice. A voice may be natural; yet, if it has the monotonous pace that confined reading gives, it soon loses grip. In an earlier day reading aloud was a king of indoor sports. Perhaps we have to our great loss allowed it to become a lost art. The fact is, however, that today few people like to be read to. Some radio studios do make a real effort, when they get the chance, to help the occasional speaker to get rid of the reading voice, which most nonprofessional speakers bring to the reading of a manuscript. There is a different cadence when one is reading, a steady drone which either irritates or puts to sleep, a draining out of excitement from the voice. To say this is not for a moment to forget that some of the most effective preaching done today in the

196

United States is done by preachers with a complete typed manuscript in front of them. But such preaching is not reading. The reading voice never gets into it at all.

One special thorn in the flesh of delivery is dropping the voice at the end of the sentence, frequently allowing to drop down through the floor the very words which would have given the congregation a clue to what it was all about. To those who have suffered from this habit —and made congregations suffer—there may seem to be no way to exorcise this evil spirit except prayer and fasting. It is interesting to learn that this particular fault of preachers was one of the burdens that Sir Christopher Wren carried while he was building St. Paul's Cathedral and other London churches. He always made allowance for the sermon as an essential part of Christian worship. He estimated that a preacher of average voice might be heard fifty feet in front, twenty behind, and thirty on either side, provided he did not drop his voice at the end of the sentence. Wren contended that the French preachers were heard farther than the English because they raised their voices at the end of the sentence, just where the words often required particular emphasis to express the meaning. The radical, and only effective, cure is to learn to breathe correctly. But a person who has been breathing for forty years finds it hard to begin over again.

Three practical suggestions have helped some of the afflicted: More than one man has carried into the pulpit and set up where he could see it plainly a card on which is written the words of command, "For heaven's sake, keep your voice up!" Another occasional help is the frequent use of questions, which encourage or even compel a rising inflection at the end of the sentence. The periodic sentence has helped others to land on the last part of the sentence with vocal force. The periodic sentence has a form like this:

> When Duty whispers low, Thou must,
> The youth replies, *I can.*

The last half of the sentence literally cries for emphasis.

One of the most important remembrances for the delivery of a sermon is that preaching to a congregation is a two-way traffic. Good delivery depends on receiving communications from the audience as well as on making them. If the preacher pays little real attention to his audience—if the center of gravity is down on the printed page, or in the hippodrome of his mind, around which he is chasing a fleeting idea or form of words, instead of out in front of him in the audience —his voice and eyes will show it. The audience will know it, and the interest will drop. The cadence of natural talk will give way to the dull tones of preoccupation; a vibrancy will be missing. He will be like a tennis player with nobody to play with; no balls coming back briskly from the audience side of the court. Dr. G. Glenn Atkins speaks of "that untranslatable word, 'rapport.'" It is untranslatable, and also indispensable. One means of achieving *rapport* is the habit of watching an audience with an attention so intense that one becomes adept in interpreting its smallest motions and most fleeting expressions.

Implied in this conception of preaching as a two-way traffic is a closely related truth, often forgotten. That truth is: the eye is an organ of speech. Lovers know it; but preachers often forget it. One of the heaviest handicaps that the habit of close reading puts on a speaker is that it sends him into battle with an audience bereft of the help of his most powerful ally—the eye. Recall Coleridge's Ancient Mariner: "He holds him with his glittering eye." The Ancient Mariner is a great teacher of public speaking. His eye waged a war with the ear—the ear of the man whose attention he wished to hold:

> The Wedding-Guest here beat his breast,
> For he heard the loud bassoon;

but the glittering eye won. The eye is needed desperately in every communication. For the eye does radiate energy. In London in 1921 an invention called the "lookatmeter" was displayed. It was a dramatic exposition of the scientific fact that the human eye radiates an appreciable amount of energy. Even a casual glance would deflect the sensitive plate.[3] Dr. James Black, of Edinburgh, Scotland, has written in some detail of this eye power as an organ of speech:

Every effective speaker uses his eye-power much more than he himself imagines; and the same is true of singers, teachers and leaders. This has been impressed on me, as never before, in reading that remarkable book by Dr. Alfred Hollins, *A Blind Musician Looks Back*. I was particularly interested in Dr. Hollins's view that a blind person can scarcely become a first-rate singer—and that chiefly by the lack of eye expressiveness. Here is a very interesting and thoughtful passage. "The magnetism of the eye is nearly everything to a conductor. I referred to this difficulty when, a few pages back, I wrote of the blind solo singer, and I think the blind conductor's handicap is even greater. If I heard two singers, one blind and the other sighted, one after the other, I believe I could tell which was the blind one, and it would be the same with conductors.[4]

Rhythm is another element of delivery which runs far beyond the province of voice production and control. Rhythm is not singsong. That, in the pulpit, is an offense against both God and man. When the minister's voice drones a metrical singsong, that is good excuse for wanting to clear it out of the pulpit altogether. True rhythm is something else. It is essentially a harmony between man's pulse and his ear drums. Nature marches to rhythm. The measured beat is in seedtime and harvest, day and night, the rise and fall of the tides, and in the contraction and expansion of the heart. Effective speech moves at times to this march of nature. Sentences that do not mill around one another and push and jostle, but march to an orderly drum tap, find harmony with the tap in the ear drums. Sentences that do not race along in a breathless fashion, like a man running to catch a bus, that allow for pause and measure, give movement and dignity. They march their way into the memory with a rhythmic tread.

Perhaps as needed a practical word as any is a caution against a premature adoption of a method of delivery. Unless there is a continued experimentation, trying now this, now that, the first habit of speaking that one accidentally falls into is liable to settle on him like a hard shell preventing future growth. Kipling makes an observation which he calls an "old law": "As soon as you find that you can do anything, do something you can't." That will break up ease and a long mental nap, often extending over the years; but it is a word of salvation. When you find you can preach readily from notes, learn to read well. After that, try, for the many occasions when it is necessary for a preacher to do so, to master speaking without notes at all.

The man who always needs an ecclesiastical setting for his speaking, as many do, and who, away from his pulpit, flounders like a fish out of water, has needlessly limited his possible range and influence. Keats's picturesque words on trying new experiments ought to fire the preacher with daring: "In Endymion I leaped headlong into the Sea, and thereby have become better acquainted with the Soundings, the quicksands, and the rocks than if I had stayed upon the green shore, and piped a silly pipe, and took tea and comfortable advice." [5]

The mood of the preacher at the time of delivery has an immeasurable contribution to make to the power of his sermon. The time comes, on Sunday morning, when the preacher can do no more with the sermon. But he can still do a great deal more with himself. What he does to the sermon directly at that time will not amount, in most cases, to more than fidgeting with it. It ought to be committed, without further tinkering, into the hands of God. But he can still do much to induce or create in himself the mood which will give wing power to his words. What a man does with himself at the last hour often counts enormously. He can open a door to an access of power which will quicken one's eagerness to preach. One man does it with private prayer, another by reading aloud prayers which he has found are able to move him deeply. Some who can play the piano, and can go from parsonage to church, do it with the music of some loved hymns. Some get a real enhancement of spirit through reading lyric poetry. For all, in creating the mood for persuasive preaching, there is an all-too-often-neglected means of grace—the active sharing of the worship service, so that the minister is not only the leader of worship but himself a worshiper. The main thing is to find, by the use of whatever means, the mood by which the word is given the momentum of the breath of God.

Deepest of all reliances is the preacher's own conception of the sermon. If it is to him just another speech by himself, he had better look carefully to his rhetoric, cadences, and gestures. The mood will not help him. The word will be with power when he looks on the sermon as the meeting place of the soul with God.

XIX. MAKING THE UNCONSCIOUS MIND
AN ALLY

THAT SLIPPERY PHRASE "THE UNCONSCIOUS" IS HERE USED WITHOUT ANY psychological exactitude whatever. It is the loose designation of a shadowy land of the mind. This is under continuous exploration, and valuable reports are being brought back by psychologists. But while it is a land of deep shadows, it is a real one. The terms "the subconscious" or "the unconscious mind" indicate all that goes on in the mind below the threshold of conscious attention. No doubt a more accurate picture is that of the "fringe" of consciousness which surrounds our focal consciousness as the sun's "corona" surrounds that body. Thus William James writes: "Let us use the words *psychic overtone, suffusion,* or *fringe,* to designate the influence of a faint brain-process, upon our thought, as it makes it aware of relations and objects but dimly perceived." [1] The resemblance of the mind to an iceberg, in the fact that a large part of both lie buried beneath visibility, is one of the valid truths demonstrated by a measureless range of human experience. It is one of the most important truths in the whole life and work of the literary creator, be he novelist, dramatist, essayist, or preacher. The writer cannot change the facts, the mysterious and uncharted ways in which the mind moves beneath the level of observation or conscious direction. But if he recognizes the way in which the mind, to use a phrase of Jesus', seems to "bear fruit of itself," and adjusts his activities to that as to something which can be confidently depended upon, he will add enormously to his productivity as a creative writer and to the ease of the creative process.

The use which a preacher can make of this hidden life and work of the mind does not depend on a theoretical understanding of it from psychology. It is no more necessary than a knowledge of the cause of the ocean tides was necessary to their use. Men used their power for centuries before there was any general knowledge that their cause is the attraction of sun and moon. A thing can be used effectively without any knowledge of its nature or causes if there is adjustment to it—just as a child, completely innocent of any knowledge of electricity, can adjust himself to it and use it by pushing a button. The dependableness of this mental ally, working silently in the dark without conscious direction, is one of the greatest assets of the preaching ministry. Without it, the audacious enterprise of preaching week after week, year after year, in the same place, would be so formidable as to be terrifying. Whether it could be done effectively at all is open to question. Yet it often fails to receive the attention which its major importance demands.

The working of this ally can be described in a few sentences which would have no place in a textbook of psychology but which do fit the experience of a multitude of literary workers. There are two stages. The first is to get a theme, a question, an idea to be developed, rammed down so deeply into the mind that the "unconscious" can go to work on it while the attention is otherwise engaged, probably even during sleep. From this basement workshop of the mind, with its machinery running so silently that it never intrudes, the results of the work will be "shoved up," as it were, for the conscious attention to examine, weigh, and pass upon. That may sound like a fairy tale, but it is true. The heart and lungs are not the only organs continuously active. Part of the brain works on a twenty-four-hour shift.

The second stage is to give to the unconscious mind time to take up the question and produce its results. It does not start with the trigger and is as balky as a mule if one tries to hurry it. The problem must be posed early enough to allow time for the work.

A homely and a far too simplified analogy is to be found in placing an order for a meal in a lunchroom where the kitchen is on the floor below. The order is called down the dumb-waiter shaft, and unseen hands put the order on the stove. After an interval it is sent up to the floor above. Mental creation is never that simple! But it frequently follows that pattern. A question on which a person is brooding is given sufficiently hard thinking and exploration to amount to an "order" and sent down to the unconscious for some material on it. After an interval, during which the mind's attention is given to other things (the interval may be a night, a day, a week, or much longer), something is·"sent up" to the light of attention in response to the order so vigorously and effectively placed by hard preliminary thinking.

Now turn from this crude analogy to a scientific description of the processes of "incubation" by a philosopher, Graham Wallas. The best description of this whole matter is to be found in his book *The Art of Thought,* in the chapter entitled "Stages of Control." Here is his description of the four steps or stages:

Helmholtz, . . . the great German physicist, speaking in 1891 at a banquet on his seventieth birthday, described the way in which his most important new thoughts had come to him. He said that after previous investigation of the problem "in all directions . . . happy ideas come unexpectedly without effort, like an inspiration. So far as I am concerned, they have never come to me when my mind was fatigued, or when I was at my working table. . . . They came particularly readily during the slow ascent of wooded hills on a sunny day." Helmholtz here gives us three stages in the formation of a new thought. The first in time I shall call Preparation, the stage during which the problem was "investigated . . . in all directions"; the second is the stage during which he was not consciously thinking about the problem, which I shall call Incubation; the third, consisting of the appearance of the "happy idea" together with the psychological events which immediately preceded and accompanied that appearance, I shall call Illumination.

And I shall add a fourth stage, of Verification, which Helmholtz does not here mention. Henri Poincaré, for instance, in the book *Science and Method,* . . . describes in vivid detail the successive stages of two of his great mathematical discoveries. Both of them came to him after a period of Incubation (due in one case to his military service as a reservist, and in the other case to a journey), during which no conscious mathematical thinking was done, but, as Poincaré believed, much unconscious mental exploration took place. In both cases Incubation was preceded by a Preparation stage of hard, conscious, systematic, and fruitless analysis of the problem. In both cases the final idea came to him "with the same characteristics of conciseness, suddenness, and immediate certainty." Each was followed by a period of Verification, in which both the validity of the idea was tested, and the idea itself was reduced to exact form. "It never happens," says Poincaré, in his description of the Verification stage, "that unconscious work supplies *ready-made* the result of a lengthy calculation in which we have only to apply fixed rules. . . . All that we can hope from these inspirations, which are the fruit of unconscious work, is to obtain points of departure for such calculations. As for the calculations themselves, they must be made in the second period of conscious work which follows the inspiration, and in which the results of the inspiration are verified and the consequences deduced. The rules of these calculations are strict and complicated; they demand discipline, attention, will, and consequently, consciousness." [2]

The "catch" in all this is largely found in the first stage, which Helmholtz called "preparation." That is what keeps it from being a lazy man's free pass to heaven. The unconscious will not work for a lazy man who merely wants inertly for things to pop into his mind. Valuable ideas and suggestions do "pop" into the mind; but they come only on urgent invitations issued in the form of hard, continued thinking about the subject. Bishop Francis J. McConnell has given, out of his own experience as a student, a vivid and persuasive testimony on that point:

When I was in college, I confronted one evening at eight o'clock a proposition in algebra on which I would be expected to recite the next morning. I worked as hard as I could until midnight, and then gave it up. The next morning, as I was walking down the street, admiring the beauty of the spring foliage, the solution suddenly flashed clear-cut into my mind. After I had made a perfect recitation in class, I asked myself what sense there was in all that work the night before. So I made up my mind that with the next problem I would not work till midnight, but would wait for the understanding to flash upon my mind. Something detained the flash, with disastrous consequences to my record in the class. I was about seventeen years old, but I have never forgotten the lesson which I learned then: the sudden inspirations that amount to anything come from patient toiling which has not much of flash or suddenness about it.

There is no illumination without the investigation in all directions. In that respect the process follows the injunction of Jesus. "Ask, and it shall be given you; seek, and ye shall find; knock, and it shall be opened unto you." That is a law of mental life as well as of religious experience. We "ask" and "seek" by intense thinking; we receive in the emergence of ideas and thoughts from our secret ally.

Illustrations that this does work are literally innumerable. Stuart Cloete, for instance, the contemporary South African novelist, speaks for a multitude of fiction writers in his conviction that all fiction writing, if it be well done, is done by the subconscious:

The front of your mind is continually drifting about—prying into what your intentions are toward unpaid bills, and deciding whether you're hungry or not hungry, and thinking up clever lines to answer the argument that was ended last night. Meanwhile your subconscious is slogging along trying to complete the job that your conscious mind is hindering.[3]

Johann Strauss says of his musical compositions: "At first there comes to me an idea—theme. This rests with me for months; . . . while I am busy the idea is fermenting of its own accord. Now and then I bring it distinctly to mind to see how far it has progressed."

Out of the mouth of a babe, if not exactly a suckling, comes a description of the same experience, put in the imaginative language of childhood. It is the observation of a five-year-old child recorded in Walter de la Mare's fascinating book on children, *Early One Morning in the Spring*: "I've got heaps of seeds of stories in my head, and they take a long time to sprout. *They get little shoots on them.*" That is profound wisdom for a preacher. Sermons that are really fruitful must grow like fruit. Time must be given for them to put out "little shoots" —of themselves, as far as any conscious willing is concerned.

Consider two other statements from personal experience. The first is from Robert Louis Stevenson, analyzing his own mind's working, as clearly as anyone can report that difficult field of observation:

You might send me early proofs, as they are sent out, to give me more incubation. I used to write slow as judgment; now I write rather fast, but I am still a "slow study" and sit a long while silent on my eggs. Unconscious thought, there is the only method: macerate your subject, let it boil slow, then take the lid off—there it is, good or bad. But the journalists method is the way to manufacture lies; it is will-worship,—if you know

205

the luminous Quaker phrase, and the will is only to be brought in the field for study, and again for revision. The essential part of work is not an act; it is a state.[4]

That phrase "sit a long while silent on my eggs" is the perfect description of incubation and its sure results.

The other writer, J. B. Priestley, while giving practically the same description of the working of the unconscious mind, adds an interesting speculation, that of the reinforcement of his mind which was not due to the conscious activity or direction of his own will, the contact of his own mind with a greater mind—something a bit close to the mystery of inspiration, to the prophet's conviction that the word of the Lord "came" to him, and to the Christian faith in the inspiration of the Holy Spirit. Thus Mr. Priestley:

I believe, then, that during these few hours of effortless but extremely rewarding creation, I was able, without being then aware of it, to "tap" a reservoir of creative energy and skill, which reservoir is really the source of all so-called inspiration. Into my mind came flooding a much greater mind. Do not mistake me here. I am not claiming that a play of mine was really the work of some world-mind. This would be a monstrous impertinence. The play itself, the people and scenes in it, all these are coloured and shaped by my own ego, and exhibit all my own particular weaknesses and merits. But that triumphant rush of energy and skill, enabling me to run across the dramatic tightwire effortlessly, just for this one act, was not really my own doing, and owed its existence to the fact, which might or might not be the product of chance, that this immensely greater mind could for the time being sustain my own mind. I was indeed not so much a creator myself as an instrument of creation. Such skill as I had was a mere sharpening of the pencil that this mysterious hand might suddenly use.[5]

The inferences of all this for preaching are obvious and need not be stressed at any length. But to one who has never paid much or any attention to it, the rearranging of his ways of thinking so that he may get continuous help from this potential ally will mark a new stage in his fertility and creativeness. For without the aid of the unconscious, which begins in our own determined exploration and continues through incubation, we are all just "half-wits"; that is, we are using just half our wits, neglecting that half which will "bear fruit of itself" if the seed is sown.

Some practical suggestions may be of use.

Enough stress has already been laid on the necessity of getting the unconscious mind into active working on a definite problem by our conscious thinking on it. This partner in the dark of our mind is not lightly moved. We have to send him a definite S.O.S., expressed by the intensity of our own exploration.

Another point important to remember is that the mental activity below the floor of attention does not respond to a general feeling of need. It needs a definite problem, question, theme, or text, carried far enough to become specific. To a preacher's general feeling, "I wish I had a good sermon for next Sunday," it stands aloof with an un-ruffled indifference. But suppose a preacher has decided to preach on a definite theme—the priority claims on the pocketbook of world-wide missions in wartime—and asks, "What exactly are they—these claims which can pull with force?" Then—give it time—the whole of the mind will get to work. Later, from the "fringe," suggestions will come: "Does this idea apply?" or, "You will remember, now that I call it to your attention, that you read last summer that the churches of Holland, ground under the conqueror's heel, had given more to missions than ever. Does that fit? Anyway, I'll be back tomorrow."

Robertson Nicoll, writing of Joseph Parker, gives point to the need for a specific subject. He writes: "Parker read much in the Bible, and texts started out of his pages. When he found a text and finally chose it, he brooded over it in his solitary walks till he reached the heart of it. Once that was discovered, illustrations crowded upon him and his work was practically done."

It is not enough for a preacher, for instance, to worry because he has to preach a Thanksgiving service, and make inward groanings which sound like St. Paul in reverse, "Woe is me that I have to preach the gospel!" Help delays until a specific terrain for the battlefield is chosen and the attack is actually launched. Suppose it were something like this—What are some of our particular habits and moods which blot out the mood of thankfulness and take away from life the blessings which gratitude to God bring? That, at least, is a detailed demand on the subconscious to go through the storehouse of the mind with a search warrant and a light. Or suppose the preacher has chosen a more national theme: What are the elements of hope in a day when it is so easy to fall into a limp, defeatist mood? Elmer Davis has given a good lead in writing that when Benjamin Franklin ran his kite and silk thread up in an electrical storm, he brought good news from bad weather; and he added that that was not the first or the last time that was done. Very well, then. Here emerges the definite question, the sort of demand to which all the mind, its visible and invisible forces, will respond—"What truly good news has come or may come out of our bad weather?" To put the question thus precisely is like giving a scent of the desired prey to hunting hounds. They are off—and may bring back something.

It is essential, also, to remember that the unconscious mind, in the loose sense of the term which we have been using, has no clock or calendar. It scorns a deadline; in fact it has never heard of one. That is the reason one frequently thinks on the way home from the meeting of the things he ought to have said in his speech. Or later still, three or four days later, the unconscious comes hurrying up the stairs, waving excitedly an idea it has dug up, and cries excitedly, "Eureka! Here it is—just the thing you were looking for." And so it often proves to be. If it had only come three days earlier! And one can only exclaim, "If the miserable thing only had a calendar!" It hasn't. That is part of the "given" of mental life. But there is a far better strategy than futile wails against fate, or bitter tears. That is the comparatively simple matter of putting the problem, theme, or text to the unconscious a long enough time ahead for it to have the leisure in which to work and bring in its results.

"Monday, not later than Tuesday," some teachers of preaching in other days, and many preachers, used to recommend solemnly as the time to get at next Sunday's sermon. It sounded like a counsel of perfection; and nothing should be disdained merely because it is a counsel of perfection, for the injunction comes with high authority, "Be ye therefore perfect." This counsel, however, is more than an ideal; it runs parallel to the natural grain of the mind. Translated into

208

the practical language of our present concern, it means, "Give the submerged part of your mind plenty of time to do its work." For that reason many ministers find it fruitful to devote the time given to sermon preparation in any one week, not to the Sunday looming immediately ahead, but to the Sunday after that. It simply moves the schedule up a week. After one gets started on it, it is no more difficult than preparing for the Sunday three or four or even two days ahead. In fact, it is easier; it removes a sense of nervous strain, with the absolute deadline pushed a week farther away; it gives an air of comparative leisure in which to work; it gives the fructifying processes of the deeper levels of the mind a longer season in which to mature.

This is also true of a longer time stretch. Often the best Advent or Thanksgiving sermons are not done wholly in November; they are definitely placed on the mind's agenda in August. And that Lenten series will have less of an air of breathless, improvised haste if it has grown out of the normal processes of study months ahead.

It is doubtless true that most men work best under some pressure. In sermons that come out of a busy life there is a warmth and reality and closeness to people which carefully carved statues produced in an infinite leisure cannot match. Particularly we should be on vigilant watch against being touched by the "island complex"—that is, the feeling that if we were only on a desert island, away from the incessant interruptions of a crowded life, *then* we would do something worth while. That is a dangerous illusion. We should remember that the best story of a desert island was not written on one; it was written in a busy life in London, by a man, Daniel Defoe, engaged in keeping one jump ahead of the sheriff. On this persistent illusion of the "ideal" location and conditions for creative work, H. V. Morton has written words of wisdom, with a glint of humor running through them:

What a haven of rest! It is the place which women friends instantly declare as the perfect spot for any writer of their acquaintance to "settle in" and produce a book. As I looked at the veranda, the eucalyptus trees and the sunlight, and as I listened, hearing only a mule going past on the road and a bird singing in the trees, I could imagine the sound of those decisive, ringing tones that have plagued many a poor man's soul: "What a lovely place to settle down and write—so quiet, so peaceful, nothing to distract you. . . ." And, flinging myself into the basket chair, I apostrophized the misunderstanding shade: "Madam," I said, "it has been proved time and again that the perfect place for a writer is in the hideous roar of a city, with men making a new road under his window in competition with a barrel organ, and on the mat a man waiting for the rent.[6]

True enough; but the pressure is much more productive when it is not to find the theme or project the question or do the whole course of thinking but to finish the job that has been laid out. Then the knowledge that the time is shortened and the thing must be done, even amid distraction, acts as a stimulus.

XX. "TO TOIL LIKE A MINER UNDER A LANDSLIDE"

THE QUOTATION WHICH SERVES AS A TITLE ABOVE COMES FROM BALZAC. It was relayed and applied to preaching by Dr. Arthur J. Gossip, who says that the preacher must "toil like a miner under a landslide." This chapter is just a footnote to that vigorous figure of speech. It enlarges on two axiomatic propositions—that the preaching ministry must rest on a life of study, and that real study and the creative work coming from it and running along with it are painfully hard. If a realistic, even slightly cynical, reader concludes that the strained earnestness of this chapter is due to sharp twinges of the writer's conscience, there is only one answer: "He is right."

Yet perhaps the words here, especially those quoted, may give some momentum and quickening to others, particularly those at the beginning of their work in the pulpit and pastorate. Any sustained preaching ministry must be built on the foundation of mental diligence and discipline. There is a text in Jeremiah, which, when applied to a preacher's work in the study, has a filling ring of doom about it— "Cursed be he that doeth the work of Jehovah negligently." Someone has well called the man who, in a parable of Jesus, said shamelessly, "I cannot dig," the shabbiest character in the Gospels. The man who says, "I cannot dig," using that word in the sense of mental digging, is just as shabby. Preparation for preaching is plowing the mind, turning it over so that fresh growth may appear. It is a long furrow. But whoever puts his hand to the plow and is not willing to go on to the end, with taut physical and mental muscles and a determined grip on the plow handles, is not worthy of the ministry.

For preaching is a terribly demanding profession. We are surrounded by a great cloud of witnesses, who have walked in the joy of the Lord, yes, but who have also brought themselves under the severity of a relentless standard of workmanship. There have been in the history of the church many dark betrayals; but there has been a golden chain of great lives who have shed on the ministry the luster of a demanding discipline, of high standards of skill.

It is on the equipment of a skilled profession that we rely in medicine. In hours of crisis we are grateful that the physician has undergone terrifically hard and pitiless discipline in the laboratory and study and clinic. Amiable good wishes are not enough in the operating room. They are not enough in the pulpit. A woman facing an operation once said to her pastor, "I do hope I have a sympathetic surgeon." The pastor replied, "I wouldn't worry, if I were you, about the surgeon's being sympathetic; what counts is whether he knows what to do and how to do it. When I am wheeled into the operating room, I don't want a surgeon whose eyes are so blinded by sympathetic tears that he cannot find the right place at which to begin the opening exercises." Sympathy in the ministry, also, can never take the place of intellectual discipline and toil.

Phillips Brooks once said to a congregation, "When all your faculties go up to the sanctuary to praise the Lord, do not leave your intellect at home to tend to the dinner." Those words may well serve as a plea to the preacher to bring his whole intellect, continuously exercised by study, to the offering in the sanctuary, and not make a mere maid-servant out of it to carry out routine, practical tasks. For if a minister is to "stand on his head"—and nothing else is strong enough for him to stand on—for an enduring ministry, he must first of all have a strong and dependable head to stand on.

Mary Lyon used to tell the girls at the "Female Seminary," which became Mt. Holyoke College, "Learn to sit with energy." As imagination pictures the little girls trying to "sit with energy" enough to satisfy the high, scholarly ideals of Mary Lyon, tears of sympathy almost start. She had the right idea, the first step in mental achievement. That is a first step which some preachers never take. There is a world of difference in "sitting with energy," with every faculty "all there" ready for a real battle, and lolling about in a comfortable slouch. The devil in-

212

vented the easy chair, as far as a preacher's morning hours are concerned. That was one of his masterpieces, when the damage it has done to the Lord's work through his preachers is computed. For the easy chair has a subtle way of turning into a grave. A good picture of the opposite of the easy chair, and of the energy demanded by real study, is that of young Richard Whiteing, the novelist, getting down on his knees before the bed with his book spread out for reading because that uncomfortable position was the only one in which he could be sure of not going to sleep. That was a last full measure of devotion, reading as a painfully active affair.

If we read the Gospels with any care, we can hardly escape the contempt of Jesus for slipshod work, his scorn, as one has put it, "for shiftless, make-it-do people. The patch on an old garment, the misuse of old wine-skins, the building of a house without proper foundations, the crazy hopefulness about a half-filled lamp." [1] There are too many of these to be ascribed to accident. Surely there is something in them reflecting the scorn of the competent craftsman for the conscienceless jerry-builder. All these scorns of Jesus apply to slipshod and lackadaisical study by the preacher.

One of the severe sayings of Jesus about the obligations of a servant, a saying which has a harsh ring about it, can, without any undue stretching, be made to apply to a pastor's obligations in the study, as well as out in the field, in the parish. Here it is: "But who is there of you, having a servant plowing or keeping sheep, that will say unto him, when he is come in from the field, Come straightway and sit down to meat; and will not rather say unto him, Make ready wherewith I may sup, and gird thyself, and serve me." [2] The servant had obligations in the house as well as in the field. The fact that he had been active and faithful in tending the sheep was no excuse for shirking the additional duties within the house. The pastor has responsibilities in the field, in the parish, looking after his flock as a good shepherd. But great as that task may be, it is no legitimate excuse for omitting or doing with a relaxed casualness the equally urgent work within the house, which, in the pastor's case, is in the study.

This is an important word of Jesus for a pastor to remember; for there is no more common excuse for failing to take study with an

213

intense seriousness than the feeling of the preacher that he has been so busy in the field that he has no time or strength for the further work in the house, the intellectual work in the study. "No time for reading or study" is the opiate of the preacher. The refuge of that unexamined excuse, repeated until one comes actually to believe it, has an attraction as false and deceptive as opium. One of the persistent self-delusions that a pastor must be able to recognize and fight is the fooling of himself into thinking that motion of the feet, necessary as it may be, can take the place of movement in the head, in the mind. The chief "end" of man, in a parish as elsewhere, is the head, not the feet. Unless one can spot this self-deception, he will land in that sorry stage of a mind breaking down, where any interruption of study is welcomed, no matter how trivial it may be, if it furnishes an excuse to get away from the grinding labor of sitting in a chair at a desk and thinking. Such a man will deserve the epithet suggested by H. W. Nevinson,

> His soul lies mouldering in the grave
> But his body goes marching on.

This continuous intellectual toil of the minister is particularly imperative because of a danger that lies in wait for one who is deeply interested, as he should and must be, in the practical success of his church and its organizations. That is the danger of becoming merely a promoter, sometimes with very little to promote.

There is no need to draw up another list of the various fields of study on which the preacher should be engaged through the years. Not much that is human is foreign to the good minister of Jesus Christ. The Bible, a measureless world in itself; the history of the church and of Christian thinking; the golden treasury of devotional writing; history, biography, poetry, fiction, science, and that rapidly growing mass of material in books and periodicals which help a man to understand the realities of his complex economic, social, and international world—all these are the preacher's domain. The main thing is not the relative place these have on a preacher's program of study, or the particular items in each class. The main thing is that something be *now* happening in the preacher's mind. That will communicate itself to the congregation by a new verve and power, like the kindling of a fire on which fresh fuel has been laid. The opposite of that will also be felt by a congregation, when the preacher is merely turning the yellowed pages of the old minutes of the last meeting of his mind with an idea, which happened some years ago.

Look for a moment at what may happen to a preacher—and, alas, has happened to many—in respect to the major task and opportunity of his lifetime—his understanding of Jesus. There is a high sense of the great words, "Jesus Christ the same yesterday, and to day, and for ever." But let us remember, in the fear of God, that there is also a very low sense of the words in a preacher's life—Jesus Christ, just the same, no deepening of understanding of him during the years. No new knowledge of the soil out of which he grew; no fresh grasp of the forces which played upon him or against which he contended; no clearer apprehension of the contemporary meaning of his words, or of what he has meant in the experience of men and the thought of the church—nothing of all this—still a notion of a boy scout Christ—even after preaching twenty years. That question of Jesus may come with cutting power, "Have I been so long time with you, and yet hast thou not known me?"

John Jay Chapman has a word of acute penetration and warning that throws light on this danger. He writes: "I read Shakespeare a good deal from year's end to year's end and always with the instinct that if I should draw all points together and put him in an essay I should draw up my own understanding—my own essay would be all that I could see in Shakespeare thereafter." [3] That is exactly what some preachers have done! They have imprisoned Jesus within their own early sermons. His figure has become static. Their "treatment" of the subject has written "Finis" to exploration.

The words "study" and "reading" have been used so far almost interchangeably. That has been intentional. A minister's serious reading should be study, with a pencil or pen on picket duty. Ellen Glasgow has given a good description of active reading, when it is not a drug but an alarm clock. "Although I am not in any sense a scholar," she writes, "I am, in every sense of that abused word, a reader. And by 'every sense' I mean you to understand that I read not with the eyes alone, but with the imagination, the heart, the nerves, and the blood-stream." [4] That is a vastly different sort of reading from the kind ascribed by his fellow journalists to William Jackson, editor of the *Literary Gazette* of London in the early nineteenth century. They said he acquired knowledge of books sent in for review by cutting the leaves and smelling the paper knife! There has been much smelling of the paper knife as a substitute for real reading.

The habit of studious reading, like the spirit of the Lord, can depart so unobtrusively that we wist not that it has left us. Paul's question to the Galatians, "Ye were running well; who hindered you?" must be faced by many in whom the eagerness of youth has slowed down to a spiritless trudge, as far as learning is concerned. No one, surely, has ever pictured more arrestingly the intellectual tragedy which occurs when intellectual quest dies down than has Irwin Edman in the familiar words in his *Philosopher's Holiday*:

I have seen spirits destroyed; youthful lovers of literature turned into pedants, some of them now quite respected in academic circles; lovers of wisdom petrified into classroom exponents of doctrine; passionate revolutionaries turned into reactionaries, or, perhaps even more sadly, passionless liberals. I have seen the word become deadened by the flesh, and the letter kill the spirit. . . . But George was mistaken in thinking the greatest stultification comes in the academy; one sees it worse outside. The students I knew best at college are shocking to meet sometimes ten years after. They were awakened at and by college, by ideas and imagination. The world, not the academy, killed them.

. . . .

I expect, somehow, that a student ten years after college will still have the brightness and enthusiasm, the disinterested love of ideas, and the impersonal passion for them that some develop during their undergraduate days. Time and again I have run into them, and wondered what the world has done to them that that passionate detachment should have gone. I know some of the things, brutal or familiar enough to the point almost of banality: a family, the struggle for a living, a disillusion with the status of contemplation in the nightmare of a violent world. But it is not revolution or disillusion that surprises me; both are intelligible. It is the death-in-life that assails the spirits of young men who had been alive when I knew them at college.[5]

On the subject of reading, a word may be permitted emphasizing a counsel made earlier. That is on the value of reading something which assails or denies the things we most deeply believe, but which shakes us out of our complacency. A minister whose reading is predominantly that to which he can give a sevenfold choral amen soon loses his realization that Christianity is having a desperate battle in the world. His wits, both for attack and defense, lose agility and grow rheumatic. No one does a man's mind a larger service than a vigorous and dangerous challenger. Many preachers have had too much of Robert Browning and too little of Thomas Hardy; too much of their favorite theologian and too little of Bertrand Russell. Some others, yearning for the role of Defender of the Faith, fight again battles that were won a generation ago.

Writing, an essential part of the life of genuine study, which deals with real issues, plowing the mind, is always toil mixed with pain. Francis Thompson has a fitting prayer for the creative writer:

> That my tone be
> Fresh with dewy pain alway.

The records that have been left by a multitude of writers, of struggle in creation that has had sheer agony mixed in with it, ought to be a rebuke to all to whom the writing of sermons is a "sheer delight" and to whom ink is not something resembling at times spilled blood, but just an intoxicating drink. Here is Joseph Conrad, for instance, telling of the joys of writing a novel:

All I know is that for twenty months, neglecting the common joys of life that fall to the lot of the humblest of this earth, I had, like the prophet of old, "wrestled with the Lord" for my creation, for the headlands of the coast, for the darkness of the Placid Gulf, the light on the snows, the clouds in the sky, and for the breath of life that had to be blown into the shapes of men and women, of Latin and Saxon, of Jew and Gentile. These are perhaps strong words, but it is difficult to characterize otherwise the intimacy and the strain of a creative effort in which mind and will and conscience are engaged to the full, hour after hour, day after day, away from the world, and to the exclusion of all that makes life really lovable and gentle—something for which a material parallel can only be found in the everlasting somber stress of the westward winter passage round Cape Horn.[6]

Every sermon cannot be the storm and stress of Conrad's experience with this particular book. But all preachers may well ask, "Have I ever done *anything* in this spirit of sacrificial and dedicated workmanship?"

Here is Flaubert: "How often I have fallen back to earth, my nails bleeding, my sides bruised, my head swimming, after having to climb straight up this marble wall."

French emotionalism? Some, perhaps; yet Flaubert's whole life bears out the essential truth of that painful quality of his toil with words. It ought to shame and sting those of us who have had little or no experience of "nails bleeding" from a craftsman's struggle. If an Emma Bovary is worth such self-dedication, how about the task of presenting a portrait of Christ?

Too much stress has doubtless been laid on study as involving toil, weariness, and pain. As unnumbered multitudes can testify, literary work has a southern exposure as well as a bleak one on the northeast. Its gardens and its goodly walks

> Continually are green,
> Where grow such sweet and pleasant flowers
> As nowhere else are seen;
> Right through the streets, with silver sound,
> The living waters flow.

James M. Barrie expressed this with characteristic imagination when speaking at a farewell dinner given to him toward the close of his life. "As for myself," he said, "I leave to you the most precious possession I ever had—hard work. She is not at all heavy-jowled and weary. She is the prettiest thing in literature." That may sound like Barrie's whimsey, but it is a truth by which men live.

A very partial and inadequate idea of a minister's work in his study would be conveyed if the impression were given that it is all made up of reading and writing. That is only a part. A minister's task in the study is not only to prepare sermons but to prepare himself. The matter of creating and recapturing the mood out of which helpful preaching comes has been presented, at least briefly, above. Here one special aspect of work in the study is emphasized with the conviction, even the knowledge, that it has been of real help in the experience of some preachers. This has to do with the primary fact that the sermon is to be spoken and not merely read with the eye. Hence, words that originate on the lips, rather than on the ends of the fingers, have a quality of spoken talk that is not often captured by merely writing the words. That which originates on the lips, comes from the lips at the time of delivery with a greater force as spoken language. In practice this means that often the most effective parts of a sermon are those which the preacher has first talked to himself in the study. To suggest that a preacher talk to himself in his study is not the prospectus of a society for the promotion of lunacy. It is just passing on the experience of some preachers who have found it to be, quite literally, "sound sense"—that is, a carefully developed sense of sound. When one puts into spoken words those climaxes of the sermon where he leans forward and seeks to win assent, the words carry farther and with greater power if they have been born on his lips rather than on a piece of paper. They can be reshaped and enlarged later on paper. But if, at the time when the thought takes fire in the mind, the words to convey the thought are spoken, they will come to the ears of the hearers as more natural and moving language. One minister has gone so far as to say that if he can sit down at his desk and quietly, with unruffled calm and perfect poise, write his sermon, he will know without trying it that it is a "dud"—a shining, beautifully shaped affair, but a nonexplosive shell, not really a weapon in God's Holy War. What has the promise of moving other people is that which has first moved him, moved him to excitement, moved him to get up from his chair, walk around the room, and in his imagination speak a part of the sermon to living hearers. Thus the passage finds its first form on the lips, moves naturally to the ear, and through the ear to the mind.

We are told in the Psalms that the Lord taketh no pleasure in the legs of a man. Dr. Charles E. Jefferson once said that this was certainly true as far as a man's walking around the pulpit is concerned. But we may say with some confidence that the Lord does take pleasure in the legs of a man when he uses them to walk around his study, giving to his thought the cadences of speech, and its warmth. For as water rises no higher than its source, so the glow of an idea is often no warmer than at the moment when it first dawns on a preacher and literally lifts him to his feet and starts him speaking it as he would to an audience. Something like that truth lay behind the remark of a Scottish preacher that the greatest help in preparing sermons that he had ever found was a stout pair of boots. When brooding on a sermon he would go out and walk and talk; and the resulting sermon had, when delivered, the directness and warmth of speech. The ideas, when born, had not been first carefully drowned in a bottle of ink.

A closing word may sound like an anticlimax; but it is not. No fruitful study can be continuous. An unrelaxed strain of mental effort is the shortest line that can be drawn between the study and the sanitarium for nervous breakdowns. Caution has been made earlier against having the sermon move on a tautly stretched line. It is a caution for the maker of the sermon as well. There must be the alternating "back stroke" as well as the "out stroke." Let Emerson have the last word: "If you do not quit the high chair, lie quite down and roll on the ground a good deal, you become nervous and heavy-hearted. There is health in table talk and nursery play. We must wear old shoes and have aunts and cousins."

XXI. THE PASSING PARADE OF HISTORY

IN CONSIDERING THE SOURCES OF PREACHING IN CONTEMPORARY HISTORY, or at least the task of preaching set before the background of current events, it might be well to look into the pit which yawns in front of preachers like a Grand Canyon. It is to be found in an Associated Press dispatch in the summer of 1942. Here it is:

Taos, N. M., June 16. The mountain village of Questa has modernized the Town Crier. A loudspeaker system serves the residents. Father Glynn Patrick Smith, pastor of the parish of St. Anthony, felt that his parishioners were not getting enough of the world's news, so, with a battery-operated amplification system and a pair of loudspeakers mounted on the roof of the rectory, he broadcasts each night at nine-thirty all the war news and war regulations for the people of the village.

There, but for the grace of God, go all of us if in preaching on the passing parade of history we become mere broadcasters. Henry Ward Beecher, when he was the problem child of Litchfield, Connecticut, used to delight in ringing the church bell, at hours other than those of church services, for the purpose of turning in a false alarm of fire. Any church bell is a false alarm when it rings merely to call people to another broadcast by some amateur commentator.

Yet contemporary events as themes for preaching are deeply set in the tradition of Judaism and Christianity and in the history of the church.

Poetry, in its great hours, has been not private speech but public speech. Poets have been prophets from Isaiah's day until now. Wordsworth's line, "Milton! thou shouldst be living at this hour," was not spoken in remembrance of any "Quips and Cranks, and wanton

Wiles," or neatness of pastoral poetry, as in *Comus,* but of organ tones —"manners, virtue, freedom, power."

Stephen Spender, writing of poetry, has stated also the preacher's commission. He writes: "The poet's problem is to understand the nature of contemporary events, and to transform them into a lucid language of the imagination, reflecting the truth of reality." That is the preacher's task, from the days of Amos up to last Sunday morning, to transform today's history into a lucid language and to examine it from the vantage ground of the nature and the will of God. If we neglect that as one source of preaching, or at least as the backdrop of preaching, the church will develop pernicious anemia. Peter Drucker has written of the church in Germany in the late 1920's and 1930's up to the tragic climax of September, 1939: "Preoccupied with doctrine and polity, it failed miserably in understanding the crucial problems of a dissolving society." That is the epitaph waiting in the cemetery for any church that turns its face away from the large issues of its world.

It would be a futile impertinence to attempt to give, even in the briefest space, any propositions purporting to be the Christian interpretation of contemporary history or the implementation of the Christian gospel in the complex and controversial issues of our chaotic world. All that is attempted here is to find some considerations that might well be held in mind in bringing Christian revelation to bear on current history.

Certainly one piece of common ground for preachers of the most widely different opinions is the agreement that preaching on the passing parade of history must be *preaching,* that is, theological preaching. A woman arranging a community Christmas "sing" consulted a neighboring pastor on what she called her "problem." She wanted help in choosing hymns. Most of the Christmas hymns, she said, were, "too distressingly theological." The pastor pointed out that Christmas itself was a rather "distressingly theological" affair. So is Christian preaching.

This whole matter finds a good analogy in the advice on street preaching given by Thomas Jackson, a veteran of fifty years of experience in outdoor preaching in London. "Always stand," he said, "at least eighteen inches above your crowd and always speak toward a

222

building, and not into a void if you can help it." That is also sound advice for indoor preaching—"Always stand at least eighteen inches above your crowd." That is, speak from a spiritual elevation; do not rehash the slogans of the street. The injunction of Isaiah is pertinent: "O thou that tellest good tidings to Zion, get thee up on a high mountain." The other injunction, "Speak toward a building," can be fairly translated, "Speak to a church, toward a concrete implementation of the mind of Christ in the world, and don't just spray the universe with words."

That means theological preaching, interpreting the passing day under the aspect of eternity. The recovery of a God-centered outlook and message is the chief mark and the chief gain of Christian thinking in this generation.

As has been frequently observed, in times of prosperity Christians tend to become Greek in their theology; in times of adversity they again become Hebrew. The movement from Greece to Judea has assumed the proportions of a great trek. Because of experience the emphasis has shifted from the immanence of God to his transcendence, from rationalism to revelation. The process might be put into old words, that "man's extremity is God's opportunity." There has been a compulsion to find other sources of salvation than those we have looked for in the ingenuities of a secular civilization.

Today words of purely secular hope have a musty flavor. They bring little more heartening than do embossed bonds in a company which has gone bankrupt. Witness Harry Elmer Barnes's words: "It is too much to believe that Homo sapiens, who has brought forth a Leonardo, a Shakespeare, a Beethoven, an Einstein, will allow fanatical obscurantism to plunge him, after a million years, into the suffering darkness of the subman." But is it too much to believe? Especially if one reads the newspapers three days in succession? For the "sapiens" part of "Homo" has gone under a bit of a cloud. Homo has a remarkable gift for turning every one of his advances into one of the world's diseases. If all our hope is in Homo sapiens, that is nothing to sing about. Any real hope must be found in that other music: "He shall reign for ever and ever."

There is a phrase in Bellamy Partridge's reminiscences of his youth,

Big Family, which throws a light on the changing emphases in religious thinking since 1914. He writes that his mother "cleared out a lot of Victorian junk from the parlor and replaced it with older and sounder items from the attic." A good deal of "Victorian junk" has been cleared out of preaching and replaced by older and sounder "items," antiques from New Testament times. Take this Victorian "junk," for instance, from Herbert Spencer: "Progress is not an accident, but a necessity. What we call evil and immorality must disappear. It is certain that man must become perfect." Much water has passed under the bridge since then, water colored red with blood. The gospel of the inevitablity of progress has been largely replaced by a Christian conception of sin. The evolutionary escalator has ceased to run. We are not saved by progress or culture or that modern development of grand larceny called geopolitics. We are saved by grace. No preaching can come close to contemporary problems in any vital way which does not begin as far away from them as possible, that is, with God.

A deep-drawn sigh in one of H. G. Wells's novels, *The New Machiavelli,* forcibly expresses the world's need for an approach to its great problems which is above that of earth-bound opportunism, or that of a calculating shrewdness which takes in only mundane factors: "The broadening of human thought is a slow and complex process. We do go on, we do get on. But, . . . O God, one wants a gale out of Heaven, one wants a great wind from the sea." Preaching should have just that—a gale out of heaven, the wind, the spirit of God. (If one should object that no writer ever needed a "gale out of Heaven" more than H. G. Wells, with his pathetic trust in panaceas, such as science, or an aristocracy of engineers, or a samurai breed of aviators, or a world encyclopedia, that only makes the plea all the stronger.)

But the God who is far away must be brought close, in specific relation, to the world's needs. For that reason one of the most deceptive and dangerous of all phrases frequently used by preachers is "getting back to God," when, as often happens, both the nature of God and what it would really mean to "get back" to him are emptied of ethical content. In that case the phrase simply adds fog to darkness, and a vague "return to God" becomes a means of evading the critical issues of the world. It is right here that the preacher must give the hardest thinking he can render as his reasonable and sacrificial service. There is no economic or political or international blueprint for building a new world to be found in the New Testament. There is no passage which declares, "This is God's way in the tangled forest of tariff barriers, or the stabilization of international currency; walk ye in it." What one must do is to find the principles of Jesus, the supreme values in human life and society, and then, by the use of the fullest knowledge he can get and by doing the clearest and most realistic thinking he can do, to decide on the specific actions and institutions and legislation which appear to give the most promise of bringing the mind of Christ more fully into the life of the world.

Take, as one illustration, the task of preaching in wartime. The preacher cannot run away from it: it besets him behind and before. It is the great backdrop before which every drama of this generation is played out. Every minister will have his own interpretation of war and the response of his conscience to it. Surely it is his duty to let that interpretation appear in his preaching. But are there not some principles in preaching in wartime and on war issues which can be taken as common ground, not as the least common denominator but as the greatest common sharing by men who differ widely in their own attitudes? Here follows an attempt to find some convictions which may fruitfully guide:

Certainly one agreement should be on the comparative futility of a "fighting speech." Let it be remembered that a "fighting speech" can be delivered on behalf of pacifism as well as for supporting a war. No matter how fervent such a speech may be, it rates very low as a means of persuasion. The Archbishop of Canterbury has well said: "You can never persuade anybody of anything unless you first recognize the truth in the position he holds. If you begin by saying he is wrong, he will reply by saying you are wrong; and there will ensue, as a result, the ordinary political dogfight." There is much to ponder in Shaw's description of Lady Britomart, in *Major Barbara,* "whose conscience is clear and her duty done when she has called everybody names." That may give a certain intoxication, but it is never preaching.

All would agree, surely, to the very great danger of patriotism's be-

225

coming a force making for a chauvinistic, aggressive nationalism, one of the worst things in the world.

Alfred Austin, the English poet, once wrote that his idea of heaven was to sit in a garden and receive constant telegrams announcing alternately a British victory on land and a British victory on the sea. Poor Alfred would have had many unheavenly hours in the past five years. But such a banal statement illustrates the real danger for many of substituting that kind of heaven for the Kingdom of God.

Another principle is to preach so that we do not have to change our entire message when the war is over. The people who will have a hearing after the war is over, and deserve to have it, will not be those who must say: "I have something brand new to give you now. It has been buried for years, but here it is again." Rather, it will be those who can say: "I have nothing to give you but the same old message—Jesus Christ the same yesterday in war, today in peace, and forever in any future that comes."

Those who feel most deeply compelled to support the war or to take part in it may join in the solemn affirmation of the futility of victory in itself. We have had victories before, sweeping victories. Among the saddest and most ironical words in the world are two sentences with which Woodrow Wilson announced the armistice, November 11, 1918: "The object of the war has been attained and with a sweeping completeness that even now we cannot realize. Armed imperialism is at an end." The boy born on November 11, 1918, was just old enough to be conscripted in the next war against armed imperialism, which was "at an end" on the day of his birth. Victory, just in itself, can guarantee no permanent human good, neither peace nor justice nor welfare.

A large multitude of thoughtful Christians, who felt conscientiously compelled to support the second World War, nevertheless refused to identify the cause of the United Nations completely with the cause of God. Among those who have refused to do this and have warned of its moral and spiritual dangers is Reinhold Niebuhr.

Again, all sensitive Christian people will stand solidly against the merely instrumental use of God, as a help in building morale and winning a war. Reference has already been made to the danger of prostituting religion by making it a means to some other end rather

226

than preserving it as an end in itself. Here all that is necessary is to point out the inevitable, insidious danger of religion's being heralded and patronized as a means of keeping up morale. Of course religion builds morale. But that is not the reason for accepting it. One of the broadcasting companies announced in 1942 the organization of a new department of religion, congratulating itself for performing a great service on the ground that "religion is a great factor in winning the war."

Christ is the Alpha and Omega, the Lord of Life, and not a minor subdivision of the Office of Civilian Defense.

In this whole realm of God's will in relation to contemporary history the preacher must be, in Hamlet's words, a creature of "large discourse, looking before and after." He must look himself, and direct the gaze of his hearers, at what went *before* the global disaster of war. He must look *after* the war, considering what, in the providence of God, in policy and action, might shape a world more nearly in accord with the divine will.

Looking backward, then, one field for continuous illumination in preaching is some causes of the second World War. This does not call for a series of sermons, or even sermons on that particular theme. It does call for helping people to see war and its calamities as moral judgment of God on communal sin. It does call for saving people from that gullibility of mind which finds emotional refuge in the "devil" theory of war, or the scapegoat sacrifice, loading all our sins on Hitler and stoning him out of the camp into the desert. If one succumbs to the mood, "Why dig up the past now? Let's get on with the war"—and a very common and superficial mood it is—the answer is that there is a sound medical reason for this study of history. The world is desperately sick. Any cure depends on recognizing the causes of the fatal infection and a courageous willingness to have them dealt with. A map-publishing company has devised a slogan for its atlas, "The Book Behind the Headlines." The Bible is the profound book behind the headlines of a shattered world. The relation between God and the news gives continual material for preaching. There is a world of needed preaching in that somber sentence of Robert Louis Stevenson's: "Sooner or later we all sit down to a banquet of consequences."

227

And what a banquet it has been, the consequences of 1914-39! We sit down to that grim, unescapable feast because we live in a moral universe.

The pulpit must help people think with their minds rather than with their emotions. That is hard. As one character in H. G. Wells's little story *The Croquet Player* says: "I do realize that the present world is going to pieces; I'm ready to fall in with anything promising. But if I'm to think, that's too much!" Mr. Wells's pathetic little figure speaks for millions of people. Clear thinking about war cannot be done unless there is a sharp remembrance of the blunders of the democracies in making war more probable while pursuing what they deemed to be the interests of their social and economic class and their supposed nationalistic interests.

A photograph printed in the *New York Times* at the beginning of the second World War showed workmen piling up sandbags around the Bank of England. Under the picture was the caption "Sandbags come among the moneybags." An unintended but deep and terrible truth lies in the caption. The sandbags in London today are in a very real degree due to blunders in British and French policy coming from the devotion of the ruling class to the moneybags. It can almost be stated as a general truth: Cling long and exclusively enough to moneybags, and the sandbags of war will inevitably follow.

Here are the words of Sir Nevile Henderson, written before 1939, which are a terrible commentary on an old text, "The love of money is a root of all kinds of evil":

Germany must dominate the Danube-Balkan zone, which means that she is to dominate Europe. England and her Empire is to dominate the seas along with the United States. England and Germany must come into close relations, economic and political, and control the world. . . . France is a back number and unworthy of support. Franco is to control Spain.[1]

What a banquet of consequences came from such "realism." Catch the echo of the word "dominate" through those sentences, like the harsh ring of thirty pieces of silver. Nor should we allow ourselves to forget that the onset of a world depression, in which we all had a part, helped greatly to set Japanese imperialism going on its bloody trail

228

over the Orient. Indeed, there has been a picture for the twenty years' interval between two wars, a demonstration by the nations, our own emphatically included, of the parable of the rich young ruler, turning away from opportunity and duty because "he had great possessions."

The purpose of this look backward is not at all to indulge the hollow pleasure of recrimination, but to warn and arouse, that the hopes of people of the world shall not be mocked and betrayed by the frenzy for "loot."

There is another deep need for the backward look—to save us all from a blind self-righteousness, to convict us of a sense of shared sin. That is the starting point of repentance and a turning away from sin. The conviction of communal sin which the world so desperately needs was put in humble and persuasive form by T. S. Eliot, the poet, in words written a few days after the Munich pact was signed in 1938:

I believe there must be many persons who, like myself, were deeply shaken by the events of September, 1938. The feeling, which was new and unexpected, was a feeling of humiliation, which seemed to demand an act of personal contrition, of humility, of repentance and amendment: what happened was something in which one was deeply implicated and responsible.

That mood is not far from the Kingdom of God. Any hope for a "just and durable peace" depends, to a degree few realize, on a preliminary repentance, joined in by millions, "God be merciful to me a sinner."

Hamlet's creature of "large discourse" looked also ahead. One of the tremendously encouraging things in the whole church picture today is the impressive amount of actual study and vigorous thinking which is being done by a wide variety of church groups, and community groups, on the problems and needs of the postwar world. Nothing quite like this has ever occurred before in history. In this the pulpit is having, and will have, its inescapable part.

Among the many emphases to be made by the preacher, two may be singled out and presented without detail here.

The first is the opportunity of drawing on the expression of the world's need of a spiritual foundation of life, which is coming in great volume from unexpected sources. This is a very different thing from the rather pathetic excitement which many ministers have shown over any kind word tossed to religion and the church by scientists, philosophers, or public figures of any sort. This joy over any endorsement of religion from an outside source is really an evidence of an inferiority complex about the validity of their gospel and faith. A Christian attitude of indifference to so many who now play the part of a "Johnny come lately" to a recognition of religion is that of Dr. George A. Buttrick. Speaking of Mr. Walter Lippmann's belated discovery that religion might be a support for democracy, he says, "His denials did not dismay: his sudden avowals do not exalt." [2]

But that is a vastly different thing from listening to the sincere report of many minds that something desperate happens to the world when God and a spiritual order of life drop out of man's thinking. Such reporting is becoming a rapidly growing library. It underlines that tremendous word of Amos that God will cause the sun to go down at noon. There is an increasing number of first-class thinkers who have come to realize that the sun has gone down at a high noon of scientific achievement. Two characteristic quotations will suffice. The first is from Jacques Barzun, discussing what he deems the disastrous effect of Darwin and Marx in banishing the sense of purpose from man's view of himself and the universe. He writes:

The world was made a place of dancing atoms, without purpose, mind or creativity. Consequently, mechanical materialism has destroyed ethics, made Machiavellianism the dominant morality and substituted the search after power for the brotherhood of man. [3]

Here is another man who is certainly without bell, book, or candle, Waldo Frank, ascribing the calamities of Europe to the forsaking of what he calls "the Great Tradition":

Europe has been in rough waters ever since it broke with the Great Tradition, which is the Christian tradition which had enormously enhanced the individual with pride of immortality and a God come down to Earth, and the Hebrew tradition of justice and brotherhood. The Great Tradition is the sense that the individual has purpose and direction and dignity and value because God is in him. [4]

230

The second emphasis is the large and compelling one which springs from the truth that God "hath made of one blood all nations of men for to dwell" together. Deeper than the need of exact blueprints of the means of bringing about an international order of justice and peace is the deep desire that such an order be devised. It must be a stout desire if it is to withstand the rising tide of isolationism with its old theme song, "Let the rest of the world go by," or the newer brand of isolationism which includes the expansion of an American empire. Preaching must achieve the characteristic miracle of Jesus, opening the eyes of the blind. It must open their eyes to the realization that in our world no one nation can provide for its own defense or its right to live. The second World War has demonstrated that men and nations rise and fall together. Let men shout to the skies, "We are interested in nothing but our own little back yards at home"; but their sons have gone out to die on Pacific islands which a year before most of them had never heard of. The children of the men and women who in the 1920's and 1930's said, "We are out of Europe for good," have gone back to Europe in the 1940's, many of them to lay down their lives. There is no isolation from death in a world that is bound together "for better for worse, for richer for poorer, in sickness and in health." Every screaming headline in a screaming world proclaims that truth. The most hopeful thing in the world today is that an increasing number of people are coming to see that we live on one globe and that as the nations are working out strategy for global death, so they must work out strategy for global life.

XXII. SOCIAL AND ECONOMIC QUESTIONS

As in the preceding chapter, there will be no attempt made here to set forth the content of the preacher's message. There is no dotted line of orthodoxy in the social implications of the Christian gospel. As each man works out his own salvation in fear and trembling, so each man in the pulpit works out with God and his own conscience, aided by his own experience and learning, the message he brings to the economic and social issues of the times. More than that, the social issues change with the years so that no conceivable body of static truth will continue to be living truth. A man's thinking must move with changing situations. A man can go from a daring radicalism in economic issues to an extreme conservatism by the simple and easy process of standing still. A great host of ministers have done it, often without realizing it. They have been so busy repeating their views that they have had no time to acquire new ones, or to take that fresh, unbandaged look at their world, local or national, which would yield the facts that demand new thinking and views. They go on fighting bravely the battles of their youth, a generation ago, battles which were either won or rendered obsolete by changing conditions. Often it is said of such ministers that they have "slipped back." Sometimes that is true; but more often the truth is that they have failed to get aboard a moving world.

The purpose here is not to announce, in a pontifical manner, an orthodoxy, either for radical or conservative, but to look at some problems and suggestions for the maker of sermons that touch on economic and social questions. They are simply listed, discussed very briefly, and left in the hope that they may prove stimulating for further thinking.

1. There are certain great issues such as labor, housing, temperance, social hygiene, race and religious discrimination about which the

preacher, if he is really doing his job seriously, will be talking, from time to time, all of his life. He cannot escape them. Surely, then, it is his reasonable service to study them until he can speak out of knowledge and thus be concretely helpful. The man who can bring no solution to any complex problem of our time except to recommend acting in "the spirit of Christ" has healed very slightly his people's diseases. He simply repeats platitudes, instead of facing problems, and ends up in a pious fog. Fog is a poor instrument of social welfare.

2. It is assumed that the preacher is striving to preach a whole gospel—not two gospels, but one—for the saving of individuals and also of communities, nations, and society. Those two aspects of one gospel hath God joined together; let no man put them asunder. The pianist Rubinstein once rebuked a favorite pupil of his, who had performed brilliantly as a concert piece one movement from a concerto. "If you ever again," he cried, "perform one movement without giving all the movements, I shall disown you." All the movements of the Christian concerto are to be played. Sometimes just the ecclesiastical movement is played—a vital part of the whole, but a fraction. It was such a rendering that infuriated Matthew Arnold—a rendering that enabled so many of the Tractarians to be mighty warriors for the doctrine of the apostolic succession of the priesthood while they remained decently reticent before the awful spectacle of working-class misery.

3. In the preaching of the gospel as it bears on social and economic questions, there must be the fullest recognition that there is a difference between the technical and moral questions. The preacher need not, should not, become an amateur arbiter of technical questions. Old age security, for instance, he can support ardently on moral and religious grounds as being an imperative of social welfare. He has, ordinarily, no technical wisdom enabling him to proclaim what proportion in a genuinely good scheme of old-age security should be borne by the four factors—employers and employees, state and federal governments. Christianity is not a book of answers to the problems of legislation and business. Competent knowledge is needed as well as moral insight and Christian devotion.

All this is granted freely, yet two things may pertinently be said: The first is that one need not be a technical expert to see the human results of many policies and to make a Christian criticism of them. Here is the tariff, for instance, a highly technical question in the hands of tariff makers all through American history. Shall the preacher, then, retire, saying with perverted modesty, "I leave all that to the technical experts"? If he does so, he evades a moral responsibility. For tariffs are moral and religious matters in that so often they determine life and death. Here is Sumner Welles, for instance, certainly no soft-hearted evangelist, on the moral aspects of tariffs:

> Our high-tariff policy reached out to virtually every corner of the earth and brought poverty and despair to innumerable communities. . . . Many foreign countries, which had not recovered from the shock of our tariff increases in 1921 and 1922 and were tottering on the brink of economic and financial collapse, were literally pushed into the abyss by our tariff action of 1930. Throughout the world this withering blast of trade destruction brought disaster and despair to countless people.[1]

Those words "disaster and despair to countless people" describe a field from which Christian preaching cannot retreat. Nor does it take a technical expert to see the relation between the lust for profits which raised towering tariff walls and disaster to millions.

The second thing to be said, and the emphasis can hardly be too strong, is that the conscientious preacher must not allow himself to be browbeaten into vague, harmless generalities on the ground that the Chamber of Commerce or the National Association of Manufacturers are the only bodies wise enough to issue oracles on economic questions. Let any preacher who feels an inferiority complex coming on look up the records of many such pronouncements set beside what actually happened. Too many preachers have been like the cowed Israelites across the valley from Goliath, trembling at the reverberations of his authoritative voice. There have been, however, praise God, many Davids, unafraid of bellowing, who have picked up five smooth stones known as facts and hurled them with deadly aim and effect. Washington Gladden, Walter Rauschenbusch, Francis J. McConnell, and hundreds of others have stood in this Davidic succession, whirling a wicked sling in the might of the Lord.

To be effective, dealing with economic issues must be done in spe-

234

cific and detailed terms. Merely to say that we ought to be loving to all people is a poor way of letting a congregation know that what we passionately desire to get accomplished is the passage of the anti-poll-tax measure. George Macdonald, in a familiar verse, has a phrase with great meaning for preaching and teaching:

> Where did you come from, baby dear?
> Out of the everywhere into the here.

The Christian message for society must be brought "out of the everywhere into the here"—out of the empty spaces of rhetoric, without latitude or longitude, into the here of explicit statement. As long as we stay in the everywhere, we are safe—and null. When we get into the "here," we are in the realm of dangers but also in the realm of social salvation.

4. This leads into the preacher's self-examination. There is much to ponder carefully in the record of John the Baptist's discomfort over the seeing the Pharisees and Sadducees flock to his baptism. He seemed to go out of his way to antagonize them, or at least to make it clear that his message was something quite beyond their traditions. "O generation of vipers," he cried, thus breaking all the laws of good taste and effective persuasion. It sounds as though he was worried about his success. Something was wrong; perhaps he was not clear enough; they did not get his meaning. So he made sure that they did get it, even though he had to call in vipers to his aid. It is a good thing for a preacher to scrutinize his successes. Does the placid reception which he gets, or the enthusiastic one, mean that the sharp edges of the message have been blunted? Whether a preacher starts a riot is of course, no valid test of the forthrightness of his message on controversial questions. But it should cause real worry

> If, on a quiet sea,
> Toward heaven we calmly sail

all the time. We cannot be in the succession to those who came to upset the world if our sweet reasonableness never upsets a teacup.

5. One reason why much preaching on the economic implications of the Christian faith does not receive the favorable reception desired is

235

so simple that it is easily overlooked. The reason is that it is not really preaching. When the minister preaches on immortality and prayer, he really preaches. But if the subject might be the rights of labor or a larger measure of social control of the common resources, he frequently lectures, reads statistics, or—scolds. To ears accustomed to sermons, this sounds like something quite different. Some people (one may call them old-fashioned if he likes, or reactionary if he is feeling particularly bitter about it; yet they are the people to be persuaded) look up and feel, "Jesus I know, and Paul I know; but who are you?" That question must be answered, not so much by lectures on economic subjects, but by preaching which sets these human needs in the midst of the gospel as an inescapable part of the compulsions laid upon Christ's disciples by God's love for the last, the least, the lost. A man is never preaching when he is merely indulging in the exhilarating experience of "getting something off his chest"; he is preaching when he is seeking and yearning to see Christ formed in the lives of his hearers, with all the social consequences of that new creation.

Under this general caution may well come mention of the truth, demonstrated by wide experience, that often the most effective social preaching is not on economic subjects at all. It comes in as an implication of a wide truth, perhaps an illustration, by which the application to social conditions is tied in with the very truth which is already accepted by the hearer. Thus Jesus' most effective sermon on race relations was not really a discourse on that subject at all. It was the parable of the good Samaritan, which applies to the whole complete circle of life. It has the wideness of the sea. But the hero is made a despised and unjustly treated member of another race, a Samaritan. That is indirect and superb preaching on appreciating and honoring other racial groups. Jesus did not make a frontal attack; he made a strategic flank movement. So a preacher often gets farther into the minds of his congregation, not by announcing and preaching another sermon on the Negro problem, but by using, as an illustration in his sermon on courage, a Negro performing an act of great courage. He will not have to look far for that!

6. The whole case for preaching which reaches into the social consequences and imperatives of the gospel is both intensified and com-

plicated by the wave of reaction which is rising over many parts of the country and population and will undoubtedly continue to rise and strengthen for years to come. On this whole subject one is tempted to have the mood which possessed Thoreau when he wrote of some subject, "My only fear is that I shall not be extravagant enough." When the slightest turn in the fortunes of war occurred, when Great Britain, for instance, no longer had its back to the wall, as it did in the tense days of 1940 and 1941, many selfish interests, which were sternly "hush-hushed" in those days, began to come out from cover and speak clearly and roughly. It was like the first warm days of spring when many crawling things begin to come out from under the boards where they have been hidden. With great clearness from many sources declarations were made that the main purpose of the second World War was "the preservation of free enterprise" or "the American way of life"—phrases never clearly defined, for that would have given away the drive for profits, but phrases wrapped gracefully around with the stars and stripes. This preservation of the principle of unhampered competition (which, of course, is the last thing on earth that monopolists really want) is easily made into a holy cause. The most vigilant wakefulness is demanded.

Two special forms of reaction grow in wartime and the complex period following. One is nostalgia for an earlier day, which takes the place of religion and increased effort for social welfare. An Associated Press dispatch direct from Denver, March 6, 1942, presented a vivid symbol of the yearning to return to the past, under which the desire for the preservation of privileges makes itself felt. Here it is in part:

John ———, whose irresistible desire to walk backwards landed him in the neurological ward at Denver General Hospital last week, was back to normal today. "He was stricken with a strange mental ailment which caused him to walk backwards," the doctor explained. He was described by psychiatrists as the victim of a form of hysteria.

There are a good many victims of hysteria who insist on walking backwards into the golden age of unrestricted profits, of little or no social control of monopolies, of mild and ineffectual labor laws, back to the happy days of the Pullman strike.

237

This nostalgia often comes with such tearful, sentimental overtones that it affects the pulpit, and the only forward march of religion seems to be a backward trail to the 1870's. Nostalgia is a self-protective device, a defense against the painful horrors of thinking, which constantly recurs in times of crisis. It is an alluring, though futile, attempt to escape the perplexities of an upset world rather than face the demanding task of taking basic Christian principles into the contemporary world.

Here, for instance, is an excerpt from a sermon preached in an American city a few years ago, as reported by a newspaper of that city: "Our fathers gave us a happy, prosperous country. Instead of keeping it in that way we became 'experts' in education, in nutrition, in housing, in welfare." (Evidently, to the mind of the preacher as it longingly conjures up the light of other days, all these things are abominations!) He goes on: "Think of the years before the era of 'experts': a small town on Sunday, with everything closed down, everybody in church, hymns resounding down Main Street, the Sunday dinners. People in those days believed in paying their bills, and never thought of getting something for nothing or something that didn't belong to them."

So beautiful that it brings tears to the eyes! But if there were a Pulitzer prize given for the most striking imaginative distortion of history, that would certainly get it! When was this happy day? In the preacher's youth, in the high days of Warren Gamaliel Harding? Perchance the days when people "never thought of getting something for nothing" were back fifty years before, in what has been called "the age of the dinosaurs." The period of the greatest corruption in American history here trotted out solemnly as the golden age to which we should return! Just get enough hymns floating down a Main Street that is closed tight as a drum on Sunday, and all will be well!

That is a sort of Currier and Ives religion. Its true symbol is not a cross but "the old oaken bucket, the iron-bound bucket," and the moss-covered sermon that hung in the pulpit. The tragedy of this kind of sentimental orgy is that, when called by the name of religion, it blocks the action of genuine prophetic faith.

7. Another remembrance to be kept in mind, covering a field so big

238

that it can only be mentioned here, is that in the twentieth century foreign policy grows from the internal policy and structure of a nation. It is not too much to say that foreign policy is a function of internal economy. If the nations, including our own, continue to have the same internal policies that have produced two world wars and a world-wide depression in twenty-five years, policies based largely on the preservation of profits and the extension of trade, there is very little hope of any greatly different future, no matter how fervent their salute to an association of nations. One pathway out of the recurring decimal of war is the recognition that the true end of production is consumption—not merely a limited consumption such as will bring a maximum profit to investors, but a standard of living for all people that accords with the wealth-producing capacities of our time. If production is motivated by meeting human need, then there is a way out of a contracting economy and its circle of unemployment. We hear, for instance, much stress on equal access of nations to raw materials. It deserves stress. But what hope is there in it if the access is just to those moneyed groups within nations who are seeking gain on investments? But genuine international co-operation will be a possible adventure in a world "in which policy is governed by the aspirations of common men and women rather than by the vested interests of monopoly corporations."

8. Should some preachers and laymen feel that such territory as is here glimpsed, dimly and through a telescope, is not the proper field for preaching and the church, that the true field is spiritual development and character building, there is a short and effective answer. Spiritual life and character building are the concerns of the church, but neither is ever produced in a social vacuum. The attempt to do so has gone on long enough to leave no possible doubt on that point. Christlikeness grows in human relations; and a church which acquiesces, without protest and struggle, in wrongs which deny the Christian purpose and revelation, becomes, in the true sense of the word, disintegrated. It does not attain the psychological unity which comes when every thought, including those about racial discrimination, labor, and wages, is brought into captivity to Christ. The ac-

239

quiescing church becomes a split personality. Much of the comparative weakness of some churches today comes from that cause.

9. Preaching dealing with these issues must be done in fear and trembling before God, lest the tone defeat the purpose. It is so easy for that to happen that nothing will avail except the constant prayer, "Deliver us from evil." J. J. Chapman says that "Carlyle was a man of words whose profession was snarling." He snarled well; but it is a poor profession, no matter how well it is done. It is a very different profession from that of the Christian ministry. We are all familiar with earnest apostles whose tone defeats their purpose. Pacifists have listened to other pacifists so rigid and denunciatory that they have almost rushed to the nearest recruiting office to enlist. Thoughtful liberals have almost been made into hard-shell conservatives by some speeches demanding the very positions they have agreed with. It is a comforting principle of the art of verbal warfare that you do not need to denounce or vilify an opponent. You can usually do something far worse—you can quote him.

The alternative to a snarl, a rant, or a denunciation is not limited to a honeyed sweetness which evades all collisions. There is a clear and courageous forthrightness which can speak all the more effectively because it speaks in the accents of love and respect. Such accents make it clear that the preacher's desire is not to "put something over" or to indulge in the false heroics of denunciation, but patiently to persuade people, for the sake of God and his Kingdom, to adopt attitudes and perform actions that seem to the preacher to be definite agencies of that Kingdom.

REFERENCES

I. BEHIND THE MINISTER

1. Isaiah 22:15.
2. Jeremiah 45:4.
3. From *The Harp Weaver and Other Poems,* Harper & Bros., 1923.
4. Judith Cladel, *Rodin,* Harcourt, Brace & Co., 1937.
5. Charles Scribner's Sons, 1911, II, 147.
6. Richard Curle, *Caravansary and Conversation,* Frederick A. Stokes Co., 1937, p. 135.
7. *Op. cit.,* I, 220.

II. THE MINISTER HIMSELF

1. Luke 14:28-30.
2. Quoted in Louis Untermeyer, *From Another World,* Harcourt, Brace & Co., 1939.
3. *The Saturday Review of Literature,* Feb. 20, 1937.
4. Untermeyer, *op. cit.,* p. 153.

III. SERMONS ARE TOOLS

1. *Blood, Sweat and Tears,* G. P. Putnam's Sons, 1941, p. 297.
2. Luke 15:1-2.
3. *The Heart of Hawthorne's Journal,* Houghton Mifflin Co., 1929.
4. *The Congregationalist and Herald of Gospel Liberty,* Dec. 15, 1932.
5. "Andrea del Sarto."
6. *New England: Indian Summer,* E. P. Dutton & Co., 1940, p. 163.
7. Mark 9:43.
8. Carl and Mark Van Doren, *American and British Literature Since 1890,* The Century Co., 1925, p. 90.
9. *A Writer's Notes on His Trade,* Doubleday, Doran & Co., 1930.

IV. AN ART IS A BAND OF MUSIC

1. Bliss Perry, *And Gladly Teach,* Houghton Mifflin Co., 1935, p. 270.
2. *Rain upon Godshill,* Harper & Bros., 1939, p. 164.

3. *Harper's Magazine,* Jan., 1942.
4. Van Wyck Brooks, *Opinions of Oliver Allston,* E. P. Dutton & Co., 1941, p. 30.

V. THE IMPORTANCE OF PREACHING

1. Romans 10:14.
2. *The Croquet Player,* The Viking Press, 1937.
3. *The Saturday Review of Literature.*
4. I Corinthians 1:23.
5. I Corinthians 2:2.
6. Mark 11:29.
7. *The Flowering of New England,* E. P. Dutton & Co., 1936, p. 393.
8. *On the Writing of History,* E. P. Dutton & Co., 1939.

VI. PREACHING TO LIFE SITUATIONS

1. Matthew 9:36.
2. Acts 8:30, 35.
3. *The Christian News-Letter,* Supplement to No. 70, Feb. 26, 1941, Oxford, England.
4. *Ibid.*
5. Luke 22:25-26.
6. Quoted in Mason Wade, *Margaret Fuller,* The Viking Press, 1940, pp. xiv-xv.
7. Luke 18:35-41.
8. W. Somerset Maugham, *The Summing Up,* p. 183. Copyright, 1938. Reprinted by permission from Doubleday, Doran & Co., Inc.
9. *Letters of James Denney,* Hodder & Stoughton.
10. M. A. De Wolfe Howe, *John Jay Chapman and His Letters.* Houghton Mifflin Co., 1937, p. 163.
11. Edna St. Vincent Millay, "Ashes of Life."
12. *The Advance,* May 17, 1934.
13. R. Ellis Roberts, *H. R. L. Sheppard,* John Murray, 1942.
14. *If I Had Only One Sermon to Prepare,* ed. Joseph Fort Newton, Harper & Bros., 1932, pp. 112-13.
15. T. S. Eliot, "The Hollow Men."

REFERENCES

VII. PEOPLE AS A SOURCE OF SERMONS

1. "The American Scholar."
2. *The Parables of the Gospel,* Abingdon-Cokesbury, 1937.
3. C. Gott and J. A. Behnke, *A Preface to College Prose,* The Macmillan Co., 1935, p. 529.
4. *The Great Age of Greek Literature,* W. W. Norton & Co., 1942, p. 63.
5. *A Treasury of Art Masterpieces,* Simon & Schuster, 1939, p. 18.
6. *Op. cit.,* p. 103.
7. *Kings and Desperate Men,* Alfred A. Knopf, 1942, p. 120.
8. *New York Times Book Review,* Feb. 2, 1941.
9. *The Christian Century,* April 11, 1929.
10. *The British Weekly.*

IX. IN THE BEGINNING WAS THE IDEA

1. *As We Were,* Longmans, Green & Co., 1930, p. 114.

X. THE HARVEST OF THE EYE

1. Dorothy Hewlett, *Adonais,* pp. 150-51. Copyright, 1938. Used by special permission of the publishers, The Bobbs-Merrill Co.
2. Aldous Huxley, *The Art of Seeing,* Harper & Bros., 1942. This book is immensely worth reading by the preacher and writer, not so much for its specific recommendation of strengthening the eyesight without glasses, about which there is much professional skepticism, as for the incidental and acute observations about the gift and use of eyesight and the cultivation of more acute vision.
3. Matthew 6:31.
4. Matthew 6:22.
5. "To Thomas Butts."
6. Descriptive Catalogue, 1810, "The Vision of Judgment."
7. *A Midsummer Night's Dream,* Act V, scene 1.
8. *London Times,* July 9, 1939.
9. *The Saturday Review of Literature.*
10. *Mandarin in Manhattan,* J. B. Lippincott Co., 1933.

XI. "IMAGINATION BODIES FORTH"

1. Acts 22:6.
2. Professor Theodore Spencer, of Harvard, in his *Death and Elizabethan Tragedy,* Harvard University Press, 1936, gives much specific detail on this point.
3. *The Saturday Review of Literature.*

XII. STRUCTURE AND OUTLINE

1. F. P. Morse, *Backstage with Henry Miller,* E. P. Dutton & Co., 1938.
2. *A Bad Child's Book of Beasts,* Alfred A. Knopf, 1923.
3. *The Christian Register,* May 24, 1934.
4. *The Christian World,* London, August 14, 1930.

XIII. SOME TYPES OF OUTLINE

1. Charles Scribner's Sons, 1942, pp. 30, 31, 33. See particularly chap. v, "By Way of Unreason."
2. William James, *A Pluralistic Universe,* Longmans, Green & Co., 1909, pp. 328-29.
3. Acts 26:22.
4. II Corinthians 4:8-9.
5. Job 28:12-28.
6. Luke 13:1-5.
7. G. K. Chesterton, *George Bernard Shaw,* John Lane Co., 1909, p. 165.

XIV. THE BIBLE AS A SOURCE OF PREACHING

1. G. B. Shaw, *Adventures of the Black Girl in Her Search for God,* Dodd, Mead & Co., 1933, p. 67.
2. M. A. DeWolfe Howe, *op. cit.*
3. Edwin Markham, "Lincoln the Man of the People."
4. T. H. Darlow, *William Robertson Nicoll,* Geo. H. Doran Co., 1925, p. 54.

REFERENCES

5. *The Christian World*, London.
6. *Confessions of an Octogenarian*, The Macmillan Co., 1942, p. 87.
7. "Sic Transit," from *Field of Honor*, The Kaleidograph Press, 1933.
8. *Travels in the North*, The Macmillan Co., 1939.
9. *Something of Myself*, Doubleday, Doran & Co., 1937, p. 199.
10. *Jesus the Unknown*, Charles Scribner's Sons, 1933, pp. 18-19.

XV. GETTING STARTED

1. Elmer Ellis, *Mr. Dooley's America*, Alfred A. Knopf, 1941.
2. Psalm 39:3.
3. Quoted in St. John Ervine, *Some Impressions of My Elders*, The Macmillan Co., 1922, pp. 71-72.
4. *New York Times Book Review*, Oct. 6, 1940.
5. Habakkuk 2:3.

XVI. COLLECTING AND ASSIMILATING MATERIAL

1. *Heroes of Smokeover*, Geo. H. Doran, 1926.
2. *Jesus Came Preaching*, Charles Scribner's Sons, 1931, p. 151.
3. *Op. cit.*, Harper & Bros., 1939, p. 121.
4. *Opinions of Oliver Allston*, E. P. Dutton & Co., 1941, p. 34.

XVII. "WORDS ARE THE SOUL'S AMBASSADORS"

1. *The Saturday Review of Literature*, Nov. 3, 1934.
2. Laurence Housman, *My Brother, A. E. Housman*, Charles Scribner's Sons, 1938.
3. *The Christian News-Letter*.
4. W. Somerset Maugham, *The Summing Up*, p. 31. Copyright, 1938. Reprinted by permission from Doubleday, Doran & Co., Inc.
5. Proverbs 30:19.
6. Ruth 1:16.
7. W. Somerset Maugham, *op. cit.*, p. 42. Copyright, 1938. Reprinted by permission from Doubleday, Doran & Co., Inc. Italics are mine.

XVIII. "OFT WHEN THE WORD IS ON ME TO DELIVER"

1. Stephen Vincent Benét, *Burning City*, Farrar & Rinehart, 1933, p. 57.
2. *Opinions of Oliver Allston*, p. 91.
3. Robert Graves and Alan Hodge, *The Long Week-End*, The Macmillan Co., 1941, p. 83.
4. *The Christian World*, London.
5. *Letters of John Keats*, Oxford University Press, 1931.

XIX. MAKING THE UNCONSCIOUS MIND AN ALLY

1. *The Principles of Psychology*, Henry Holt & Co., 1890, I, 258.
2. Harcourt, Brace & Co., 1926, pp. 79-81.
3. *New York Times Book Review*, Nov. 17, 1940.
4. *Letters*, II, 286.
5. *Op. cit.*, pp. 41-42.
6. H. V. Morton, *In the Steps of St. Paul*, p. 132. Copyright, 1936, by Dodd, Mead & Co., Inc.

XX. "TO TOIL LIKE A MINER UNDER A LANDSLIDE"

1. Hugh Martin, *The Parables of the Gospel*, Abingdon-Cokesbury, 1937.
2. Luke 17:7-8.
3. M. A. De Wolfe Howe, *op. cit.*, p. 113.
4. *The Saturday Review of Literature*, Jan. 23, 1937.
5. From *Philosopher's Holiday*, pp. 62, 122. Copyright, 1938, by Irwin Edman. By permission of The Viking Press, Inc., New York.
6. Joseph Conrad, *A Personal Record*, p. 160. Copyright, 1912, 1940, by Doubleday, Doran & Co., Inc.

XXI. THE PASSING PARADE OF HISTORY

1. *Ambassador Dodd's Diary*, Harcourt, Brace & Co., 1941, p. 421.
2. *Preaching in These Times*, Charles Scribner's Sons, 1940, p. 24.
3. *Darwin, Marx, Wagner*, Little, Brown & Co., 1941.
4. *Chart for Rough Water*, Doubleday, Doran & Co., 1940.

XXII. SOCIAL AND ECONOMIC QUESTIONS

1. *The World of the Four Freedoms*, Columbia University Press, 1943, pp. 19-20.

INDEX OF SCRIPTURAL REFERENCES

INDEX OF SCRIPTURAL REFERENCES

INDEX OF NAMES AND TITLES

INDEX OF NAMES AND TITLES

INDEX OF NAMES AND TITLES

251

INDEX OF NAMES AND TITLES

INDEX OF TOPICS

INDEX OF TOPICS